Lecture Notes of the Institute for Computer Sciences, Social Informatics and Telecommunications Engineering 140

More information about this series at http://www.springer.com/series/8197

Natalie Mitton · Antoine Gallais
Melike Erol Kantarci · Symeon Papavassiliou (Eds.)

Ad Hoc Networks

6th International ICST Conference,
ADHOCNETS 2014
Rhodes, Greece, August 18–19, 2014
Revised Selected Papers

 Springer

Editors

Natalie Mitton
INRIA
Villeneuve d'Ascq
France

Melike Erol Kantarci
Clarkson University
New York
USA

Antoine Gallais
Université de Strasbourg
Strasbourg
France

Symeon Papavassiliou
National Technical University of Athens
Athens
Greece

ISSN 1867-8211   ISSN 1867-822X   (electronic)
Lecture Notes of the Institute for Computer Sciences, Social Informatics
and Telecommunications Engineering
ISBN 978-3-319-13328-7   ISBN 978-3-319-13329-4   (eBook)
DOI 10.1007/978-3-319-13329-4

Library of Congress Control Number: 2014956192

Springer Cham Heidelberg New York Dordrecht London
© Institute for Computer Sciences, Social Informatics and Telecommunications Engineering 2014

Printed on acid-free paper

Springer International Publishing AG Switzerland is part of Springer Science+Business Media
(www.springer.com)

Preface

It has been a real pleasure to chair the Sixth International Conference on Ad Hoc Networks on this beautiful Rhodes Island. Following the great success of AdHocNets 2009–2013, AccessNets 2014 has again presented an exciting technical program consisting of keynote speeches, invited talks, and technical sessions. This year, AdHocNets was collocated with the QShine conference and gathered about 70 attendees in very interactive and interesting sessions, generating many fruitful discussions. The conference consisted of two awesome keynote talks, technical sessions, and an associated workshop. The technical sessions presented original and fundamental research advances while the workshops focused on development and application issues in this hot field.

We received high-quality submissions from many parts of the world, including Europe, North America, South America, and Asia. After a rigorous review process, 16 regular and invited papers were included in the technical program. The technical program included two keynote talks and five technical sessions, which presented recent advances in various aspects of ad hoc networks. In particular, the program featured two keynote addressed by Prof. Evangelos Kranakis from Carleton University, Canada and Prof. Karyotis Vasileios from National Technical University of Athens, Greece.

I would like to thank gratefully the TPC chairs Prof. Symeon Papavassiliou, Dr. Antoine Gallais, and Dr. Melike Erole Kantarci, who made a remarkable job in the etablishment of the technical program. It would neither have been possible without the help of all the TPC members and external reviewers who volunteered their time and professional expertise. I would like to take this opportunity to thank all of them for their help. We would also like to thank all the authors for contributing their quality work, and our sponsors and partners for their support, including CREATE-NET and EAI. We received excellent and reactive support from our sponsors, especially from Ruzanna Najaryan who managed the conference organization. Sincere and dedicated thanks to her.

Finally, we hope you enjoy reading these technical proceedings as much as we enjoyed the live sessions.

August 2014   Nathalie Mitton

Organizing Committee AdHocNets 2014

Steering Committee

Imrich Chlamtac	Create-Net, Italy
Jun Zheng	Southeast University, China
Shiwen Mao	Auburn University, USA

Conference Organizing Committee

TPC Co-chairs

Symeon Papavassiliou	National Technical University of Athens, Greece
Melike Erol-Kantarci	Clarkson University, USA
Antoine Gallais	Université de Strasbourg, France

General Chair

Nathalie Mitton	Inria, France

Web and Publication Chair

Jun Li	Carleton University, Canada

Publicity Chair

Razvan Stanica	INSA Lyon, France

Workshop Chair

Enrico Natalizio	Université de Technologie de Compiègne, France

Conference Manager

Ruzanna Najaryan	EAI, Italy

Contents

WAMN

ADHOCNETS

Interest-Based Forwarding for Satisfying User Preferences in Vehicular Networks

Farouk Mezghani[1], Riadh Dhaou[1(✉)], Michele Nogueira[2],
and André-Luc Beylot[1]

[1] Université de Toulouse, INP/ENSEEIHT, IRIT, France
{Farouk.Mezghani,Riadh.Dhaou,Andre-Luc.Beylot}@enseeiht.fr
[2] Federal University of Paraná-UFPR, Curitiba, Brazil
Michele@inf.ufpr.br

Abstract. Daily roadway commutes provide driving patterns in time
and in space motivating the formation of mobile vehicular groups based
on common backgrounds and interests. These groups can be used to
reduce the propagation of irrelevant and redundant information and can
be used also for group-based applications such as caravaning. This paper
investigates the groups formation behavior under the dynamic topology
of vehicular networks through different traces and synthetic scenarios.
Next, to show the impact of group on content dissemination scheduling,
a comparison of group-based scheduling with other relevant data dissemination scheduling schemes is conducted by simulations in terms of delivery ratio and latency. Simulation results show that groups can be used in
order to share information in an intelligent way such that to reduce the
propagation of irrelevant and redundant information. Additionally, this
paper shows that group-based data dissemination can enhance the delivery ratio and latency compared to other relevant scheduling schemes.

1 Introduction

The advent of mobile technologies promotes the great use of mobile devices
such as smartphones, PDAs and On-Board Units (OBUs). The growing ubiquity
has been employed to characterize roadway commutes driving patterns. Also, it
has motivated the formation of mobile vehicular communities, called Vehicular
Social Networks (VSNs) [1] composed of commutes' devices temporarily grouped
by their user's common backgrounds and interests.

Understanding the dynamics of the vehicular environment and their existing
patterns is essential to strategically disseminate relevant information to users
and propose mechanisms for network or service adaptation [2]. Vehicular networks are highly mobile and in a short period many changes may occur in the
environment, such as the neighborhood can quickly change; communication networks may become available or unavailable, and user groups can appear or dis-
appear. Content dissemination in these networks is a challenge mainly due to the
opportunistic communication between vehicles and the weaknesses on wireless
connectivity. Nodes interact when they meet geographically, thus, they have only

© Institute for Computer Sciences, Social Informatics and Telecommunications Engineering 2014
N. Mitton et al. (Eds.): ADHOCNETS 2014, LNICST 140, pp. 3–14, 2014.
DOI: 10.1007/978-3-319-13329-4_1

a partial view of the network, making hard routing and dissemination decisions. Furthermore, wireless communication technologies present constraints making some solutions infeasible because they cause an excessive overhead for the network, e.g. the Epidemic protocol [3].

Groups formation can be useful for content dissemination in vehicular networks. In one hand, groups can be used to share information in an intelligent way such that to reduce the propagation of irrelevant and redundant information. In the other hand, several applications in vehicular networks such as caravaning, collaborative gaming, platooning, and so on [4,5] require connectivity between groups of vehicles in which users can communicate among them. Works on the literature define groups in such environment where vehicles communicate using the well-known centralized entities. For instance, in [6], authors developed a prototype for voice chat groups which enables drivers in the same location and time to communicate using voice messages. However, such a centralized communication mechanism may cause high latencies and also cannot work in ares poorly covered (e.g. rural areas). Other approaches define clustering algorithms where a clusterhead is elected in order to manage the group.

In this work, two definitions of group are used for the evaluation. First, a group is defined based on the notion of clique in the network graph. Each vehicle is in direct contact with all other nodes in the same group. Second, to compare group-based scheduling with other scheduling schemes, group is defined as a set of vehicles sharing common interest.

This paper evaluates first the viability and behavior of group formation in vehicular networks. This evaluation is performed under different traffic scenarios considering real traces and synthetic models. The group formation is evaluated in terms of vehicles density, group size and group lifetime. Analysis results show that under high traffic, vehicular groups can be used to enhance the performance of content dissemination. Next, simulations are conducted to compare group-based content dissemination scheduling with other relevant scheduling schemes in term of delivery ratio and latency. Results show that group-based dissemination scheduling can achieve better latency as well as delivery ratio comparing to other schemes. Finally, this paper addresses user satisfaction under vehicular social networks (VSNs) to promote the progress in the state-of-te-art of content dissemination in VSNs.

This paper proceeds as follows. Section 2 presents a review of related work aiming to show the unique position of this paper. The evaluation results of vehicular groups' formation under the dynamic behavior of vehicular networks are presented in Section 3. A comparison of group-based content dissemination scheduling with other relevant scheduling schemes is described in Section 4. Section 5 discusses the importance of user satisfaction in VSNs. Section 6 concludes the paper.

2   Related Works

In vehicular network, nodes move very quickly, reducing their contact duration (duration they are within the range of each other) and constraining data transmission. There are several attempts to measure the contact duration and other behaviors in vehicular networks, such as neighboring dynamics [7,8]. Precisely characterizing nodes or even commutes patterns can assist in data delivery, even though there is no guarantee that a route is available for data delivery. In face of these challenges, few approaches have followed a different perspective applying Delay Tolerant Network (DTN) protocols, such as Epidemic [9] and MaxProp [10], envisioning to improve data dissemination without characterizing network behavior. These protocols are, in general, based on broadcasting routing, assuming that a large number of copies of the same message can increase the probability of successful message delivery. Their main purpose is to optimize delivery delay, delivery ratio and minimize resource utilization. These solutions achieve valuable results. However, they are very resource consuming, leading to a rapid saturation of the mobile nodes buffer, as well as the network bandwidth.

Recently, group communication has been studied in the context of vehicular networks. Some of these works has been explored using the permanent connectivity of centralized server [1,6,11,12]. In [6], authors proposed a group-based voice communication that allows drivers to join chat groups defined a priori based on location and time at a centralized server. RoadSpeak uses the cellular network and cannot work otherwise. These works define groups based on common interests and users join these groups to share information. Unfortunately, these works rely on permanent availability of a central server, which manages interactions between drivers. Hence, even communications between drivers in the same vicinity need to pass through an intermediate (i.e. the central server), in which a direct communication link can be created. Furthermore, cellular network-based systems can easily overload the network and they cannot be used in poorly covered areas. Other works focus on group communications in vehicular networks based on clustering [13] where a clusterhead is chosen to manage the connection between the members of a group.

First, to understand the behavior of groups formed based on location and time, this work defines the group based on the notion of clique in the network graph. Each vehicle is in direct contact with all other nodes in the same group. Second, to show the impact of vehicular groups on content dissemination scheduling, this paper defines group as a set of vehicles defined as destination. This paper analyses the impact of group formation only on adhoc WIFI links between nodes (i.e. V2V communications).

3   Evaluation of Groups Formation in Vanets

Groups can be used to enhance content dissemination in vehicular networks. Groups can be used to share information in an intelligent way such that to reduce the propagation of irrelevant and redundant information. Further, several applications in vehicular networks such as caravaning, collaborative gaming, platooning, and so on require connectivity between groups of vehicles in which users can communicate among them. However, vehicular groups can suffer from short-lived links due to the highly mobile vehicles communications and the intermittent connectivity. Thus, in order to understand groups behavior in vehicular networks and conduct an informed design of content dissemination methods between vehicles, it is of great importance to evaluate the formation of vehicular groups in terms of density, frequency and lifetime. For this purpose, this evaluation is conducted under various real traces and synthetic traces. The Network Simulator NS-3 [14] and the traffic simulator SUMO [15] are both employed in order to set up Scenario1 as follows.

Scenario1 (on a short period - 180 seconds):
In order to present the network dynamics, simulations are limited to a short period. 20 vehicles are selected randomly and the transmission range is set to 250 meters. Each node sends periodically a discovery message (i.e. beacon message) which contains information about the node such as the identifier (ID) for neighboring discovery. When vehicles meet opportunistically, neighbors which present the nodes directly connected between them can form a group. This section defines the group as a set of nodes that are in the range of each other as shown in Fig. 1, it corresponds to the notion of clique in the network graph.

To study the traffic road impact on the stability of groups in vehicular networks, different traces and mobility patterns are considered using high and low traffic.

- Real vehicle traffic, based on two real traces (trace 1 and trace 2) under high and low traffic already generated from different cities [16]
- Random vehicle traffic, generated in real-world map extracted from a map of the OpenStreetMap tool [17], in which two mobility model (model 1 and model 2) using high and low traffic are produced by the traffic generator SUMO.

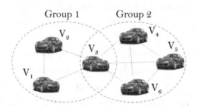

Fig. 1. Clique-based group

Scenario1 intends to analyze network density variation and show its impact on group formation, verifies the dynamic and viability of physical groups considering metrics as number of nodes per group, number of groups each node participates in, and group lifetime. The next subsections present the results.

3.1   Network Density Variation

The normalized density is calculated as the proportion of actual connections to the maximum of potential connections. The variation of the density is shown in Fig. 2, and the average values are given in Table 1. The density of nodes tends to vary more under the random mobility than under real traces. The different graphs show that the density varies with time and show sometimes

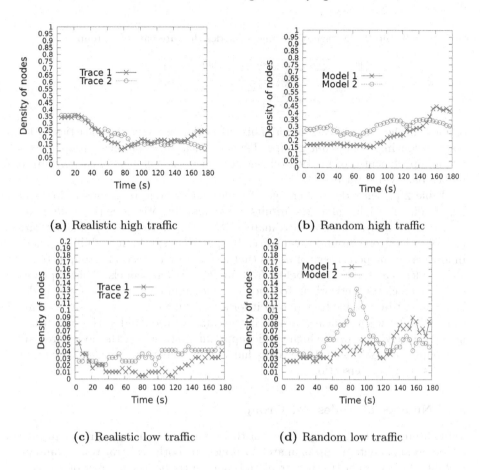

(a) Realistic high traffic   **(b)** Random high traffic

(c) Realistic low traffic   **(d)** Random low traffic

Fig. 2. Normalized density variation

Table 1. Average normalized density

Average normalized density		Low density	High density
Real vehicle traffic	Trace 1	0.019	0.21
	Trace 2	0.034	0.21
Random vehicle traffic	Model 1	0.047	0.23
	Model 2	0.058	0.3

peaks. This is explained by the fact that vehicles meet at intersections (i.e. the density increases) and then spread again all over the map (i.e. the density decreases). Average values of density are shown in Table 1.

3.2 Network Partition into Physical Groups

In order to assess if user groups based on their spatial dependence could assist to interactions between neighbor nodes on data dissemination, the network nodes are partitioned into several physical groups. A physical group is defined as a set

Table 2. Average percentage of nodes that are part of a group

Percentage of nodes that are part of group (%)		Low density	High density
Real vehicle traffic	Trace 1	31	85
	Trace 2	48	91
Random vehicle traffic	Model 1	50	91
	Model 2	57	91

of nodes in the range of each other. This subsection analyses the statistics about nodes belonging to the same groups. The identification of physical groups allows setting up efficient coordination schemes between the members of each group to reduce bandwidth waste.

Table 2 presents the percentage of nodes that belong to groups in low and high traffic. In high traffic, the results are similar in both cases (i.e. traces and synthetic models), where approximately 88% (respectively 91%) of nodes are part of at least one group in real traces (respectively synthetic mobility model). In low traffic the percentage of nodes that are part of at least one group is below 48% under real traces, and below 57% under random models. This explains, in low traffic, the network is fragmented, the communication between nodes being almost impossible to maintain it for a long time (i.e. a low density making connection between vehicles, present in the same location and at the same time, happens rarely). As for the high traffic, approximately 90% of the nodes are part of groups (i.e. vehicles in dense roads have more probability to encounter other vehicles such in intersection).

3.3   Number of Nodes Per Group

Table 3 presents the average values of the number of nodes per group. In high traffic, groups contain approximately 4 nodes for both real traces and random mobility. In low traffic, for both real and random traffic, the number of nodes in a group is fairly constant (almost time 2 and sometimes 3). Which means that a group is usually formed just between two vehicles that meet opportunistically.

Table 3. Average number of nodes per group

Average number of nodes per group		Low density	High density
Real vehicle traffic	Trace 1	2.04	3.87
	Trace 2	2.23	3.78
Random vehicle traffic	Model 1	2.13	3.96
	Model 2	2.28	4.28

3.4   Number of Groups Per Node

Tables 4 and 5 presents the average number of total formed groups and the average number of groups per node, respectively. In low traffic, most of the nodes are part of only one group at the same time. Moreover, the total number of groups is less than 6 under the random models and less than 4 with the traces. In the previous subsection, results show that there are approximately 2 nodes per group in low traffic. Therefore, in low traffic (e.g. rural roadways) it

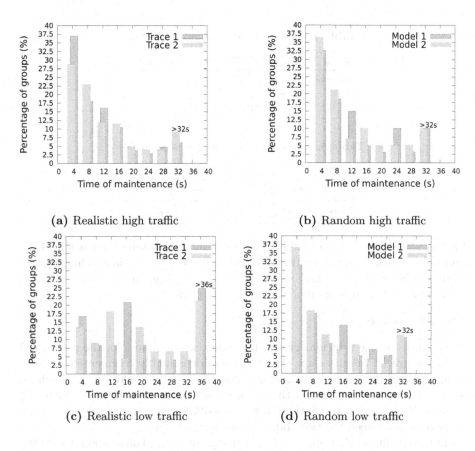

Fig. 3. Normalized density variation

is not efficient to create vehicular groups since most of the communications are between just two vehicles. Thus, a simple coordination between the two vehicles is sufficient.

In high traffic, as an average value, a node can be part of one or two groups in the same time. The results from the previous subsection show that a group contains 4 nodes. Thus, in the high traffic, a node can be in contact with 3 or with 6 nodes (i.e. a node is part of 2 groups and each group contains 4 nodes). If the node is part of 2 groups containing 4 nodes each, then it is in contact with 6 nodes. Additionally, there are more than 8 groups with random mobility and real traces. Hence, in high traffic, formation of groups can be useful to enhance content dissemination algorithms in vehicular networks if they are maintained for enough time.

3.5   Group Lifetime

The lifetime of a group gives an estimation of the maximal duration for data dissemination within the same group. Fig. 3 shows the groups lifetime for Scenario1.

Table 4. Average number of groups: Total

Average number of groups		Low density	High density
Real vehicle traffic	Trace 1	3	8
	Trace 2	4	9
Random vehicle traffic	Model 1	6	8
	Model 2	5	8

Table 5. Average number of groups per node

Average number of groups per node		Low density	High density
Real vehicle traffic	Trace 1	1.02	1.56
	Trace 2	1.00	1.49
Random vehicle traffic	Model 1	1.27	1.66
	Model 2	1.15	1.92

Results show that in high traffic there are groups maintained for a long time comparing to the simulation time. Additionally, the figure shows that groups' lifetime using real traces and mobility model are close. In low density, Fig. 3 shows also that groups are maintained for a long time.

3.6 Discussion

The analysis on the vehicular groups point out two key issues for the next work:

In low traffic, results show that the network is highly fragmented. Indeed, almost half of the vehicles are not in contact with other vehicle (i.e. a vehicle is not part of any group). Further, almost all groups formed contains just 2 vehicles. Hence, in low traffic there is no necessity to create groups since a simple coordination between the two nodes is sufficient.

In high traffic, evaluation shows that groups are formed often and almost 90% of the nodes are part of at least one group. Moreover, groups contains usually 4 nodes (average). Some nodes are part of 2 groups in the same time, thus, these nodes can be used to aid the inter-groups communication. Additionally, several groups are maintained for enough time compared to the simulation time. Thus, the formation of groups can be used to share information in an intelligent way such that to reduce the propagation of irrelevant and redundant information. Also these results promote the development of group-based applications such as caravaning, collaborative gaming that require connectivity between group of vehicles.

4   Comparison of Group-Based Scheduling with Other Scheduling Schemes

Basically, users that form a group to interact between them share common interests. Thus, users with common interests join the same group [6], and then they can socialize and exchange information when they meet opportunistically. This section investigates the impact of group-based scheduling compared to other scheduling schemes representative from the literature, under different data dissemination algorithms as Epidemic and MaxProp.

The main purpose of data dissemination algorithms in vehicular networks is to maximize the delivery ratio and minimize the latency between the source and destination. We compare the performance of Epidemic and MaxProp schemes under different packet forward scheduling. The most employed packet forward scheduling in the literature have been employed, as FIFO (First in First Out) and priority to the smallest packet. Therefore, this section analyses a hypothetical packet forward scheduling that gives priority to groups. For the analysis presented in this section, the ONE (Opportunistic Network Environment) [18] simulator is employed in order to set up Scenario2 as follows.

Scenario2 (on a long period - 12 hours):
An urban area of 4500m × 3500m has been chosen for these evaluations. The scenario considers 70 nodes equipped with a short-range wireless communication device, i.e. on board unit (OBU) or a smart-phone, to detect other users' devices and to communicate or share content. For the sake of simplicity, vehicles are divided into three different types: car, buses, and pedestrians in order to create different groups. Each type follows a specific mobility model appropriate for the node type. The different groups are set with features significantly closer to reality. The first type contains 40 cars that follow a synthetic mobility model [19] with a speed varying in the range of 10~50 km/h. The second type comprises 10 buses that follow a deterministic mobility model with an average speed of 10~37 km/h and stop periodically during 10~30 seconds of pause time. Finally, 20 pedestrians move randomly with an average speed of 1.8~5.4 km/h over the entire surface of the map. The node's transmission range is set to 250 m and the transmission speed is set to 2.5 Mbps. Simulations are conducted over various buffer sizes (2~20 Mb), and packet size (10~100 KB). Packets are generated randomly over random nodes each period of time in the range of $[25s, 35s]$. The TTL is set to 120 minutes.

For the group-based scheduling, each group has an identifier; pedestrians 0, cars 1, and buses 2. In the simulation, packets are assigned a priority, i.e. packets are generated with different identifier (i.e. 0, 1, or 2). When nodes encounter, using group-based scheduling, each node sends first the packets containing the same identifier as its group, then it continues sending other packets (i.e. prioritize packets that are assigned for nodes from the same group. Three scheduling schemes are compared: Packet size priority, FIFO, and groups priority. The following subsections investigate the influence of groups on data dissemination compared to other packet forward scheduling schemes. Investigations apply the delivery ratio and latency metrics for the evaluation. The delivery ratio is computed as the ratio of successfully delivered packets to the total number of packets at the end of the simulation.

4.1   Results

Fig. 4 and Fig. 5 presents the delivery ratio and latency for the different scheduling schemes under the Epidemic routing and MaxProp routing, respectively.

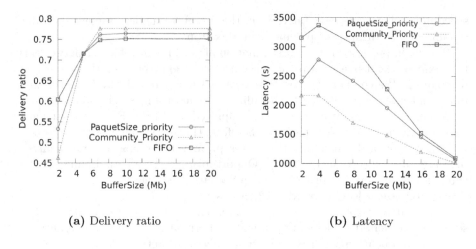

(a) Delivery ratio   **(b)** Latency

Fig. 4. Different scheduling schemes with Epidemic

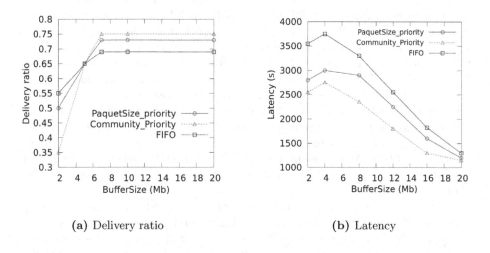

(a) Delivery ratio   **(b)** Latency

Fig. 5. Different scheduling schemes with Maxprop

Fig. 4a and Fig. 5a show that group-based priority shows an improvement over the other schemes when the buffer size is more than 5Mb, while for a low buffer capacity (less than 5Mb), group-based scheduling realizes less delivery ratio compared to other schemes. This technique allows prioritizing a group whose packets are ignored because of few contacts with the rest of the nodes. Additionally, with a large buffer capacity, the packet size priority is better than FIFO. This is because it allows the transmission of more packets during the short contact period between nodes. The most significant improvement is in terms of latency as shown in Fig. 4b and Fig. 5b. Using group priority, the packets arrive to destination faster compared to packet size priority and FIFO. As the buffer size increases, the latency decreases and the difference between the differences schemes decreases. This is because, with a small buffer capacity, a node has to send the appropriate packets in a limited contact duration before the packets are dropped due the limited buffer. Therefore, group-based scheduling schemes can improve the content dissemination and it has the same behavior under different routing protocol. Moreover, group-based dissemination enables users to share content that they are interesting first. Thus, it maximally satisfy users interests compared to other scheduling schemes that ignore the relations between users.

5   Towards Satisfying User Interests in VSN

Recently, vehicular social networks (VSNs) [1] have attracted tremendous interests in the context of opportunistic networks. Several works [2,8] have investigated social network in vehicular networks dissemination targeting to optimize both delivery ratio and fan-out delay. Such as the work in [2], authors proposed an opportunistic data forwarding scheme, named ZOOM, for fast routing. They integrate both contact-level and social-level in order to predict future contact and select the best relays. These works achieve valuable results. Unfortunately, most of them do not consider an important criterion: **user interests**. Even though these dissemination protocols can reach noticeable performance in terms of delivery ratio and delay, they might not be able to maximally satisfy users' preferences.

Those studies consider information as a black box, without handling the user's interest in the content. They consider a single type of object while there are different types of information such as traffic information and restaurant recommendation that need to be accommodated by a VSN.

VSNs constitute an environment where a large amounts of content are being generated every day. Users are seldom interested in all these content; they only want a small part of the information. Moreover, connections between vehicles in a VSN exist only during a very short period, allowing users to exchange a limited volume of data. Therefore, there is an increasing demand for efficient content dissemination in VSNs that takes user interests into consideration and that is designed to maximally satisfy user preferences. An efficient content dissemination protocol has to manage: which content objects to forward? how to schedule these objects? Additionally, there is a need for performance criterion (i.e. quantitative metric to compute how much users are satisfied) different from the classic metrics to evaluate dissemination protocols.

6   Conclusion

In this paper, we investigate the impact of traffic dynamics on temporary group creation in vehicular networks based on realistic traces and synthetic mobility models, to better understand groups behavior in vehicular networks. The analysis shows that in high traffic scenario groups can be formed with enough nodes and are maintained enough time allowing its members to communicate and share information between them. Thus, groups can be used in high traffic for groups-based applications or to enhance the content dissemination in vehicular networks. Next, we evaluate the impact of group-based scheduling on content dissemination under different routing protocols. Results show that the use of group provide, using enough buffer capacity, better results in term of latency and delivery ratio. Moreover, group-based content dissemination enables to maximize the satisfaction for users since it divide users sharing common interests in different groups. Finally, a new vision that targets on maximally satisfying user interests (specific for comfort applications) is discussed. Future works may lead us to propose an innovate protocol that exploits the formation of group based on common spatio-temporal and common interests between vehicles.

References

1. Smaldone, S., et al.: RoadSpeak : Enabling Voice Chat on Roadways using Vehicular Social Networks, SocialNets (2008)
2. Zhu, H., et al.: ZOOM: Scaling the Mobility for Fast Opportunistic Forwarding in Vehicular Networks. In: Proc. INFOCOM, pp. 2832–2840 (2013)
3. Vahdat, A., Becker, D.: Epidemic Routing for Partially-Connected Ad Hoc Networks, Duke University Technical Report (2000)
4. Kuklinski, S., Wolny, G.: CARAVAN: a context-aware architecture for VANET. Applications. In: Tech, Ad-Hoc Networks (2011)
5. Gerla, M., Kleinrock, L.: Vehicular networks and the future of the mobile internet. Computer Networks **55**(2), 457–469 (2011)
6. Han, L., Smaldone, S., Shankar, P., Boyce, J., Iftode, L.: Ad-hoc Voice-based Group Communication, In: Proc. IEEE PerCom, pp. 190–198 (2009)
7. Raw, R., et al.: Comprehensive Study of Estimation of Path Duration in Vehicular Ad Hoc Network, ACITY (2), pp. 309–317 (2012)
8. Qin, J., et al.: POST: Exploiting Dynamic Sociality for Mobile Advertising in Vehicular Networks. In: Proc. INFOCOM (2014)
9. Tian, D., et al.: Optimal epidemic broadcasting for vehicular ad hoc networks, International Journal of Communication Systems (2014)
10. Burgess, J., et al.: MaxProp: Routing for vehicle-Based Disruption-Tolerant Networks. In: Proceedings INFOCOM, pp. 1–11 (2006)
11. WAZE. https://www.waze.com/
12. Sha,W., et al.: Social Vehicle Navigation: Integrating Shared Driving Experience into Vehicle Navigation, ACM HotMobile 2013 (2013)
13. Di Felice, M., Bedogni, L., Bononi, L.: Group communication on highways: An evaluation study of geocast protocols and applications. Ad Hoc Networks **11**(3), 818–832 (2013)
14. Network Simulator NS3. http://www.nsnam.org/
15. SUMO. http://sumo-sim.org/
16. Vehicular traces. http://www.lst.inf.ethz.ch/research/ad-hoc/car-traces/
17. Open Street Map. http://www.openstreetmap.org/#map=5/51.509/7.603
18. Keränen, A., Ott, J., Kärkkäinen, T.: The ONE Simulator for DTN Protocol Evaluation, SIMUTools (2009)
19. Keränen, A., et al.: Simulating Mobility and DTNs with the ONE. Journal of Communications **52**, 92–105 (2010)

Traffic-Aware Access-Points Deployment Strategies for VANETS

Amine Kchiche[✉] and Farouk Kamoun

ENSI CRISTAL Lab, University of Manouba, Manouba 2010, Tunisia
amin.kchiche@gmail.com, farouk.kamoun@sesame.com.tn

Abstract. Using WLAN-hotspots to provide access to mobile users has proven its feasibility and interest in many cases such as mesh and vehicular networks. Nevertheless, VANETs are still looking for deployment strategies that would ensure a maximum data exchange and a well balanced access. The high mobility and density of users and the impossibility to provide a full coverage make such requirements a hard challenge.

In this paper we make a quick review of the commonly used deployment schemes and show their limits regarding real VANETs constraints. We analyze the deployment problem taking into account the vehicular density and the resulting contention problem. We formalize the problem and provide a centrality-based deployment aiming a global service-access optimization and a p-center based deployment aiming fairness as a second objective. We evaluate through simulation the performance of our proposed schemes and show their efficiency and benefits in comparison to other deployment strategies.

Keywords: VANET · AccessPoint deployment · Coverage problem

1 Introduction

VANET is best known for V2V (vehicle-to-vehicle) communications; Nevertheless, many recent studies revealed the importance of V2I (vehicle-to-infrastructure) communication not only as a gateway to external resources (internet access, content sharing...) but also as an indispensable support for V2V communication. The Drive-Thru-Internet [1] was one of the first projects which evoked and demonstrated the feasibility of such communication even at high speed. Thenceforth, many projects showed the benefits of using V2I communication in many application field such as traffic congestion monitoring, accident tracking, Geo-Routing support and many others [2]. Developing dedicated deployment strategies becomes hence essential.

In this paper we provide an overview of, so far, proposed deployment strategies for VANETs. We show that most of them reveal to be ineffective since neglecting the contention problem caused by vehicular density.

In the second part we introduce a novel view of the coverage problem for VANETs and define more accurate and effective deployment objectives.

© Institute for Computer Sciences, Social Informatics and Telecommunications Engineering 2014
N. Mitton et al. (Eds.): ADHOCNETS 2014, LNICST 140, pp. 15–26, 2014.
DOI: 10.1007/978-3-319-13329-4_2

The third part of this paper, introduces a composed model which takes into account vehicular density and traffic load followed by a detailed analysis to address both global optimization and fairness requirement. We show through theoretical analysis that the deployment problem could be reduced to an evolved form of centrality-based classification for the global optimization and a complex form of the *p-center* problem [3] for the fairness consideration. Based on this model, we develop two deployment strategies aiming at efficiency and fairness.

Finally, we evaluate in paragraph 4 the performance of our deployment schemes and show that they perform significantly better than random deployment and other centrality-based strategies, confirming hence the theoretical analysis.

2   Overview of Deployment Strategies

Many ITS projects have integrated the use of access points [2,4] to provide internet access or any kind of sharing and communication services, unfortunately without any care for the choice of their location and the impact it could have on the efficiency and validity of their results.

Several works have progressively tried to address the VANET access-point deployment problem. Using open Wifi, was a starting point for such efforts [4,5]. Many works used then the intuitive idea of placing APs on intersections as to improve the number of covered vehicles [2,6,7].

A better and deeper understanding of the role of infrastructure on application level pushed researchers then to develop application-oriented schemes such as those presented in [8] and [9]. In the first work [8], a cooperative downloading scenario was intended. The deployment aimed at maximizing the potential for collaboration among vehicles i.e., the probability of meeting between downloader and prospective carriers of information. In the second work [9], AP-positions were selected with regards to the benefit (i.e. time saving), vehicles may gain from the knowledge of real-time road traffics.

Works [6] and [10] formulated the problem in a more abstract way. The first work [6], formulates the problem as a Maximum Coverage Problem (MCP) [11], so as to maximize the number of vehicles that get in contact with deployed access points. The second work [10] tries to ensure a regular contact opportunity at maximal pre-configured distance. A deployment provides a so-called 'α-coverage' of distance α if any path in F (set of paths) is covered by at least one access point. The authors modeled the problem as a vertex multicut problem whose solution corresponds to the sought after access point locations.

Despite the importance of all these efforts, most of them are reducing the coverage notion to a simple meeting opportunity (for vehicles) [6–9] or even to a belonging-test (to streets which are then considered to be well covered!) [10,12,13]. In spite of the idea of [12] and [13] to account for the distance, the relative position and the time spent in contact with the access point in order to get a better evaluation of the quality of the *opportunity* metric, we think that considering any "contact" with an access point as an 'opportunity' to establish an appropriate communication is unfortunately untrue in VANET conditions.

It is well known that the wireless channel is shared among all participants and could be even inaccessible in contention scenarios. Such a deployment scheme is hence only relevant and valuable in low density environments.

The problem was thus reduced to a simple geographical coverage by having overlooked the traffic load and the vehicular density and the resulting contention they may cause in such type of communication.

In a recent study, F.MA et al. [14] attempted to address the contention problem by proposing a modeling that prohibits simultaneous communications of neighboring nodes and evaluates the proposed deployment strategy based on the aggregate throughput instead of a simple metric. In spite of this important step towards a consistent and coherent modeling of the deployment problem, we think that a more abstract and application-independent model should be used. In fact the last work gets around the problem of contention by presenting a model which prohibits concurrent communications. Apart from pure dissemination-oriented scenarios, where access points broadcast application-related information to vehicles, concurrent communications do exist and do affect the average throughput of the whole system and should be therefore taken into account instead of being pushed aside.

In the next paragraph we will redefine the concept of coverage for VANETs and formalize the problem in such a way to take into account the key factors contributing to the fulfillment of a valuable deployment scheme.

3   The Coverage Problem

The above presented approaches may be relevant in download direction (dissemination scenarios) where density does not much affect the overall data transfer. They are, however, unsuitable for upload scenarios and could even be counterproductive because they do not take interference and contention problem into account. In the rest of our work, we will thus consider the difficult side of the problem namely the optimization of the deployment with regard to the upload direction.

In the following, we present a model which focuses on this aspect and allow us to move from a loose metric 'the contact opportunity' to a very precise metric "the data volume" and from global scenarios to two tailored scenarios with different constraints.

Definition 1. *A trip t, is a Set of successively connected edges; so for a graph G(V, E) representing the roads plan, $t = \{e_i; e_i \in E\}$ We note thereby the set of predefined considered trips as π.*

Definition 2. *A deployment provides a maximum coverage, if the average data volume (in the uplink direction) is maximized (global optimisation) for the overall considered trips or if possible for each considered trip (fairness consideration).*

This new formulation of the problem reveals the importance of vehicle traffic and data traffic incorporation in the deployment problem. In order to take these factors in consideration, we propose the following modeling:

1. We are considering a predefined set of trips denoted by π (where π_{AB}^k, is the kth considered trip between A and B).
2. A set of candidate deployment positions is given, denoted S_{AP}
3. We consider an average vehicle traffic of γ_{AB}^k veh/sec on each trip π_{AB}^k.
4. We consider an average data traffic load of λ packets/s for each vehicle.
5. We are only considering traffic in the uplink direction (V2I).

The first assumption reflects the fact that vehicle-traffic is usually a mixture of vehicle flows driven by origin to destination paradigm [15,16]. The third point applies different traffic arrival rates for the considered trips which truly maps the real state on roads. As it is stated by the last assumption, we will focus on the uplink traffic as it fully accounts for the contention problem we are trying to address.

Based on these assumptions, the following definitions and theorems will lead us to formalize the problem and to define valuable objective functions.

Lemma 1 (Average Density). *Let $\eta(i)$ denote the average number of vehicles in the range of access point (i). Applying little's law and summing the different traffics of vehicles passing through (i), we get the following result:*

$$\eta(i) = \sum_{\pi_{AB}^k, i \in \pi_{AB}^k} \frac{2r}{v_i} * \gamma_{AB}^k \tag{1}$$

r being the radius of the communication zone and v_i the average vehicle velocity within the communication zone of (i).

The traffic load generated by each vehicle being equal to λ packets/s, the total offered load for an access point (i) is then defined as:

$$\lambda_i^{Total} = \lambda * \eta(i) \tag{2}$$

Theorem 1. $\mathcal{TH}(i, v)$ *being the effective throughput offered to a vehicle v in the range of the access point (i), $\mathcal{TH}(i, v)$ depends only on the access point position (under constant vehicular density in its communication zone).*

Proof. Bianchi [17] showed that the effective throughput per vehicle $\mathcal{TH}(i, v)$ depends only on the total offered load and the number of contending stations. Or, the total offered load for an access point (i), noted λ_i^{total}, depends only from the position of that access point (Eq. 2) and of the average number of contending vehicles in its range. This last one depends in our case also only on the access point position (lemma 1); So the average effective throughput depends only on the access point position. We note it for simplicity $\mathcal{TH}(i, v) = \mathcal{TH}_i$.

Hence, knowing the vehicle traffic, we can deduce the effective throughput for each candidate access point position (formally [17,18], experimentally or by simulation as we did). The corresponding vector (to S_{AP}) is noted $\mathcal{TH}_{AP}$.

Based on this estimation, we can now calculate the average data volume per km $\mathcal{NB}(\pi^k_{AB})$ that could be sent from a vehicle taking a Trip π^k_{AB} from A to B through a set of chosen access-points noted AP:

$$\mathcal{NB}(\pi^k_{AB}) = \frac{1}{|\pi^k_{AB}|} \sum_{i \in AP} (\mathcal{TH}_i * \frac{2r}{v_i}) * \chi_{\pi^k_{AB}}(i)$$

$$\text{with} \quad \chi_{\pi^k_{AB}}(i) = \begin{cases} 0 \text{ if } i \notin \pi^k_{AB} \\ 1 \text{ if } i \in \pi^k_{AB} \end{cases}$$

This formulation reflects the simple fact that a vehicle will have the opportunity to send data through each access point belonging to the trajectory of its trip from A to B assuming an effective throughput of $\mathcal{TH}(i)$ along the communication zone. This value is then normalized over the trip length (noted $|\pi^k_{AB}|$).

We can now define the average data volume per km that can be successfully sent by a vehicle taking a trip on the network as $\mathcal{NB}(F)$:

$$\mathcal{NB}(F) = \sum_{p \in \pi} \frac{\gamma_p}{\gamma_{total}} * \mathcal{NB}(p) \text{ with } p = \pi^k_{AB}. \tag{3}$$

where γ_{total} represents the total arrival rate for the whole network (all considered trips: $\gamma_{total} = \sum_{p \in \pi} \gamma_p$. This average is obtained by considering the vehicle traffic rate for each trip.

The deployment problem being now well formalized, we can henceforth tackle the optimization problem. In the following two sections, we investigate the global optimization version and the fairness version of the deployment problem.

3.1 Global Optimization

In this section the following problem is considered: given a set of candidate access-point positions S_{AP}, we are looking for the optimal subset of p positions AP^* that maximizes $\mathcal{NB}(F)$.

Theorem 2. *The optimal set of p positions that maximizes $\mathcal{NB}(F)$ is the set having the maximal group betweeness centrality.*

Proof. According to equation (3)

$$\mathcal{NB}(F) = \frac{1}{\gamma_{total}} \sum_{p \in \pi} \{ \frac{\gamma_p}{|p|} \sum_{i \in AP} (Th_i * \frac{2r}{v_i}) * \chi_p(i) \}$$

$$= \frac{1}{\gamma_{total}} \sum_{p \in \pi} \frac{\gamma_p}{|p|} \{ \sum_{i \in AP} \mathcal{C}_i * \chi_p(i) \} \tag{4}$$

with $\mathcal{C}_i = Th_i * \frac{2r}{v_i}$ which only depends on the access point position (Theorem 1 and r being constant).

The obtained form (Eq. 4) corresponds to a scaled group betweeness central-ity [19] defined in its simplest length-scaled form [20] for a subset $G \in V$ as

$$C_B(G) = \sum_{s,t \in V} \frac{1}{dist(s,t)} \frac{\sigma(s,t|G)}{\sigma(s,t)}$$

where the numerator $(\sigma(s,t|G))$ counts the number of shortest $(s,t) - paths$ containing any vertex of G as an inner vertex.

In our case, paths are restricted to the set π and not limited to shortest paths, so group betweeness can be written in a more general weighted form:

$$C_B(G) = \sum_{p \in \pi} \frac{\gamma_p}{|p|} \chi_p(G) \quad \text{where } \chi_p(G) = \begin{cases} 1 \text{ if p contains any vertex of G} \\ 0 \qquad\qquad \text{otherwise} \end{cases}$$

This formulation reflects the social consideration that connections of the group to other members are counted once. This is in our case not true, as each member (access point) contributes to the group by its own connection (repre-sented by C_i in our model) even to the same client.

We can hence extend the group betweeness definition by redefining:

$$\chi_p(G) = \sum_{i \in G} C_i * \chi_p(i) \quad \text{with } \chi_p(i) = \begin{cases} 1 \text{ if i belongs to p} \\ 0 \quad \text{otherwise} \end{cases}$$

Finally we obtain : $C_B(AP) = \sum_{p \in \pi} \frac{\gamma_p}{|p|} \sum_{i \in AP} C_i * \chi_p(i)$ which corresponds to $\mathcal{NB}(F)$ confirming hence Theorem 2.

The next theorem will allow us to shift toward individual betweeness to avoid the complexity of group betweeness algorithms which are difficult to scale [21].

Theorem 3. *The optimal set of* p *positions that maximizes* $\mathcal{NB}(F)$ *is the set of* p *positions with the highest betweeness centralities.*

Proof. Coming back to equation (4) and considering the maximum:

$$\max_{AP \subset S_{AP}} (\mathcal{NB}(F)) = \frac{1}{\gamma_{total}} \cdot \max_{AP \subset S_{AP}} (\sum_{p \in \pi} \{ \sum_{i \in AP} \frac{\gamma_p}{|p|} * C_i * \chi_p(i) \})$$

$$= \frac{1}{\gamma_{total}} \cdot \max_{AP \subset S_{AP}} (\sum_{i \in AP} \{ \sum_{p \in \pi} \frac{\gamma_p}{|p|} * C_i * \chi_p(i) \}) \quad \text{commutative property}$$

$$= \frac{1}{\gamma_{total}} \cdot \sum_{k=0..p} \max_{i_k \in S_{AP}} (\sum_{p \in \pi} \frac{\gamma_p}{|p|} * C_{i_k} * \chi_p(i_k)) \quad \text{independance of the max operands}$$

Fortunately, $\sum_{p \in \pi} \frac{\gamma_p}{|p|} * C_{i_k} * \chi_p(i_k)$ corresponds to the weighted beetweeness of the node i_k in the graph π. So we can formalize as:

$$\max_{AP \subset S_{AP}} (\mathcal{NB}(F)) = \frac{1}{\gamma_{total}} \cdot \sum_{k=0..p} \max_{i_k \in S_{AP}} \{ \mathcal{CB}_\pi(i_k) \}$$

$\mathcal{CB}_\pi(i_k)$ being the centrality betweeness of node i_k regarding the graph π.

Hence, the optimal solution (which maximizes $\mathcal{NB}(F)$) corresponds to the positions with the highest betweeness centralities.

3.2 Fairness (Maximizing the Minimal)

In this section we consider the fairness side of the problem: given a set of candidate access-point positions, we are looking for the optimal set of p positions that maximizes the minimal achievable data transmission among all trips (paths) of the considered network:

$$\max_{AP \subset S_{AP}} (\min_{p \in \pi} \mathcal{NB}(p, AP))$$

Assuming D is the distance matrix $d_{ij} := [d(ap_i, p_j)]$ which associates to each access point ap_i its distance to the path p_j defined as:

$$d(ap_i, p_j) := \mathcal{NB}(p_j, ap_i) = \frac{1}{|p_j|} * C_i * \chi_{p_j}(ap_i)$$

Definition 3. *We define and consider the following objective function:*

$$center(AP) := \min_{p_j \in \pi} \mathcal{NB}(p_j, AP) = \min_{p_j \in \pi} \sum_{i \in AP} \frac{1}{|p_j|} * C_i * \chi_{p_j}(i)$$

$$= \min_{p_j \in \pi} \sum_{i \in AP} d(ap_i, p_j)$$

$$= \min_{j=1,..,m} \sum_{i=1}^{n} d_{ij} * x_i \qquad (5)$$

n being the number of candidate access-point positions, m the number of paths to be covered and x_i the decision variable whether access point i is selected or not. Our deployment problem can be hence formulated as:

$$\max_{AP \in S_{AP}} center(AP) \quad \text{subject to:} \begin{cases} 1. & \sum_{i=1}^{n} x_i \le p \\ 2. & x_i \in \{0,1\} i = 1..n \end{cases}$$

This category of problems is known in the literature as the *'p-center localization problem'* [3] which aims in its dual form to minimize the maximal distance of a set of p service points to a set of demand points. The only difference lies in the definition of the distance metric (The sum of all distances in our case, while it is aggregated to the minimal distance in the p-center problem).

The p-center problem being classified in the NP-Hard category [22], we use the p-center heuristic proposed in [23] as a basis to determine locally optimal positions. The two-stage heuristic (Algo.1) is adapted to take into account the above mentioned difference (the definition of the distance between a client and a set of service points and the corresponding objective function).

The first stage uses a greedy approach that looks for the 1-center solution in each iteration and updates iteratively the resulting objective function. The distance matrix is updated in such a way that each column represents the 'distance' of each path to the so far chosen access point group. The obtained set is then used in the substitution stage as a starter pack.

Algorithm 1. P-center adapted Heuristic

Greedy phase : 1-Center

1: Pick the access point ap^* that maximizes the objective function: $Center(ap^*) = max_{ap_i \in S_{AP}} Center(ap_i)$ (the column that has the largest minimum)
2: Modify the distance matrix by setting $d(ap_i, p_j) = d(ap_i, p_j) + d(ap^*, p_j)$ $\forall i, j$
3: Repeat until obtaining an initial set of **p** points.

Substitution Phase

4: Let p_{min} be the least served path.
5: Pick the, not yet selected, access point ap^+ which improves at most p_{min}.
6: Look for an access point ap^- to be replaced, such that the objective function get not decreased $Center(AP \cup ap^+ \setminus ap^-) \geq center(AP)$.
7: If none found goto 5 Else replace ap^- with ap^+ and Goto 4

The second stage, tries to improve the performance for the less served routes (paths) by exchanging access points, one-by-one, until no movement of single access-points can improve the objective function.

The two-stage heuristic provides a locally optimal solution. Better results can be surely achieved using globally optimal solutions built on different exhaustive p-center heuristics and algorithms [23,24].

4 Performance Evaluation

4.1 Access-Points Throughput Estimation

To evaluate the performance of the proposed deployment schemes, we estimated in a first stage the effective throughput $\mathcal{TH}(i, v)$ offered to a vehicle v with a constant speed v_i in the range of an Access point (i) under constant density conditions. According to theorem 1, this value depends only on the vehicular density within the communication zone.

Simulation scenarios consist of an access point placed on the side of a rectilinear road. Vehicles have been injected on each trip with a fixed inter-arrival rate ranging from $2s$ to $200s$ and a fixed average speed ranging from 2.5 to $15m/s$. A CBR traffic transmitting 1250 Byte packets at a $10Mb/s$ rate has been configured on each vehicle (to ensure a maximum load). The simulator OMNET++ was configured to use the 802.11b protocol with a communication range of about $300m$ (802.11b was employed with the idea of using the widely deployed and freely accessibles Wifi Access-Points. The simulation can be, however, straightforward extended to dedicated norms for VANETs namely the 802.11p).

In Figure 1, we show the average successfully transmitted data per vehicle for different speeds ($10..15m/s$) and different inter-arrival times. The number of packets successfully received by the AP reaches its maximum for an inter-arrival-rate of about $60s$ which corresponds to a communication with no concurrent vehicles ($60s * 10m/s = 600m$ inter-distance).

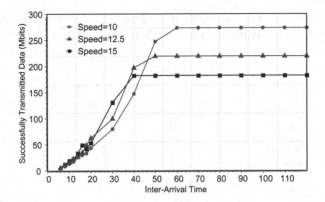

Fig. 1. Successfully Transmitted Data per Vehicle According to Inter-Arrival

The left part of the figure shows the negative impact of a high arrival rate (vehicular density) on the transmission, confirming our evaluation of deployment strategies made in paragraph 2. The speed has no direct impact on the quality of transmission but only on the duration of communication phase, which explains the constant gap between the three scenarios in the latter phase ($> 60s$).

4.2 Effective Throughput

To evaluate the proposed deployment strategies, we simulated a vehicular traffic over a $35km$ x $40km$ road-network using the SUMO simulator. Microscopic models implemented by SUMO are Krauss' car-following model [25] and Krajzewiczs lane-changing model [26] which faithfully mimic realistic driver's behavior. The macroscopic model is based on an O/D matrix [origin to destination paradigm], forming a set of about 90, randomly chosen, paths (denoted as π).

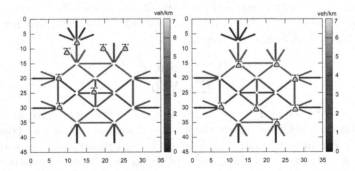

Fig. 2. Access Point Deployment Strategies (Global (left) Vs Fairness (right))

Vehicles have been injected with an average arrival rate of 1 vehicle each $200s$ on each path. Figure 2 illustrates the network topology, chosen to highlight the centrality of nodes as a key factor of our deployment strategy. Vehicular density varies up to $7veh/km$. At intersections, higher densities are obviously recorded.

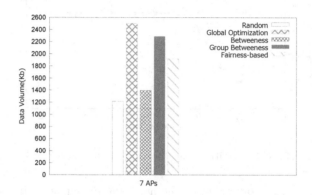

Fig. 3. Average Sent Data per Vehicle per km

Figure 3 evaluates the global approach by comparing the average amount of data successfully sent per vehicle per km according to five different deployment approaches: our approaches, denoted as *"Global"* and *"Fairness-based"* in addition to a betweeness, group-betweeness and a random based repartitions.

The 'global' approach presented in section 3.1 aiming to maximize $\mathcal{NB}(\mathcal{F})$ (the average data volume successfully sent per vehicle per km), achieves the best average value ie of $2,5Mb/km$ per vehicle. As stated in theorem 2 and 3 the 'global' deployment schema corresponds to a fine-parameterized form of the betweeness and group-betweeness centrality, which well explains the relative good performance achieved by these deployment approaches.

Fairness, being the second objective of our work, we evaluated and compared the fairness degree of the proposed deployment strategies reflected through the Jain's Fairness Index [27]. The Jain's Fairness Index of a data exchange vector $\mathcal{NB} = (\mathcal{NB}(p_1), ..., \mathcal{NB}(p_n))$ is given by:

$$\frac{(\sum_{i=1}^{n} \mathcal{NB}(p_i))^2}{n * \sum_{i=1}^{n} \mathcal{NB}(p_i)^2}$$

Intuitively, the Jain's Fairness Index of a data exchange vector is 1 if it is perfectly fair (i.e., vehicles realizes the same performances among all trips), and is $1/n$ if it is completely unfair (i.e., only one trips is covered all others are not).

Figure 4 shows that the fairness-based deployment outperforms indeed all other schemes and realizes a good performance by reaching an index of about 75% followed as expected by the group-betweeness approach, which favors as explained in 3.1 a collective behavior towards clients.

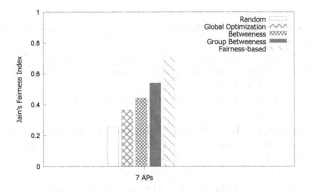

Fig. 4. Fairness Assessment for Deployment Strategies

5   Conclusion

In this article, we made a thorough review of classical coverage approaches and showed that these cannot be effective without taking into account the contention problem and without differentiating between download and upload directions.

Combining routes topology with both data and vehicle traffic, we proposed a consistent model and an accurate estimation of the average sent data among considered trips. Two objectives have been considered: maximizing the average successfully sent data and maximizing the minimal successfully sent data among different trips as a matter of fairness.

The analysis conducted us in the first case to a sophisticated form of betweeness centrality and in the second case to a complex form of the *p-center* problem. This led us to develop two deployment schemes, which demonstrated significant performance improvements in term of fairness and efficiency.

The simulation was performed using realistic mobility models and one of the most reliable simulators(SUMO). This should allow a straightforward application of our approaches on real maps and using even more realistic mobility traces.

References

1. Ott, J., Kutscher, D.: Drive-thru internet: IEEE 802.11b for automobile users. In: INFOCOM (2004)
2. Gerla, M., Zhou, B., Lee, Y.z., Soldo, F., Lee, U., Marfia, G.: Vehicular grid communications: The role of the internet infrastructure. In: 1st International Conference on Genetic Algorithms and their Applications (2006)
3. Tansel, B.C., Francis, R.L., Lowe, T.J.: Location on networks: A survey. part i: The p-center and p-median problems. Management Science (1983)
4. Marfa, G., Pau, G., De Sena, E., Giordano, E., Gerla, M.: Evaluating vehicle network strategies for downtown portland: opportunistic infrastructure and the importance of realistic mobility models. In: MobiOpp MobiSys workshop (2007)
5. Bychkovsky, V., Hull, B., Miu, A., Balakrishnan, H., Madden, S.: A measurement study of vehicular internet access using in situ wi-fi networks. MobiCom 2006 (2006)

6. Trullols, O., Barcelo-Ordinas, J.M., Fiore, M., Casetti, C., Chiasserini, C.-F.: A max coverage formulation for information dissemination in vehicular networks. In: WIMOB (2009)
7. Trullols, O., Fiore, M., Casetti, C., Chiasserini, C.F., Ordinas, J.M.B.: Planning roadside infrastructure for information dissemination in intelligent transportation systems. Computer Communications, 33
8. Fiore, M., Barcelo-Ordinas, J.M.: Cooperative download in urban vehicularnetworks. In: IEEE MASS (2009)
9. Lochert, C., Scheurman, B., Wewetzer, C., Luebke, A., Mauve, M.: Data aggregation and roadside unit placement for a vanet traffic information system. VANET (2008)
10. Zheng, Z., Sinha, P., Kumar, S.: Alpha coverage: Bounding the interconnection gap for vehicular internet access. In: INFOCOM (2009)
11. Nimrod, M., Eitan, Z., Hakimi, S.L.: The maximum coverage location problem. SIAM Journal on Algebraic and Discrete Methods, 4(2) (1983)
12. Cataldi, P., Harri, J.: User/operator utility-based infrastructure deployment strategies for vehicular networks. In: Vehicular Technology Conference (2011)
13. Liang, Y., Liu, H., Rajan, D.: Optimal placement and configuration of roadside units in vehicular networks. In: Vehicular Technology Conference (2012)
14. Malandrino, F., Casetti, C., Chiasserini, C., Fiore, M.: Content downloading in vehicular networks: What really matters. In: INFOCOM (2011)
15. Uppoor, S., Fiore, M.: Large-scale urban vehicular mobility for networking research. In: IEEE Vehicular Networking Conference (VNC) (2011)
16. Uppoor, S., Fiore, M.: Insights on metropolitan-scale vehicular mobility from a networking perspective. In: Proceedings of the 4th ACM international workshop on Hot topics in planet-scale measurement, pp. 39–44 (2012)
17. Bianchi, G., Fratta, L., Oliveri, M.: Performance evaluation and enhancement of the csma/ca mac protocol for 802.11 wireless lans. In: PIMRC'96., volume 2
18. Li, J., Blake, C., Couto, D.S.J.D., Lee, H.I., Morris, R.: Capacity of adhoc wireless networks. In: Proceedings of the 7th annual international conferenceon Mobile computing and networking, MobiCom '01
19. Everett, M.G., Borgatti, S.P.: The centrality of groups and classes. Journal of Mathematical Sociology 23(3), 181–201 (1999)
20. Brandes, U.: On variants of shortest-path betweenness centrality and their generic computation. Social Networks, 30(2) (2008)
21. Puzis, R., Elovici, Y., Dolev, S.: Fast algorithm for successive computation of group betweenness centrality. Physical Review E, 76(5) (2007)
22. Kariv, O., Hakimi, S.L.: An algorithmic approach to network location problems :the p-centers. SIAM Journal on Applied Mathematics, 37 (1979)
23. Mladenovic, N., Labbe, M., Hansen, P.: Solving the p-center problem with tabu search and variable neighborhood search. Networks, 42
24. Elloumi, S., Labbé, M., Pochet, Y.: A new formulation and resolution method for the p-center problem. INFORMS J. on Computing, 16
25. Krauss, S., Wagner, P., Gawron, C.: Metastable states in a microscopic model of traffic flow. Physical Review E, 55(5) (1997)
26. Krajzewicz, D.: Kombination von taktischen und strategischen einflüssen in einer mikroskopischen verkehrsflusssimulation (2009)
27. Jain, R.: The Art Of Computer Systems Performance Analysis: Techniques for Experimental Design, Measurement, Simulation, and Modeling. Wiley India Pvt, Limited (2008)

A Social-Based Approach for Message Dissemination in Vehicular Ad Hoc Networks

Alexandra Stagkopoulou, Pavlos Basaras, and Dimitrios Katsaros(✉)

University of Thessaly & CERTH, Volos, Greece
{alstagop,pabasara,dkatsar}@inf.uth.gr

Abstract. The spreading of messages in a vehicular network is an important task and finds many applications in Intelligent Transportation Systems (ITS). A common problem to this direction is to select an appropriate set of vehicles that on behalf of a sender will further rebroadcast the message and reduce redundant retransmission. Of particular interest is the use of social inspired metrics to identify potent vehicles which can set the right path for the spreading of messages and cover a wide range of a vehicular network. In this work we propose a novel approach for selecting vehicles based on the *Probabilistic Control Centrality (pCoCe)*, which accounts for the number of directed and diverse paths emanating from each individual vehicle. We evaluated our approach and compared with the standard IETF, *Optimized Link State Routing Protocol (OLSR)*. Our experimental results show that *pCoCe* outperforms its competitor in various network conditions by at least 10%.

Keywords: Multipoint relays · Broadcasting protocols · Influential spreaders · Vehicular ad hoc networks · OLSR

1 Introduction

Vehicular ad hoc networks (VANETs) provide peer to peer communication between vehicles Some of the most challenging fields in VANETs include the routing of information messages among vehicles as well as the reliability in package delivery due to their dynamically changing topology. Traffic congestion phenomena, the increased number of car accidents, the environmental impact in CO_2 emissions etc. urges for the use of inter vehicle communications to increase safety, comfort and ensure a greener road environment. There are plausible circumstances were one to all communications is a great asset and may affect the entire network topology. Consider cases were a driver near a parking lot broadcasts a message concerning limited free spots. Nearby interested drivers may decide to follow to this location whereas further away vehicles are less likely to do so. Generally vehicles informed of unfavorable road conditions, for example of blocked roads, traffic jams or accidents will take prompt actions to alternate their route in order to avoid those locations and thus save time and fuel. To this direction the effective dissemination of messages (i.e., broadcasting a message to the largest possible portion of the vehicular network) plays an essential role.

© Institute for Computer Sciences, Social Informatics and Telecommunications Engineering 2014
N. Mitton et al. (Eds.): ADHOCNETS 2014, LNICST 140, pp. 27–38, 2014.
DOI: 10.1007/978-3-319-13329-4_3

The main goal of broadcasting (one-to-all communications) is to deliver a message to the entire network or to a sufficiently large portion, while keeping the number of redundant retransmissions at minimum. This domain has rich literature. Centralized broadcasting (each node is aware of the entire network topology) [1] comes with unacceptable communication cost for maintenance, and thus cannot be utilized in dynamic networks such as VANETs. Geocasting [2] is another broadcasting approach for the delivery of messages to wireless nodes located in a specific geographic region, data dissemination and warning notifications. Other studies include the use of connecting dominating sets (CDS) as proposed in [3] to extract a 'backbone' image of a network. Nevertheless, in vehicular networks with high mobility and intermittent connections maintaining an accurate backbone image is a costly strategy. More sophisticated approaches include those studied in [4]. Here a vehicular network is divided in groups of neighbors called clusters. For each cluster a leading vehicle, the cluster head (CH), is elected and assigned with specific functionalities i.e., rebroadcasting. When a vehicle has a message to send, it communicates with his CH who is then responsible to rebroadcast the message to neighboring CH's (or *gateways*) and so on until the entire network is covered. In this study we are interested in methods which do not induce significant additional communication costs such as by using CDSs or CHs.

Flooding a message throughout the network is a frequently used technique in wireless ad hoc structures. The simple flooding algorithm however causes the broadcast storm problem [5]. Other flooding based approaches include cases where nodes decide whether or not to rebroadcast a message based on some probability p. However this may results in occasions with either too few or too many retransmissions, which renders this flooding approach unreliable. In [6] the authors collected a list for the literature of small and large scale routing protocols and broadcasting methods. Among other studies, VDEB [7] and BPAB [8] are mentioned for selecting appropriate nodes to forward a message. However these approaches are not further modified for implementation in roads which include intersections.

OLSR [9] and also our competitor in this work, is a proactive or table-driven routing protocol i.e maintains a list of destinations and routes by periodically exchanging topology messages and is widely used in mobile and vehicular ad hoc networks. This protocol relies on employing selected nodes to retransmit a message among the nodes of the network instead of pure flooding. The selected nodes are called multipoint relays (MPRs).

In this article we exploit social inspired techniques for selecting appropriate sets of relay vehicles. We introduce the *Probabilistic Control Centrality (pCoCe)* as a one-to-all communication protocol with performance metric the total number of vehicles informed at the end of a notification message event. As a competing method we utilize the MPR set selection mechanism of the IETF standard *OLSR*. Our experimental results show that there are many occasions, where the minimum selected set of relays as identified by our competitor is not necessarily propitious to reach a sufficiently large part of a network. The rest of this article is organized as follows. Section 2 binds the work of influential spreaders with the relay selection process, further explains our proposition and broadly reviews the competitors. Experimental design and results are thoroughly illustrated in section 3 and finally in section 4 the conclusions.

2   Influential Nodes in Complex Networks

The analysis of complex networks has recently gathered the interest of the research society. A very important aspect lies in the identification of influential entities, i.e., detect those node-entities in a complex structure where by exploiting their connection patterns, or their topological position in a graph, a sufficiently large portion of the network can be influenced. These 'super spreaders' will be used to either boost spreading in case of fast dissemination of messages. Vehicular networks are also complex networks since their constantly changing topology creates network structures with non-trivial topological features. Our objective in this study is to use vehicles that according to some criterion play an important role in a network and exploit them to maximize the spreading of messages. In [10] the authors argued that nodes positioned in the "core" of the network as identified by the k-shell decomposition algorithm are capable of achieving the most efficient spreading; different and more local approaches are proposed in [11].

As mentioned earlier for vehicle networks the fast dissemination of a message that covers the largest possible portion of a network is a very important issue and finds fertile ground in many applications, from safety and precaution mechanisms to comfort and fuel saving applications. In this article we leverage metrics from complex network theory used for the identification of influential nodes and particularly we propose a novel method the $pCoCe$ based on *Control Centrality* [12] that efficiently detects potent vehicles for disseminating messages.

2.1   Control Centrality

In [12] the authors introduce the concept of *Control Centrality* with view to identify nodes with the ability to 'control' (drive to a specific state) a directed network based on an initial input and a 'control goal'. To further investigate on the issue let us first note some definitions. A *stem* on a directed graph, is a directed path consisting of n nodes and $n-1$ edges where no node appears more than once e.g. $i \rightarrow j \rightarrow k \rightarrow l \rightarrow m$. A *cycle* is noted as a *stem* ending on the initial node: $i \rightarrow j \rightarrow k \rightarrow i$. A *stem-cycle disjoint subgraph*, is a subgraph of the directed network where stems and cycles have no nodes in common. For any node i its control centrality is defined as the largest number of edges among all possible stem-cycle disjoint subgraphs.

The purpose of this article is to exploit vehicle-nodes with high $pCoCe$ values for use as multipoint relays. The intuition lies on the idea that those selected relays will rebroadcast a message on behalf of the initial sender and will likely cover a sufficiently large part of the vehicular network.

2.2   From Control Centrality to pCoCe

As a first step we must define incoming and outgoing neighbors in vehicular networks. Since all connection links among vehicles are considered bidirectional, we use the relative direction between them to classify them either as in or outgoing neighbors. Generally vehicle A is considered an outgoing of vehicle B when A is moving either in front of B or away from B in a different direction. For instance in Figure 1 and for vehicle 7 the set of it's outgoing neighbors includes vehicles 1,3 and 6 while the rest synthesize it's ingoing vicinity.

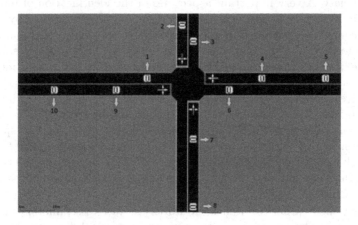

Fig. 1. In and out neighborhoods of a typical vehicular network

With this consideration we can define stems and cycles in VANETS. However the use of cycles to enhance a vehicle's importance in a vehicular network is very likely to overestimate the vehicles ability in disseminating a message to a large part of the network. Hence from here on we account only for stems, created from vehicle paths.

The original control centrality algorithm is computed with stems and cycles which cover the entire range of a network. However in VANET's due to their constantly changing topology and connection pattern (neighbor vehicles increase or decrease their distance in and out of the communication range or in-neighbors become out and vise versa) we cannot utilize the method in full range. In this study we confined our selves to a range of two and three hops distance (*2pCoCe, 3pCoCe*).

Note that *pCoCe* uses all stems within our specified range and there are occasions were different stems have common edges. These stems will all contribute in the final *pCoCe* value for a vehicle-node and form it's final index. At this point we would like to note that our new method is a novel approach that considers and combines different stems emanating from a particular vehicle and define its significance in the network.

The last part of *pCoCe* accounts for the strength of connections between vehicles (*stem power*) and incorporates this attribute in the formed stems. Depending on the quality of the connection for each out-neighbor we assign a weight value between 0 to 1 depicting the strength of connection between the two vehicles. Weights close to 1 depict a perfect communication link whereas values close to 0 depict an almost absent connection. The *stem power* is computed as follows:

$$Sp = S \cdot PW \tag{1}$$

where S depicts the size of a stem in edges and PW is the product of the weights that form it. In this work we consider all weight values to be equal to 1. Further investigation for the strength of connections and its incorporation in Sp is a very interesting task, but it's beyond the scope of this study.

Finally in order for a vehicle to accumulate its final $pCoCe$ index it sums all the different Sp's to a final value which will characterize its importance within its vicinity:

$$pCoCe(x) = \sum_i Sp(i) \tag{2}$$

where i denotes the different stems emanating from vehicle x.

2.3 pCoCe Relay Set Selection

$pCoCe$'s algorithm for selecting relays is straightforward. Every vehicle sorts its out one hop neighbors in descending order of their $pCoCe$ values. The neighbor with the maximum value is selected as a relay. In the sequence the next highest neighbor is examined. If additional out two hop neighbors are reached, this vehicle is included in the relay set and so on until the entire two hop neighborhood is covered. At this point we should note that only the out one and two hop neighbors are considered for the selection process. The pseudocode is given in Algorithm 1. One final modification of the $pCoCe$ is needed in order for a sender to select an appropriate relay set. Some of the accumulated Sp's that are used in order to form the $pCoCe$ value may be incoming stems to the sender i.e., the final vehicle on a stem may be an incoming neighbor. Those vehicle stems should be excluded from the computation of the final index. To this end when a vehicle needs to broadcast or rebroadcast a message it dynamically asks from its out one hops to compute and respond with their $pCoCe$ values excluding stems incoming to the sender. Finally the returned values are multiplied by the number of the two hops covered by each respective out-neighbor. Note that at this point we introduce an additional communication phase and thus an additional delay before sending the message.

2.4 OLSR MPR Set Selection

The notion of in and out going neighbors is also induced into the MPR selection process of OLSR in order to select relays from identical vicinities in both approaches and thus only out one and two hop neighbors are considered. OLSR

Result: Select appropriate relay set
x : a vehicle
$N(x)$: set of one hop out neighbors
$N^2(x)$: set of two hop out neighbors
$MPR(x)$: multipoint relays for x
$Vector_x$: neighbor pCoCe values in descending order
if *Notification Event* **then**
> $MPR(x) = \emptyset$
> $Vector_x = \emptyset$
> Request one hop out neighbor pCoCe values.
> $MPR(x) \leftarrow Vector_x[0]$
> Delete $Vector_x[0]$
> **while** $\exists$ *vehicle in* $N^2(x)$ *not covered by* $MPR(x)$ **do**
> > $MPR(x) \leftarrow Vector_x[0]$
> > Delete $Vector_x[0]$
>
> **end**

end

Algorithm 1. Pseudo-code for pCoCe relay set selection

first selects vehicles who provide unique access to some two hop neighbors. In the sequent the vehicle that covers the maximum remaining two hop vicinity is selected and so on until the entire two hop neighborhood is reached. The pseudocode for the MPR selection process is given in Algorithm 2.

Result: Select appropriate mpr set
x : a vehicle
$N(x)$: set of one hop out neighbors
$N^2(x)$: set of two hop out neighbors
$MPR(x)$: multipoint relays for x
Compute Mpr Set:
$MPR(x) = \emptyset$
Select those one hops from $N(x)$ that are the only neighbor of some vehicle in $N^2(x)$.
while $\exists$ *vehicle in* $N^2(x)$ *not covered by* $MPR(x)$ **do**
> $\forall y \exists N(x)$ & $y \not\in MPR(x)$: compute the number of vehicles that each y covers among the uncovered vehicles of $N^2(x)$.
> Add to $MPR(x)$ the vehicle with the maximum number.

end

Algorithm 2. Pseudo-code OLSR MPR set selection

3   Performance Evaluation

For the evaluation purposes and for our experimentation we use the open source vehicular network simulation framework, VEINS [13], which uses SUMO for the traffic simulation and OMNET++ the network simulation framework.

3.1 Simulation Design

Grid Network. We evaluated the performance of $pCoCe$ in a grid road network topology (3X3). The network includes road segments with two direction flows and every $2km$ there are intersections with traffic lights providing a coordinated traffic flow. The competitors where evaluated under different circumstances concerning the range of communication, the velocity of vehicles and the density of cars on the road network. Particularly we experimented with vehicle velocities of 14, 20 and $28m/s$ and range of communication at 250 and $500m$. For the density of the scenarios we introduce a vehicle every 1, 5, 10 and 15 seconds, ranging from very dense to very sparse network topologies. The average number of vehicles to the corresponding frequencies is 950, 250, 170 and 120 cars respectively. Vehicle flows enter the simulation from different road segments of the grid network.

Communication Between Vehicles. All vehicles are communicating through DSRC with range of communication as previously noted in 250 and $500m$. For every vehicle in order to be aware of its vicinity, beacon messages are exchanged every 1 seconds. In order to maintain an updated image of its surroundings, every vehicle that has not received a beacon message from recoded neighbors for more than two seconds i.e., missed two consecutive beacons, updates its vicinity by removing those vehicles. This ensures that each vehicle has a clear and very recent image of its neighboring cars.

Notification Message Event. The dissemination of notification messages is triggered upon notification events. A notification event is generated from a random vehicle at a random position on the road network (the same vehicle for both approaches) with only one notification existing at a time. The results are averaged over 10 different events for each competing method.

3.2 Dissemination to the Entire Grid

Experimenting on Vehicle Density, 2pCoCe. The aim of this first experimentation set is to conclude whether the conservative MPR set selection of OLSR is adequate for informing a sufficiently large part of a vehicular network. The results are illustrated in Figures 2 to 4. On the x-axis we depict the frequency to which vehicles are introduced in the simulation in seconds, while keeping the velocity constant at 14, 20 and $28m/s$ respectively. Communication range is set to $500m$. The results are given in percent depending on the number of vehicles present in the simulation at the time of the notification event.

In all but one cases OLSR fails to exceed the percentage of the vehicular network covered by $2pCoCe$. The results in Figure 2, set with the lowest speed ($14m/s$) in our experimentation, show that the frequency of vehicles does not have a significant impact on our approach. Our method manages to find the right paths for the spreading of messages and inform the vehicular network at near 80%. For our competitor the worst case performance is illustrated for the dense scenarios. This indicates that OLSR when faced with many options for selecting MPR vehicles cannot distinguish an appropriate MPR set for the most efficient spreading of messages. Considering the sparser scenarios in the same Figure, and thus with fewer choices, OLSR's performance is improved. Nevertheless the competitors show a difference in percent coverage of more than 25% for the best case of OLSR.

In Figures 3 and 4 we repeat our experimentation with increased speeds to 20 and $28m/s$ respectively. Increasing the velocity of vehicles will result in a more frequently changing topology among a vehicle's surroundings and thus a more profound selection is crucial. As illustrated *2pCoCe* is performing extensively well when dealing with a large number of potential choices for the relay set. The coverage rate rises up to more than 90%. OLSR significantly fails to keep up with our approach. In the last illustrated example for this set of experimentation, Figure 4, *2pCoCe* shows a decreasing performance as we move to sparser network topologies. This indicates a more reliable and trustworthy behavior in contrast to OLSR showing extensive fluctuations in coverage when changing the network density at a relative high speed.

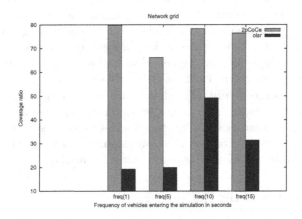

Fig. 2. OLSR Vs 2pCoCe with vehicle velocity at 14m/s

Differences in the Selected Relays. In Figure 5 we normalize the size of the network that received the message with the number of MPRs selected by each competing method, through the entire spreading process. Since OLSR makes a conservative choice for his MPRs a frequent phenomenon is that the spreading dies after a few hops (due to false relay set selection) and thus covers a significantly lower portion of the network. Since the spreading for *2pCoCe* continues in further broadcasting circles than our competitor, more vehicles are selected in subsequent steps as relays.

As far as the average number of MPRs per vehicle is concerned OLSR selects the minimum set of relays. However as shown through our experimentation in many cases OLSR results into very poor spreading compared to our approach. For the dense scenarios with vehicles entering the simulation every 1 or 5 seconds, *2pCoCe*'s relay set is greater than OLSR's by one or two vehicles whereas for the

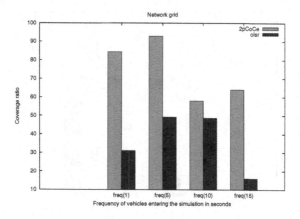

Fig. 3. OLSR Vs 2pCoCe with vehicle velocity at 20m/s

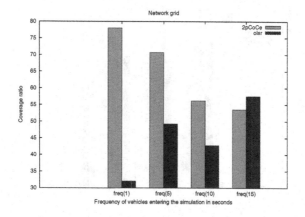

Fig. 4. OLSR Vs 2pCoCe with vehicle velocity at 28m/s

cases of 10 and 15 seconds we have either equal sets or our set is greater by one. By equal or greater sets we are merely referring to the number of relays selected by each method. Indeed there are occasions were the competitors select similar sets of vehicles, however on average different relays are chosen as identified by each algorithm. Reviewing the differences in coverage rates for both methods in Figures 2 to 4 one or two additional relays is a good trade-off when a significantly larger part of the network is reached.

Increasing the Range of pCoCe to 3 Hops Distance. In this set of experiments we evaluate the performance of *pCoCe* when increasing the distance of interest from 2 to 3 hops. The results are illustrated in Figure 6. When vehicles enter the simulation every 1 seconds, regardless of their velocity, *3pCoCe* covers a greater percent of the vehicular network than *2pCoCe* and thus greater than OLSR. This indicates that *3pCoCe* (and also *2pCoCe*) performs extensively well

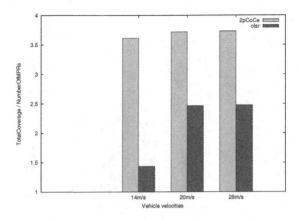

Fig. 5. Normalize coverage by number of selected mprs of each method

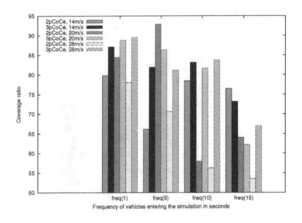

Fig. 6. Comparing pCoCe's performance with 2 and 3 hops distance

in very dense scenarios by selecting potent vehicles for rebroadcasting with total percent of coverage over 85%. For vehicle frequencies of every 5 and 10 seconds as shown in our experimentation, *3pCoCe*'s coverage is constantly higher than 80%. Our algorithms performance seems to start getting affected by the vehicle velocities when examining the sparse scenario where vehicles enter the simulation every 15 seconds. Nevertheless the coverage percentage reached by *3pCoCe* is about 63% for the worst case of its performance and up to approximately 73% at best. For OLSR the best coverage rate in this scenario rises up to about 56%.

Reducing the Range of Communications to 250m. Considering only out one hop vehicles as potential relays can be considered a 'hazardous' approach. As noted in section 2.2 out going neighbors are those who either move away from a sender to a different direction or positioned ahead of a sender and moving towards the same direction. Thus these are the vehicles which are most likely to 'exit' the communication range of a sender, sooner than other neighbors. In Figure 7 we illustrate the obtained results with vehicle frequency set at 1 seconds and communication range at $250m$. Excluding results at $28m/s$, $pCoCe$ provides a wider range of the network coverage than OLSR for 2 and 3 hops distance stems. Analogous results were obtained for 5 seconds frequency, however both the algorithms performance drop below 10% when considering the sparser scenarios. Let us elaborate a little more on the impact of the communication range on $pCoCe$. As mentioned earlier our approach calculates stems of vehicles of 2 or 3 hops distance from a sender car. These stems are composed of outgoing neighbors (excluding paths incoming to the sender) and thus further expand the hazardness of outgoing vehicles to additional hops. Therefore $pCoCe$ when limited to a very short communication range performs best in minimum stem distance, i.e., 2 hops.

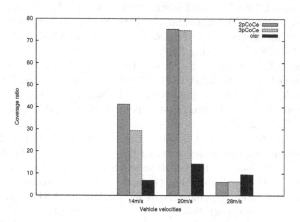

Fig. 7. Communication range at 250m for frequency of vehicles every 1 seconds

4   Conclusion

In this paper we presented a novel approach for the selection of relay vehicles based on metrics from complex network theory and the identification of influentials. We proposed a novel broadcasting protocol which induces minimum additional communication cost and performs extensively well when dealing with a large number of potential relay choices. Our competitor fails to provide both an adequate coverage rate and reliability as illustrated under diverse simulation parameters. As future work incorporating the quality of links in the 'stem power' will provide valuable insights in broadcasting a message under harsh communication environments and different road topologies.

Acknowledgments. Part of research supported by the project "REDUCTION: Reducing Environmental Footprint based on Multi-Modal Fleet management System for Eco-Routing and Driver Behavior Adaptation", funded by the EU.ICT program,

Challenge ICT-2011.7. Dimitrios Katsaros acknowledges the support of ERC08-RECITAL project, co-financed by Greece and the European Union (European Social Fund) through the Operational Program "Education and Lifelong Learning" - NCRF 2007-2013.

References

1. Gaber, I., Mansour, Y.: Centralized broadcast in multihop radio networks. Journal of Algorithms **46**, 1–20 (2003)
2. Daraghmi, Y.A., Stojmenovic, I., Yi, C.W.: A taxonomy of data communication protocols for vehicular ad hoc networks, Mobile Ad Hoc Networking: Cutting Edge Directions pp. 517–544 (2013)
3. Stojmenovic, I., Khan, A., Zaguia, N.: Broadcasting with seamless transition from static to highly mobile wireless ad hoc, sensor and vehicular networks. International Journal of Parallel, Emergent and Distributed Systems **27**, 225–234 (2012)
4. Vegni, A.M., Stramacci, A., Natalizio, E.: SRB: A selective reliable broadcast protocol for safety applications in VANETs. In: Proc. of Intl. Conf. on Selected Topics in Mobile & Wireless Networking (2012)
5. Ni, S.Y., Tseng, Y.C., Chen, Y.S., Sheu, J.P.: The broadcast storm problem in a mobile ad hoc network. In: ACM/IEEE MOBICOM, pp. 151–162 (1999)
6. Daraghmi, Y.A., Yi, C.W., Stojmenovic, I., Abdulaziz, K.: Forwarding methods in data dissemination and routing protocols for vehicular ad hoc networks. IEEE Network **27**, 74–79 (2013)
7. Tseng, Y.T., Jan, R.H., Chen, C., Wang, C.F., Li, H.H.: A vehicle-density-based forwarding scheme for emergency message broadcasts in VANETs. In: IEEE 7th International Conference on Mobile Adhoc and Sensor Systems pp. 703–708 (2010)
8. Sahoo, J., Wu, E.H.-K., Sahu, P.K., Gerla, M.: Binary-partition-assisted AMC-layer broadcast for emergency message dissemination in VANETs. IEEE Transactions on Intelligent Transportation Systems **12**, 757–770 (2011)
9. Jacquet, P., Muhlethaler, P., Clausen, T., Laouiti, A., Qayyum, A., Viennot, L.: Optimized link state routing protocol for ad hoc networks. In: IEEE International Multi topic Conference pp. 62–68 (2001)
10. Kitsak, M., Gallos, L.K., Havlin, S., Liljeros, F., Muchnik, L., Stanley, H.E., Makse, H.A.: Identification of influential spreaders in complex networks. Nature Physics **6**, 888–893 (2010)
11. Basaras, P., Katsaros, D., Tassiulas, L.: Detecting influential spreaders in complex, dynamic networks. IEEE Computer magazine **46**(4), 26–31 (2013)
12. Liu, Y.-Y., Slotine, J.-J., Barabasi, A.-L.: Control centrality and hierarhical structure in complex networks, PLOS One **7**(9) (2012)
13. Sommer, C., German, R., Dressler, F.: Bidirectionally coupled network and road traffic simulation for improved IVC analysis. IEEE Transactions on Mobile Computing **10**(1) (2011)

Intelligent Transportation Systems – Maybe, But Where Are My Agents?

Thierry Delot[1], Sergio Ilarri[2],
and María del Carmen Rodríguez-Hernández[2(✉)]

[1] University of Valenciennes, Valenciennes, France
tdelot@univ-valenciennes.fr
[2] University of Zaragoza, Zaragoza, Spain
{silarri,692383}@unizar.es

Abstract. Significant advances in wireless communication technologies and mobile devices have led to their widespread use. For example, the so-called Intelligent Transportation Systems (ITS), which encompass a wide range of advanced applications for transportation, have attracted a lot of attention. In this context, one could think that software agents, which can have properties such as intelligence and autonomy, are expected to play a key role. But is this the case? Are they being used in work related to ITS and/or vehicular networks? Could they really provide benefits? In this paper, we analyze the state of the art and draw some conclusions about the potential interest of mixing these two fields.

Keywords: Intelligent Transportation Systems · Vehicular networks · VANETs · Software agents · Mobile agents

1 Introduction

Today, the car is indisputably the most heavily used mode of transportation. Unfortunately, its popularity has been accompanied by numerous problems, for example, in the areas of safety and the environment. Despite significant efforts to reduce the number of persons dying on the road, this number remains quite high, mainly due to the human factor (e.g., accident-prone behavior or impaired reaction time). To reduce the number of accidents, a variety of programs, generally involving *Intelligent Transportation Systems* (ITS) [1,2], have been initiated in Japan, Europe, and the United States, attracting the interest of researchers both in academia and in industry.

On the other hand, in the field of Artificial Intelligence (AI), *software agents* [3,9,10] represent a fundamental major effort to provide intelligence in the form of software programs that somehow mimic the behavior of people and act as their virtual representatives in the computer world. They exhibit features such as autonomy, social ability, reactivity, and pro-activeness. In other words, they are not merely passive objects but active pieces of software that pursue their own goals and behave in an intelligent way.

© Institute for Computer Sciences, Social Informatics and Telecommunications Engineering 2014
N. Mitton et al. (Eds.): ADHOCNETS 2014, LNICST 140, pp. 39–50, 2014.
DOI: 10.1007/978-3-319-13329-4_4

Apparently, the aforementioned capabilities of agents make them a good fit to bring the intelligence that Intelligent Transportation Systems need. The interest of applying agents in the field of transportation is also highlighted in other papers. For example, [4] indicates that many problems in traffic management and control are inherently distributed and that many actors in transportation (drivers, pedestrians, traffic experts, and even intersection and traffic light controllers) could be considered as autonomous agents, and [5] indicates that the "autonomous and distributed nature of multi-agent systems is well-suited to the transportation domain which is dynamic and geographically distributed".

But what is the real impact of software agents on ITS? Are they really made for each other? In this paper, we try to explore this question and provide some insights that could help to understand the current state of the art. The structure of the rest of the paper is as follows. In Section 2 we provide an overview of the technological context that is relevant in this work, that is, ITS and agents. In Section 3 we describe the analysis of the literature that we have carried out to discover the existing relation between agents and ITS. In Section 4, we briefly describe some proposals that are based on the use of mobile agents. Finally, in Section 5, we provide some conclusions.

2   Technological Context

In this section, we provide a basic overview of the two topics whose relation we try to analyze. First we will focus on ITS (including vehicular networks), and then we will consider software agents (including mobile agents).

2.1   Intelligent Transportation Systems

ITS have attracted significant research attention. Independently of the specific technology used, the key point is that ITS tries to provide "intelligence" to improve the efficiency of transportation, the safety of the passengers, and the convenience of travelers.

Thanks to the resulting research, Advanced Driver Assistance Systems (ADAS) and Advanced Traveler Information Systems (ATIS) were born. Some of them are already available on the market (e.g., navigation systems, warning systems to alert the driver when he/she is about to fall asleep), and many others are under development. Nevertheless, ITS continues to be a hot spot of research and a major focus in initiatives and projects around the world, also as an important element of the so-called *smart cities*.

Within the context of ITS, *vehicular ad hoc networks* (*VANETs*) [6], where vehicles dynamically set up a network using short-range wireless communication technologies (e.g., WiFi, Bluetooth, or WAVE) to exchange different types of data, are expected to play a key role. Thanks to short-range wireless communication devices, the vehicles can quickly exchange data with others and even to transmit queries (i.e., requests of data) in a peer-to-peer way (i.e., without the need to deploy a costly support communication infrastructure and without incurring the economic cost derived from the use of technologies such as mobile telephony networks). Whereas this scenario opens up a number of opportunities for the development of interesting applications and services, several difficulties also arise, as this is a highly-dynamic network subject to frequent changes in its topology (e.g., two vehicles driving in opposite directions at high speeds will be within range of each other only during a short period, and therefore they should exchange data very quickly).

2.2 Software Agents

In this section, we first describe the general concept of *software agent* [3,9,10]. Then, we present a specific type of software agents that have the movement capability, which are called *mobile agents* [7,8].

Generic (Static) Software Agents. Wooldridge defines an agent as a software-based computer system that exhibits certain properties (which conform what he calls the *weak notion of agency*) [3]: autonomy (agents have control over their internal state and behavior), social ability (they interact with each other, using a certain agent communication language, and potentially also with humans), reactivity (they perceive their environment and are able to react to changes), and pro-activeness (they are not only reactive, but they can also act to pursue their own goals, even in the absence of changes in the environment). Moreover, a *stronger notion of agency* would imply attributing agents other features usually applied only to humans, such as their ability to have knowledge, beliefs, intentions, and desires.

Despite the existing controversy regarding the right definition of agent [9], most authors agree that autonomy is a required feature of an agent whereas other capabilities could be absent in some cases, and this autonomy requires some form of intelligence [10]. Although it is difficult to establish a precise definition of intelligence in this context, it is usually assumed that it should involve learning from past experiences to improve the behavior along time. There is also a strong emphasis on the cooperation aspects of agents, as they can accomplish complex task when composing *multi-agent systems* (MAS) [11]. For the development of agent-based applications, many *agent platforms* have been developed (e.g., see [12,13]), being JADE [14] one of the most popular ones nowadays.

Agents and multi-agent systems have been around for more than 20 years [15] and provide a nice abstraction suitable for the development of certain software systems, which gave rise to the emergence of the *Agent-Oriented Software Engineering* (AOSE) paradigm [16].

Mobile Agents. Mobile agents are software agents that have the capability to move from one execution environment (hosted in a certain computer or device) to another [7,8]. Thus, a mobile agent can stop its execution at a device, move to another device, and resume its execution at the destination. Thus, they are not bound to the computer where they were created; instead, they can move freely across different computers and devices along their lifetime. Only a specific middleware, called *mobile agent platform* [8], which is a server process that supports the execution of agents and provides them specific services (e.g., communication with other agents, security, a movement facility to support their mobility, a naming or directory service to search for agents, a persistence service, etc.), is required in the involved computer/devices.

The mobility capability makes mobile agent technology an ideal solution to design solutions for distributed and mobile computing environments [17]. Thanks to their mobility, mobile agents offer many interesting benefits [18], such as: *encapsulation* (they encapsulate tasks and can dynamically carry the required functionality to any device with a mobile agent platform, by moving there), *minimization of the network load* (they can move the computation to the data instead of the other way around, and therefore they can filter the data at the source in order to communicate only the data that are really relevant), *minimization of the network connections* (as they can perform their processing without accessing remote data, they minimize the amount of time during which network connections need to be kept active), *minimization of network latency* (they can move closer to a resource –e.g., a service, another agent, or a data source– in order to access it without much network delay), *asynchrony and autonomy* (a mobile agent does not need to keep contact with its source computer while performing its tasks, as it can live independently, and therefore for example the originating device can be turned off or go offline without any problem), *higher adaptability* (a mobile agent can adapt its execution, for example, by traveling to other computers/devices, due to different reasons such as to achieve load balancing).

Thanks to these features, they have also been considered as a very promising technology for mobile, wireless, and pervasive computing environments (e.g., see [19]). Therefore, they should be expected to play an important role in ITS.

3   Study of the Literature on Agents and ITS

We have analyzed several journals and international events related to both agents and intelligent transportation in order to see the relation between these two fields. Specifically, we have considered the following representative venues:

- J1: *Autonomous Agents and Multi-Agent Systems* journal (Springer).
- J2: *Transportation Research Part C: Emerging Technologies* journal (Elsevier).
- J3: *IEEE Intelligent Transportation Systems Magazine* (IEEE).
- J4: *IEEE Transactions on Intelligent Transportation Systems* journal (IEEE).
- J5: *Expert Systems with Applications* journal (Elsevier).
- C1: *IEEE Intelligent Vehicles Symposium (IV)*.
- C2: *IEEE Conference on Intelligent Transportation Systems (ITSC)*.
- C3: *Autonomous Agents and Multiagent Systems (AAMAS)* conference.
- C4: *IEEE Vehicular Technology Conference (VTC)*.
- W1: *ACM International Workshop on Vehicular Inter-Networking, Systems, and Applications (ACM VANET)*.

In Table 1 we show the number of papers that concern some aspect of ITS and agents at the same time, for each journal and conference/workshop, per year; for simplicity, we do not distinguish between different types of papers (e.g., full papers vs. posters or short papers). The symbol "–" is used for a conference/journal that did not exist yet that year or for a conference that has not been held yet (in the case of the year 2014); it should be noted that most journals will continue publishing papers in the remaining of 2014.

Table 1. Numbers of papers applying agents in transportation (sources considered)

Year	Total	J1	J2	J3	J4	J5	C1	C2	C3	C4	W1
2002	4	0	3	–	0	0	0	0	1	0	–
2003	3	0	0	–	0	0	0	1	2	0	–
2004	2	0	0	–	0	0	0	0	2	0	0
2005	13	1	2	–	0	1	0	0	9	0	0
2006	1	0	0	–	0	0	0	0	1	0	0
2007	2	0	0	–	1	0	0	0	1	0	0
2008	1	0	0	–	0	0	1	0	0	0	0
2009	5	1	1	1	0	0	0	0	1	1	0
2010	11	0	3	0	2	0	1	0	5	0	0
2011	11	0	0	0	3	0	1	0	7	0	0
2012	2	1	0	0	0	0	0	0	1	0	0
2013	5	0	1	0	2	1	0	0	1	0	0
2014	3	0	1	0	0	1	–	–	1	–	–
Total:	63	3	11	1	8	3	3	1	32	1	0

If we consider the total number of papers published in the journals and international events considered per year, we can reach the conclusion that the actual percentage of papers applying agent technology in the context of ITS is quite low.

In the following, we will show in more detail some of the different papers identified as relevant (i.e., dealing with both agents and transportation) in our study (due to the lack of space, we only select a subset of such papers). In Table 2 we show some data for the relevant papers found in the journals, conferences, and workshops selected in our study. In column "Reference" we indicate the reference to the work (a value *MA* in brackets next to the reference indicates that mobile agents are considered in that work). In column "Focus" we indicate the main concern of the work mentioned: traffic signal control and coordination, such as the coordination of traffic lights to optimize the traffic flow (value *TSC*); intelligent traffic management and coordination, such as route guidance to solve local traffic problems such as traffic congestion (value *TM*); intelligent transportation systems in general (value *ITS*); traffic information systems (value *TIS*); road safety (value *RS*); and design and planning of transportation systems (value *DTS*); it should be noted that we are not covering all the possible topics in the table, as we also identified some papers focused on simulation. In column "Infrastructure" we indicate the basic underlying infrastructure considered, such as *road*, *water*, and *air*; although we are mainly interested in terrestrial transportation, for completeness we also consider other scenarios. Finally, in column "A few key ideas" we collect some basic ideas of the proposal.

As shown in the tables, many identified proposals deal with traffic management, which basically tries to distribute traffic in the network (based on the demand, supply, and capacity at different locations) through information broadcast (to influence the route choice), control (e.g., traffic signals, variable message signs), and optimization (e.g., operational parameters of traffic lights, route planning) [4].

Table 2. Relevant papers in the journals, conferences and workshops considered

Reference	Focus	Infrastructure	A few key ideas
			Journals
[4]	TSC, ITS	road	Agentification in transportation. Survey of methods and problems.
[20]	TSC	road	Centralized vs. agent-based control. Evolutionary game theory.
[21]	TSC	air	Agent-based air traffic management. Learning. Reward structure.
[22]	TM	road	Adaptive vehicle route guidance. Ant colony behavior. Fuzzy model.
[23]	TM	road	Centralized vs. agent-based control (integrated TRYS, TRYS agents).
[24]	TM	road	Agent-based DSS (Decision Support Systems). Transport prototypes.
[25]	TM	urban roads	Generic model of a traffic regulation support system.
[26] (MA)	TM	road	Integration of mobile agents (FIPA-compliant Mobile-C) and MAS.
[28]	TM	air, road, water, rail	Survey of agent-based approaches for transportation. Logistics.
[29]	TM	air	Efficiency of communication, delays of flights.
[30]	TSC	urban roads	Linear dynamic systems. Graceful extension, localized reconfiguration.
[31]	TM	air	Air Traffic Management. Reinforcement Learning (RL). Rewards.
[32]	TM	freeway roads, streets	Distributed cooperative problem solving. Cartesius.
[33]	TM	road	Cooperative traffic management instruments, modeled as agents.
[34]	TM	road	Traffic guidance using VMS (Variable Message Signs). Based on SWARM.
[35] (MA)	ITS	road, rail and air	Survey. Modeling and simulation vs. real-world applications. Interest of MAs.
[36]	TSC	road	Multi-agent reinforcement learning. Agents as controllers of traffic lights.
[37]	TM	road	Coordination for anticipatory vehicle routing (avoid congestion). Ant behavior.
[38]	TSC	urban roads	Geometric fuzzy multi-agent system. Simulation models in PARAMICS.
[39]	TM	road	Integration of agent organizations and services for transportation management.
[40]	TM	road	Congestion Avoidance and Route Allocation using Virtual Agent Negotiation (CARAVAN).
[41]	TM	urban roads	Competitive market. Driver agents negotiate the use of intersections.
[42]	TM	air	Conflict resolution for intersecting flows. Planar space partition.
[43]	TIS	road	Architecture-centric method to develop MAS. Applied to ITS.
[44]	RS	road	Exchange info between vehicles and road nodes. Detect vehicles driving in the opposite direction.
[45]	DTS	urban roads	Demand Responsive Transport systems (DRT). Flexible optimized routes.
			Conferences and Workshops
[5] (MA)	TM	road	Classification of multi-agent techniques. Suitability for congestion management.
[46]	TSC	urban roads	Intelligent agents for coordination of traffic lights. Hierarchical architecture.
[47]	TM	urban roads	Demand Responsive Transport (DRT). Multilayer distributed hybrid planning.
[48] (MA)	ITS	road	Overview of ITS applications where multi-agent systems may impact.
[49]	TSC	urban roads	Multi-agent history-based traffic light controllers. Global fairness.
[50]	TM	air	Agents associated to specific locations set the separation required among airplanes traveling nearby. NASA's FACET simulator.
[51]	TM, RS	urban roads	Reserve space and time at intersections for safe crossing. Driver agents trade with infrastructure agents in a virtual marketplace.
[52]	TM	road	Coordinated look-ahead scheduling. Optimize traffic approaching intersection. Consider non-local impacts from indirect neighbors.
[53]	TM	air	Managing delay in airports. Autonomous partitioning of agents using system features.
[54]	TM, TSC	road	Pheromone-based traffic management model. Optimize vehicle re-routing and traffic light control. Forecast traffic conditions.
[55]	TSC	urban roads	Cooperative multi-agent fuzzy system. Decentralized traffic signal control to minimize traffic congestion. NetLogo-based traffic simulator.

It is worth mentioning that from all the papers identified as relevant, only [40] considers the use of ad hoc wireless communication technologies explicitly; other papers either do not consider it or do not mention the details of the communication infrastructure used. This scarce impact of agent technology on vehicular ad hoc networks can also be noticed if we observe the absence of relevant papers identified in W1 (see Table 1), which is a workshop focused on VANETs. It is also a bit surprising that, even though all the papers indicated consider the use of multi-agent systems, only a few of them actually mentions the use of a specific agent platform, such as:

- *MadKit* (*Multiagent Development Kit*, http://www.madkit.org/) is used in [22] for simulation purposes.
- *Mobile-C* (http://www.mobilec.org/) [56] is used in [26].
- *JADE* (*Java Agent DEvelopment Framework*) [14] is used in [24,36,40,43,44].

The reason is that in many occasions a specific platform does not seem necessary, as the proposal focuses on the application (or at least consideration) of techniques and methodologies from multi-agent systems in a real environment where the agents are the real entities involved (drivers, pedestrians, traffic lights, etc.). According to [35], most agent-based applications in the context of transportation focus on modeling and simulation.

Moreover, as can be observed in the tables, only a very reduced number of papers published in the journals and venues considered use mobile agents [5,26, 48], despite their potential interest in the context of ITS. Interestingly, the review presented in [35] emphasizes that "mobile agents can enhance the ability of traffic-control and management systems to handle the uncertainty introduced in a dynamic environment"; in particular, it indicates the interest of encapsulating functionalities within mobile agents to facilitate their dynamic deployment on remote machines. Notice also that some proposals (e.g., [42]) may also use the term "mobile agent" to refer to physical entities that move rather than to the concept of software agent that has the capability to change from one execution environment (computer or device) to another.

4   Mobile Agents in Transportation

In this section, we briefly describe some work that illustrates interesting approaches regarding the application of agents in the field of ITS. We focus on the application of mobile agents in the context of transportation because, as indicated in Section 2.2, mobile agents are software agents with the mobility capability, which in principle makes them ideal candidates to develop applications for the dynamic scenarios found in transportation. However, according to what was mentioned in Section 3, mobile agent technology has not achieved a significant impact on transportation research so far.

The work presented in [26] proposes the integration of mobile agents with multi-agent systems to improve the ability of traffic management systems to deal with the inherent uncertainty that arises in dynamic environments that are continuously changing. So, it basically uses mobile agents as a way to encapsulate updated code and algorithms that can be delivered dynamically to the intended systems as needed. The authors indicate that "to the best of our knowledge, the mobile agent technology has not been applied to this field" before. The work presented in [27] proposes the use of *context-aware migratory services* that migrate transparently due to context changes (similar to the concept of mobile agents); the authors present TJam as a proof-of-concept example that predicts traffic jams in a highway.

The proposal in [57] motivates the interest of using mobile agents in vehicular networks for environment monitoring. The idea is to exploit sensors available in conventional cars to flexibly monitor the environment. So, it tries to benefit from the fact that the number of sensors available in cars is continuously increasing: according to [58], "Today's luxury cars have more than 100 sensors per vehicle". Instead of manually deploying a set of static sensors in the area that has to be monitored, which would be expensive and time-consuming, agents travel to cars moving through the interesting area and exploit their sensors dynamically.

The proposal in [59] attempts to generalize the ideas presented in [57] by considering general query processing tasks in vehicular networks. The goal is to exploit information available on the vehicles, which are considered as data sources that can provide interesting information about events and other elements relevant for drivers (e.g., the surrounding traffic and the environment, the available parking spaces, etc.). To make this a reality, significant challenges arise from the point of view of data management: it is necessary to communicate a query to the relevant vehicles, retrieve the relevant data from such a distributed and highly-dynamic network, and bring back those data to the vehicle that originated the query. Although mobile agent technology could provide significant benefits to accomplish these tasks (thanks to the adaptability of mobile agents to mobile environments, their mobility, autonomy, and intelligence), its potential and the associated difficulties should be researched in more depth.

As short-range ad hoc wireless communications are exploited in these last proposals, mobile agents must hop from car to car until they arrive in the target area, collect measures, and then come back to the monitoring station with the data collected. A mobile agent could keep itself in a certain car while the car is within the area to monitor, but if the car gets out of the area it will have to find a way to come back to the area (again, by jumping from car to car). So, mobile agents move both thanks to the locomotion of the vehicles (by staying in a car that moves) and thanks to the wireless communications (by jumping to another car nearby). They use vehicles as "taxis" and as monitoring instruments when they have the required sensors and the vehicles are within the area to monitor.

Therefore, a key issue is the need of appropriate *jumping policies* for agents, that is, suitable mechanisms that allow agents to decide between jumping and staying, and in the case of jumping select a promising target.

5   Conclusions

In this paper, we have studied the relation between software agents and transportation. Based on our study, we agree with the conclusions from [28,35] that indicate that agent-based approaches seem suitable in the transportation domain but there are very few real deployed systems. It is also worth noticing that mobile agents have had for the moment a limited impact on the transportation field. The same can be said about the use of (generic) agents in VANETs.

The analysis presented in this paper should be regarded with certain caution, due to its limited scope (we mainly focused on a fixed set of journals and venues related to the transportation and agent fields). Moreover, it is complementary to other surveys published. For example, [35] reviews the application of agent technology in traffic and transportation systems, considering several issues affecting traffic and transportation systems (modeling and simulation, routing and congestion management, intelligent traffic control), and covers different modes of transportation (roads, railways, air). Another interesting overview of the applications where multi-agent systems could be useful is presented in [48].

Acknowledgments. This work has been supported by the CICYT project TIN2010-21387-C02-02, DGA-FSE, and a Banco Santander scholarship held by María del Carmen Rodríguez Hernández.

References

1. Dimitrakopoulos, G., Demestichas, P.: Intelligent Transportation Systems. IEEE Vehicular Technology Magazine 5(1), 77–84 (2010)
2. Zhang, J., Wang, F.Y., Wang, K., Lin, W.H., Xu, X., Chen, C.: Data-Driven Intelligent Transportation Systems: A Survey. IEEE Transactions on Intelligent Transportation Systems 12(4), 1624–1639 (2011)
3. Wooldridge, M., Jennings, N.R.: Intelligent Agents: Theory and Practice. The Knowledge Engineering Review 10(2), 115–152 (1995)
4. Bazzan, A.L.C.: Opportunities for Multiagent Systems and Multiagent Reinforcement Learning in Traffic Control. Autonomous Agents and Multi-Agent Systems 18(3), 342–375 (2009)
5. Desai, P., Loke, S.W., Desai, A., Singh, J.: Multi-Agent Based Vehicular Congestion Management. In: Intelligent Vehicles Symposium, pp. 1031–1036. IEEE (2011)
6. Olariu, S., Weigle, M.C. (eds.): Vehicular Networks: From Theory to Practice. CRC Press (2009)
7. Milojicic, D., Douglis, F., Wheeler, R.: Mobility: Processes, Computers, and Agents. ACM Press/Addison-Wesley Publishing Co. (1999)
8. Trillo, R., Ilarri, S., Mena, E.: Comparison and Performance Evaluation of Mobile Agent Platforms. In: The Third International Conference on Autonomic and Autonomous Systems, pp. 41–46. IEEE (2007)
9. Franklin, S., Graesser, A.: Is It an agent, or Just a Program?: A Taxonomy for Autonomous Agents. In: Jennings, N.R., Wooldridge, M.J., Müller, J.P. (eds.) ECAI-WS 1996 and ATAL 1996. LNCS, vol. 1193, pp. 21–35. Springer, Heidelberg (1997)
10. Wooldridge, M.J.: Intelligent Agents: The Key Concepts. In: Mařík, V., Štěpánková, O., Krautwurmová, H., Luck, M. (eds.) ACAI 2001, EASSS 2001, AEMAS 2001, and HoloMAS 2001. LNCS (LNAI), vol. 2322, pp. 3–43. Springer, Heidelberg (2002)
11. Wooldridge, M.: An Introduction to Multiagent Systems. John Wiley & Sons (2009)
12. Mulet, L., Such, J.M., Alberola, J.M.: Performance Evaluation of Open-Source Multiagent Platforms. In: Fifth International Joint Conference on Autonomous Agents and Multiagent Systems, pp. 1107–1109. ACM (2006)

13. Ricordel, P.-M., Demazeau, Y.: From Analysis to Deployment: A Multi-agent Platform Survey. In: Omicini, A., Tolksdorf, R., Zambonelli, F. (eds.) ESAW 2000. LNCS (LNAI), vol. 1972, pp. 93–105. Springer, Heidelberg (2000)

14. Bellifemine, F., Caire, G., Greenwood, D.: Developing Multi-Agent Systems with JADE. Wiley Series in Agent Technology. Wiley (2007)

15. Ganzha, M., Paprzycki, M., Omicini, A.: Software Agents: Twenty Years and Counting Guest Editors' Introduction for Special Issue. Computing Now 6(11) (2013)

16. Zambonelli, F., Omicini, A.: Challenges and Research Directions in Agent-Oriented Software Engineering. Autonomous Agents and Multi-Agent Systems 9(3), 253–283 (2004)

17. Bobed, C., Ilarri, S., Mena, E.: Distributed Mobile Computing: Development of Distributed Applications Using Mobile Agents. In: 16th International Conference on Parallel and Distributed Computing, pp. 562–568. CSREA Press (2010)

18. Lange, D.B., Oshima, M.: Seven Good Reasons for Mobile Agents. Communications of the ACM 42(3), 88–89 (1999)

19. Spyrou, C., Samaras, G., Pitoura, E., Evripidou, P.: Mobile Agents for Wireless Computing: The Convergence of Wireless Computational Models with Mobile-agent Technologies. Mobile Networks and Applications 9(5), 517–528 (2004)

20. Bazzan, A.L.C.: A Distributed Approach for Coordination of Traffic Signal Agents. Autonomous Agents and Multi-Agent Systems 10(1), 131–164 (2005)

21. Agogino, A.K., Tumer, K.: A Multiagent Approach to Managing Air Traffic Flow. Autonomous Agents and Multi-Agent Systems 24(1), 1–25 (2012)

22. Kammoun, H.M., Kallel, I., Casillas, J., Abraham, A., Alimi, A.M.: Adapt-Traf: An Adaptive Multiagent Road Traffic Management System Based on Hybrid Ant-Hierarchical Fuzzy Model. Transportation Research Part C: Emerging Technologies 42, 147–167 (2014)

23. Hernández, J.Z., Ossowski, S., García-Serrano, A.: Multiagent Architectures for Intelligent Traffic Management Systems. Transportation Research Part C: Emerging Technologies 10(5–6), 473–506 (2002)

24. Ossowski, S., Hernández, J.Z., Belmonte, M.V., Fernández, A., García-Serrano, A., de-la Cruz, J.L.P., Serrano, J.M., Triguero, F.: Decision Support for Traffic Management Based on Organisational and Communicative Multiagent Abstractions. Transportation Research Part C: Emerging Technologies 13(4), 272–298 (2005)

25. Balbo, F., Pinson, S.: Using Intelligent Agents for Transportation Regulation Support System Design. Transportation Research Part C: Emerging Technologies 18(1), 140–156 (2010)

26. Chen, B., Cheng, H.H., Palen, J.: Integrating Mobile Agent Technology with Multi-Agent Systems for Distributed Traffic Detection and Management Systems. Transportation Research Part C: Emerging Technologies 17(1), 1–10 (2009)

27. Riva, O., Nadeem, T., Borcea, C., Iftode, L.: Context-Aware Migratory Services in Ad Hoc Networks. IEEE Transactions on Mobile Computing 6(12), 1313–1328 (2007)

28. Davidsson, P., Henesey, L., Ramstedt, L., Trnquist, J., Wernstedt, F.: An Analysis of Agent-Based Approaches to Transport Logistics. Transportation Research Part C: Emerging Technologies 13(4), 255–271 (2005)

29. Weigang, L., Dib, M.V.P., Alves, D.P., Crespo, A.M.F.: Intelligent Computing Methods in Air Traffic Flow Management. Transportation Research Part C: Emerging Technologies 18(5), 781–793 (2010)

30. de Oliveira, L.B., Camponogara, E.: Multi-Agent Model Predictive Control of Signaling Split in Urban Traffic Networks. Transportation Research Part C: Emerging Technologies 18(1), 120–139 (2010)
31. Cruciol, L.L.B.V., de Arruda Jr., A.C., Weigang, L., Li, L., Crespo, A.M.F.: Reward Functions for Learning to Control in Air Traffic Flow Management. Transportation Research Part C: Emerging Technologies 35, 141–155 (2013)
32. Logi, F., Ritchie, S.G.: A Multi-Agent Architecture for Cooperative Inter-Jurisdictional Traffic Congestion Management. Transportation Research Part C: Emerging Technologies 10(56), 507–527 (2002)
33. van Katwijk, R., van Koningsbruggen, P.: Coordination of Traffic Management Instruments Using Agent Technology. Transportation Research Part C: Emerging Technologies 10(56), 455–471 (2002)
34. Shi, W., Wu, J., Zhou, S., Zhang, L., Tang, Z., Yin, Y.Y., Kuang, L., Wu, Z.: Variable Message Sign and Dynamic Regional Traffic Guidance. Intelligent Transportation Systems Magazine 1(3), 15–21 (2009)
35. Chen, B., Cheng, H.H.: A Review of the Applications of Agent Technology in Traffic and Transportation Systems. IEEE Transactions on Intelligent Transportation Systems 11(2), 485–497 (2010)
36. El-Tantawy, S., Abdulhai, B., Abdelgawad, H.: Multiagent Reinforcement Learning for Integrated Network of Adaptive Traffic Signal Controllers (MARLIN-ATSC): Methodology and Large-Scale Application on Downtown Toronto. IEEE Transactions on Intelligent Transportation Systems 14(3), 1140–1150 (2013)
37. Claes, R., Holvoet, T., Weyns, D.: A Decentralized Approach for Anticipatory Vehicle Routing Using Delegate Multiagent Systems. IEEE Transactions on Intelligent Transportation Systems 12(2), 364–373 (2011)
38. Gokulan, B.P., Srinivasan, D.: Distributed Geometric Fuzzy Multiagent Urban Traffic Signal Control. IEEE Transactions on Intelligent Transportation Systems 11(3), 714–727 (2010)
39. Fernández, A., Ossowski, S.: A Multiagent Approach to the Dynamic Enactment of Semantic Transportation Services. IEEE Transactions on Intelligent Transportation Systems 12(2), 333–342 (2011)
40. Desai, P., Loke, S.W., Desai, A., Singh, J.: CARAVAN: Congestion Avoidance and Route Allocation Using Virtual Agent Negotiation. IEEE Transactions on Intelligent Transportation Systems 14(3), 1197–1207 (2013)
41. Vasirani, M., Ossowski, S.: A Computational Market for Distributed Control of Urban Road Traffic Systems. IEEE Transactions on Intelligent Transportation Systems 12(2), 313–321 (2011)
42. Mao, Z.H., Dugail, D., Feron, E.: Space Partition for Conflict Resolution of Intersecting Flows of Mobile Agents. IEEE Transactions on Intelligent Transportation Systems 8(3), 512–527 (2007)
43. Park, S., Sugumaran, V.: Designing Multi-Agent Systems: a Framework and Application. Expert Systems with Applications 28(2), 259–271 (2005)
44. Conesa, J., Cavas-Martínez, F., Fernández-Pacheco, D.G.: An Agent-Based Paradigm for Detecting and Acting on Vehicles Driving in the Opposite Direction on Highways. Expert Systems with Applications 40(13), 5113–5124 (2013)
45. Satunin, S., Babkin, E.: A Multi-Agent Approach to Intelligent Transportation Systems Modeling with Combinatorial Auctions. Expert Systems with Applications 41(15), 6622–6633 (2014)
46. Guerrero, A., Contreras-Castillo, J., Buenrostro, R., Marti, A.B., Muoz, A.R.: A Policy-Based Multi-Agent Management Approach for Intelligent Traffic-Light Control. In: Intelligent Vehicles Symposium, pp. 694–699. IEEE (2010)

47. Jin, X., Abdulrab, H., Itmi, M.: A Multi-Agent Based Model for Urban Demand-Responsive Transport System Intelligent Control. In: Intelligent Vehicles Symposium, pp. 1033–1038. IEEE (2008)

48. Jin, Z., Hui, W., Ping, L.: Towards the Applications of Multi-Agent Techniques in Intelligent Transportation Systems. In: Intelligent Transportation Systems, vol. 2, pp. 1750–1754. IEEE (2003)

49. Balan, G., Luke, S.: History-Based Traffic Control. In: Fifth International Joint Conference on Autonomous Agents and Multiagent Systems, pp. 616–621. ACM (2006)

50. Tumer, K., Agogino, A.: Distributed Agent-Based Air Traffic Flow Management. In: Sixth International Joint Conference on Autonomous Agents and Multiagent Systems, pp. 342–349. ACM (2007)

51. Vasirani, M., Ossowski, S.: A Market-inspired Approach to Reservation-based Urban Road Traffic Management. In: Eighth International Conference on Autonomous Agents and Multiagent Systems, vol. 1, pp. 617–624. International Foundation for Autonomous Agents and Multiagent Systems (2009)

52. Xie, X.F., Smith, S.F., Barlow, G.J.: Coordinated Look-Ahead Scheduling for Real-Time Traffic Signal Control. In: Eleventh International Conference on Autonomous Agents and Multiagent Systems, vol. 3, pp. 1271–1272. International Foundation for Autonomous Agents and Multiagent Systems (2012)

53. Curran, W., Agogino, A., Tumer, K.: Partitioning Agents and Shaping Their Evaluation Functions in Air Traffic Problems with Hard Constraints. In: Fifth Annual Conference Companion on Genetic and Evolutionary Computation, pp. 183–184. ACM (2013)

54. Jiang, S., Zhang, J., Ong, Y.S.: A Pheromone-Based Traffic Management Model for Vehicle Re-Routing and Traffic Light Control. In: 2014 International Conference on Autonomous Agents and Multi-agent Systems, pp. 1479–1480. International Foundation for Autonomous Agents and Multiagent Systems (2014)

55. Daneshfar, F., RavanJamJah, J., Mansoori, F., Bevrani, H., Azami, B.Z.: Adaptive Fuzzy Urban Traffic Flow Control Using a Cooperative Multi-Agent System based on Two Stage Fuzzy Clustering. In: 69th IEEE Vehicular Technology Conference, pp. 1–5. IEEE (2009)

56. Chen, B., Cheng, H.H., Palen, J.: Mobile-C: A Mobile Agent Platform for Mobile C-C++ Agents. Software - Practice & Experience 36(15), 1711–1733 (2006)

57. Urra, O., Ilarri, S., Mena, E., Delot, T.: Using Hitchhiker Mobile Agents for Environment Monitoring. In: Demazeau, Y., Pavón, J., Corchado, J.M., Bajo, J. (eds.) 7th International Conference on Practical Applications of Agents and Multi-Agent Systems (PAAMS 2009). AISC, vol. 55, pp. 557–566. Springer, Heidelberg (2009)

58. Fleming, B.: Sensors - A Forecast (Automotive Electronics). IEEE Vehicular Technology Magazine 8(3), 4–12 (2013)

59. Urra, O., Ilarri, S.: Using Mobile Agents in Vehicular Networks for Data Processing. In: 14th International Conference on Mobile Data Management, Ph.D. Forum, vol. 2, pp. 11–14. IEEE (2013)

On the Usefulness of Information Hiding Techniques for Wireless Sensor Networks Security

Rola Al-Sharif[1], Christophe Guyeux[2]([✉]), Yousra Ahmed Fadil[2,3],
Abdallah Makhoul[2], and Ali Jaber[1]

[1] Universite Libanaise, Beirut, Lebanon
rola.alcharif@gmail.com, ali.jaber@ul.edu.lb
[2] Universite de Franche-Comte, Besançon, France
{christophe.guyeux,yousra_ahmed.fadil,abdallah.makhoul}@univ-fcomte.fr
[3] University of Diyala, Baqubah, Iraq

Abstract. A wireless sensor network (WSN) typically consists of base stations and a large number of wireless sensors. The sensory data gathered from the whole network at a certain time snapshot can be visualized as an image. As a result, information hiding techniques can be applied to this "sensory data image". Steganography refers to the technology of hiding data into digital media without drawing any suspicion, while steganalysis is the art of detecting the presence of steganography. This article provides a brief review of steganography and steganalysis applications for wireless sensor networks (WSNs). Then we show that the steganographic techniques are both related to sensed data authentication in wireless sensor networks, and when considering the attacker point of view, which has not yet been investigated in the literature. Our simulation results show that the sink level is unable to detect an attack carried out by the nsF5 algorithm on sensed data.

Keywords: Information hiding · Steganography · Steganalysis · Wireless sensor networks · Security

1 Introduction

Wireless sensor network (WSN) typically consists of base stations and a number of wireless sensors [3]. Sensors are usually small in size, have limited computing capabilities, communicate wirelessly and are powered by small batteries. These sensors are often scattered in a sensor field. Data from the sensor field are collected and sent to a base station. The base station then sends the data to the end users for analysis and strategic decisions. Base stations usually have unlimited power, sufficient memory, powerful processors and a high bandwidth link, in comparison to other sensor nodes.

WSNs are used in many fields. For example, like in military applications for monitoring friendly forces, battlefield surveillance, biological attack detection,

© Institute for Computer Sciences, Social Informatics and Telecommunications Engineering 2014
N. Mitton et al. (Eds.): ADHOCNETS 2014, LNICST 140, pp. 51–62, 2014.
DOI: 10.1007/978-3-319-13329-4_5

troop coordination, and battle damage assessments. In environmental applications, sensors can be used to detect and monitor environmental changes like tracking oil pollution. Data being transmitted are vulnerable to external or internal attacks, such as forgery, tampering, replay and selective forwarding. Data integrity is a core requirement for secure sensor data in WSN. False or malicious data would result in incorrect decisions and potentially financial losses. For instance, an intruder could insert hidden code or a message in the network with intent to do harm. On the battlefield this could result in misinformation to troops that could put them in harm's way. In a health care application, an intruder could insert code that result in the relay of false information about a patient who is being monitored. Such incidents could result in lack of confidence in the security of WSNs.

On the other hand, in an era of rising security concern, steganography (the art of secret communication) and steganalysis (attacks against steganography to discover hidden messages) have taken an increased importance. The information hiding (IH) techniques are reputed to meet both legal and illegal interests. For example, civilians may use it for protecting privacy while terrorists may use it for spreading terroristic information.

In this article, we show that this claim holds too in WSN context, by illustrating the fact that, on the attacker side, steganographiers can be used to manipulate data without being detected, while steganalyzers are useful for the sink to detect any malfunctioning behavior. Our aim is to prove that IH techniques can enrich the collection of tools useful for either guaranteeing or attacking wireless sensor networks. Therefore, we start our work by reviewing existing proposals using IH techniques for WSN security, then we propose a new context of applications with concrete examples and validated via simulation results.

The organization of this paper is as follows. In the next section, we will remind definition of steganography and steganalysis. In Section 3, a practical application of steganalysis for detecting an abnormality in a network is presented. Then, in Section 4, we present a concrete application of steganography to perform an attack on a network. This article ends by a conclusion section, in which the contribution is summarized and intended future work is detailed.

2   Steganography and Steganalysis

2.1   Steganography

Since the rise of the Internet one of the most important factors of information technology and communication has been its security. To do so, encryption has been developed as a technique for securing communications. Many different methods have been developed to encrypt and decrypt data in order to keep the message secret. But it may not be enough to keep the contents of a message secret, it may also be necessary to keep the existence of the message secret. The technique used to implement this is called steganography [2,13].

Steganography is different from cryptography. Where cryptography focuses on keeping the contents of a message secret, steganography focuses on hiding the fact that a secret message exists. Note that (1) the strength of steganography is amplified by combining it with cryptography: first the secret message is encrypted and then it is embedded into other cover content. (2) Images are the most popular carrier files for steganography, because of the way images are stored creates a great amount of redundant space, which is the ideal place to hide information. Hiding information is done through a variety of algorithms, mainly of them being based on bit-level.

2.2 Image Steganography

Researches mainly concentrate on hiding data in gray-scale or color images. Since the luminance component of a color image is equivalent to a gray-scale image, we focus on the steganography for gray-scale images. Besides, it is generally considered that gray-scale images are more suitable than color images for hiding data because the disturbance of correlations between color components may easily reveal the trace of embedding [5,13].

Spatial steganography. The common ground of spatial steganography is to directly change the image pixel values for hiding data. The embedding rate is often measured in bit per pixel (bpp). One of the most reputed tool of this kind is the so-called HUGO steganographier [10].

JPEG steganography. JPEG is one common format of the images produced by digital cameras, scanners, and other photographic image capture devices. Therefore, hiding secret information into JPEG images may provide better camouflage. Most of the steganographic schemes embed data into the non-zero alternate current (AC) discrete cosine transform (DCT) coefficients of JPEG images. As a result, the embedding rate of JPEG steganography is often evaluated in bit per non-zero AC DCT coefficient (bpac). Currently, the best frequency domain steganographier is the nsF5 algorithm [9], described in a next section.

2.3 Steganalysis

Because steganography is a technology that enables users to hide messages from unintended recipients, it can also be used by criminals to hide messages from authorities. None of these have been provenly used, but the fact that these possibilities exist makes it necessary to research methods for detecting steganography. Such methods are called steganalysis [4]. Indeed, for steganographic algorithms sometimes leave a signature in the stego-content, which can be detected by *ad hoc* artificial intelligence tools.

More precisely, steganalysis can be regarded as a two-class pattern classification problem that aims to determine whether a testing medium is a cover medium or a stego one. Steganalysis can be realized following either specific methods or universal ones. A specific steganalytic method fully utilizes the knowledge of a targeted steganographic technique and may only be applicable to such a kind of steganography. A universal steganalytic method can be used to detect several kinds of steganography. Conversely, universal methods do not require the knowledge of the details of the embedding operations. Therefore, it is also called blind method [4,5].

3   Relations Between Images and WSN

The key idea formerly presented in [17] is to visualize the sensory data gathered from the whole network at a certain time snapshot as an image, in which every sensor node is viewed as a pixel with its sensory reading representing the pixel's intensity. As a result, information hiding techniques can be applied to this "sensory data image". Specifically, they adopt direct spread spectrum sequence (DSSS) based watermarking to balance energy consumption in the network with asymmetric resources. With a simple mathematical operation (addition), each sensor node can embed part of the whole watermark into its sensory data, while leaving the heavy computation load from watermark detection at the sink. Once the aggregated and watermarked data reach the sink, this latter is able to verify the existence of the watermark and hence the authenticity of the data.

Authors of this aforementioned article adopt existing image compression schemes as aggregation functions, to reduce network load while retaining the most informative part of the data. Recall that for frequency domain compression like JPEG, an image is first divided into a number of non-overlapping blocks. Then, roughly speaking, a linear transform such as (DCT) or (DWT), is applied to each block to transform the data into frequency domain, and smallest coefficients of this transform are set to 0. Therefore it is possible to slightly alter informative frequential coefficients, in order to embed a secret message in them, which still remains after compression.

The proposal of [17] can thus be summarized as follows. Based on the block size (system parameter), a cluster of sensors is first divided into blocks, in each of which a DCT is performed by the cluster head. Once the aggregated and watermarked data reaches the sink, the sink is able to verify the existence of the watermark and hence the authenticity of the data.

3.1   Steganalyzers as Malfunctioning Detectors

Let us firstly recall a few words about steganalyzers, that is tools designed to detect the presence of hidden information into a given innocent looking cover image.

The oldest steganalytic technique is visible detection, which include human observers detecting minute changes between a cover file and a stego one. For palette-based images, if the embedded file was inserted without first ordering the cover file palette according to its colors, then dramatic color shifts can be found in the stego file. Additionally, since many steganographic tools take advantage of close colors or create their own close color groups, many similar colors in an image palette may make the image suspect [1]. By filtering images as described by Westfield and Pfitzmann in [16], the presence of an embedded file can become obvious to the human observer.

Steganalysis can also involve the use of statistical techniques. By analyzing changes in an image's close color pairs, the steganalyst can determine if LSB substitution was used. Close color pairs consist of two colors whose binary values differ only in the LSB. The sum of occurrences of each color in a close color pair does not change between the cover file and the stego file [16]. This fact, along with the observation that LSB substitution merely flips some of the LSBs, causes the number of occurrences of each color in a close color pair in a stego file to approach the average number of occurrences for that pair [1]. Determining that the number of occurrences of each color in a suspect image's close color pairs are very close to one another gives a strong indication that LSB substitution was used to create a stego file [16].

Fridrich and others proposed a steganalytic technique called the RQP method. It is used on color images with 24-bit pixel depth where the embedded file is encoded in random LSBs. RQP involves inspecting the ratio between the number of close color pairs and all pairs of colors. This ratio is calculated on the suspect image, a test message is embedded, and the ratio is calculated again. If the initial and final ratios are vastly different then the suspect image was likely clean. If the ratios are very close then the suspect image most likely had a secret message embedded in it [7].

These statistical techniques benefit from the fact that the embedding process alters the original statistics of the cover file and in many cases these first order statistics will show trends that can raise suspicion of steganography [7,16]. However, steganographic tools such as OutGuess [14] are starting to maintain the first-order statistics during the embedding process. Steganalytic techniques using sensitive higher-order statistics have been developed to counter this covering of tracks [6,8].

4   Using Steganographic Techniques for Wireless Sensor Networks

4.1   Digital Watermarking and WSN

Current technologies allow validation during data transit through the WSN, but stop after the data reaches its destination (a specific node or the sink). One of the challenges with these technologies is to preserve the source of the data once they leave the WSN. Therefore, it needs to be ensured that the data source is identifiable and the data is valid. Sensors are susceptible to various types of attack, such as data modification, data insertion and deletion, or even physical capture and sensor replacement. Hence, security becomes an important issue with WSNs. Traditional algorithms are used for securing data transmission between sensor nodes. However these algorithms need millions of multiplication instructions to perform operations, and cannot efficiently protect the copyright of the valuable sensor data. Digital watermarking techniques are one of the effective choices to overcome this challenge: a watermark is added as a second line of defense, to ensure that the data is valid.

Two manners to embed a piece of information (the watermark) into the data stream are possible. The embedding can be achieved in such a way that any change or tampering with the original data would corrupt the watermark: this type of digital watermarking is called fragile watermarking. Conversely, in robust watermarking, the added information cannot be removed without destroying the cover information. Fragile watermarking is useful to detect any attempt to tamper with sensed data, while robust watermarking serves when data authentication is required (note that cryptography provides no protection after the content is decrypted). Watermarking algorithms are much lighter and thus require less battery power and processing capabilities than cryptographic-based algorithms. Another advantage for watermarking-based algorithms is that the watermark is embedded directly into the sensor data: the payload does not increases.

4.2   Another Application of Steganographic Tools for WSNs

Using Steganographiers to Achieve WSN Attacks. Steganographic techniques are not only related to sensed data authentication in wireless sensor networks. Another application, which has not yet been investigated in the literature, is to consider the attacker point of view.

Let us suppose that this latter desires to manipulate the data in such a way that this manipulation cannot be detected in sink side. For large scale networks, such a detection and the surveillance of data provided by the wireless sensor network cannot be achieved manually. It necessitates ad hoc techniques for manipulating big data, such as data mining, information theory, or artificial intelligence. Similar techniques have been deployed for detecting artificial manipulations of images or videos, steganalyzers being among the best tools currently available. Thus it is reasonable to consider, as a first approximation, that the sink either embeds such a tool, or at least uses another device having a similar behavior.

A way to achieve such an attack is thus to consider the parallel presented in a previous section, between images and sensory data gathered from the whole network at a certain time snapshot, and to map the modifications of the area following the locations designed by the steganographic tools under consideration. Doing so using an up-to-date steganographier like nsF5 (see below) for achieving, for instance, an intrusion on an area under video-surveillance, leads to slight modifications of the sensed data very difficult to detect, and the adversary can consequently hope to achieve his attack without being detected.

In the following, we will simulate an attack on sensed data using nsF5 algorithm, and we will prove that even up-to-date steganalyzers are not able to detect any abnormal behavior in the data provided by the WSN. Let us first recall how the nsF5 works.

Presentation of nsF5. The nsF5 algorithm [9] extends the F5 algorithm [15]. Let us first have a closer look on this latter. First of all, as far as we know,

F5 is the first steganographic approach that solves the problem of remaining unchanged a part (often the end) of the file. To achieve this, a subset of all the least significant bits LSB is computed thanks to a pseudorandom number generator seeded with a user defined key. Next, this subset is split into blocks of x bits. The algorithm takes benefit of binary matrix embedding to increase it efficiency. Let us explain this embedding on a small illustrative example where a part m of the message has to be embedded into this x LSB of pixels, which are respectively a 3 bits column vector and a 7 bits column vector. Let then H be the binary Hamming matrix

$$H = \begin{pmatrix} 0\ 0\ 0\ 1\ 1\ 1\ 1 \\ 0\ 1\ 1\ 0\ 0\ 1\ 1 \\ 1\ 0\ 1\ 0\ 1\ 0\ 1 \end{pmatrix}$$

The objective is to modify x to get y s.t. $m = Hy$. In this algebra, the sum and the product respectively correspond to the exclusive *or* and to the *and* Boolean operators. If Hx is already equal to m, nothing has to be changed and x can be sent. Otherwise we consider the difference $\delta = d(m, Hx)$ which is expressed as a vector:

$$\delta = \begin{pmatrix} \delta_1 \\ \delta_2 \\ \delta_3 \end{pmatrix},$$

where δ_i is 0 if $m_i = H_{x_i}$ and 1 otherwise.

Let us thus consider the j-th column of H, which is equal to δ. We denote by x_j the vector we obtain by switching the j-th component of x, that is, $\overline{x^j} = (x_1; \ldots; \overline{x_j}; \ldots; x_n)$. It is not hard to see that if y is equal to $\overline{x^j}$, then $m = H_y$. It is then possible to embed 3 bits in only 7 LSB of pixels by modifying on average $1 - 2^3$ changes. More generally, the F5 embedding efficiency should theoretically be $\frac{p}{(1-2^p)}$.

However, the event when the coefficient resulting from this LSB switch becomes zero (usually referred to as shrinkage) may occur. In that case, the recipient cannot determine whether the coefficient was -1, +1 and has changed to 0 due to the algorithm or was initially 0. The F5 scheme solves this problem first by defining a LSB with the following (not even) function:

$$LSB(x) = \begin{cases} 1 - x \mod 2 \text{ if } x < 0, \\ x \quad\quad \mod 2 \text{ otherwise} \end{cases}$$

Next, if the coefficient has to be changed to 0, the same bit message is re-embedded in the next group of x coefficient LSB.

The scheme nsF5 focuses on steps of Hamming coding and ad hoc shrinkage removing. It replaces them with a wet paper code approach that is based on a random binary matrix. More precisely, let D be a random binary matrix of size xn without replicates nor null columns: consider for instance a subset of $\{1, 2^x\}$ of cardinality n and write them as binary numbers. The subset is generated thanks to a PRNG seeded with a shared key. In this block of size x, one choose to embed only k elements of the message m. By abuse, the restriction of the message is again called m. It thus remains $x - k$ (wet) indexes/places where the information should not be stored. Such indexes are generated too with the keyed PRNG. Let v be defined by the following equation:

$$D_v = \delta(m, D_x).$$

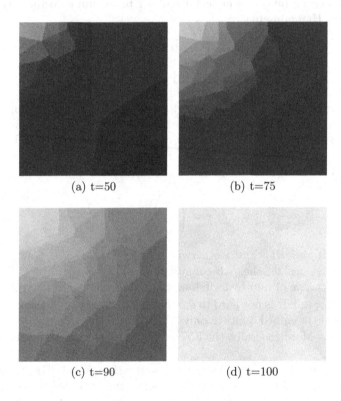

(a) t=50   (b) t=75

(c) t=90   (d) t=100

Fig. 1. The wireless sensor network at various dates

This equation may be solved by Gaussian reduction or other more efficient algorithms. If there is a solution, one have the list of indexes to modify into the cover. The nsF5 scheme implements such an optimized algorithm, that is to say, the LT codes.

Let us now apply this algorithm in order to modify locally the sensed data without being detected.

Simulation Protocol and Results. In this set of experiments, the sensors network computed using Python language is constituted by 256^2 individuals, sensing respectively the temperature (50 % of the sensors), pressure (40 %), and humidity (10 %) levels on the area under consideration. Moreover, the physical measure evolution is defined as follows. 100 particular homogeneous areas have been defined on the monitored place, on which temperature (50 remarkable locations), pressure (40), or humidity (10 locations) are constant. We then have supposed that at time t and location (x, y), and after normalization:

- temperature follows a Gaussian law of parameter $(40(1+0.005t/4\sqrt{x^2+y^2}), 5)$;
- the Gaussian parameters are $(40(1+0.01t/4\sqrt{x^2+y^2}), 5)$ for pressure;
- finally, the 10 humidity remarkable locations produce data following a Gaussian law of parameter $(40(1+0.001t/4\sqrt{x^2+y^2})$.

At each location (x, y), a color pixel is associated to the sensed value, temperature being its red component while pressure and humidity are respectively associated to green and blue. Examples of image-represented data produced by the wireless sensor network are represented in Figure 1 after gray scale conversion.

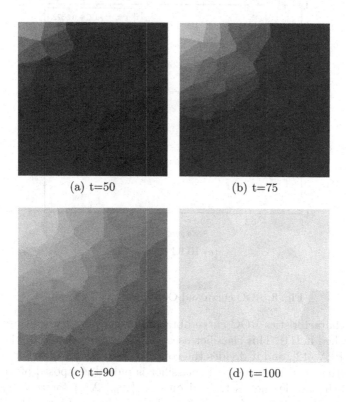

(a) t=50   (b) t=75

(c) t=90   (d) t=100

Fig. 2. The attacked wireless sensor network at various dates

An attack has then been realized on the area under surveillance on locations (physical attack of sensors) provided by the nsF5 [9] algorithm with a payload equal to 0.1 bits per non-zero AC DCT coefficient. Figure 3 contains the receiver

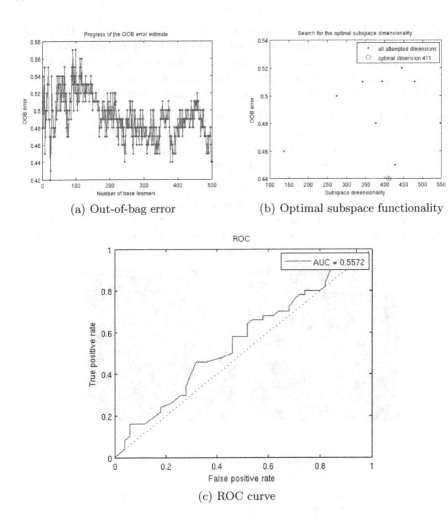

(a) Out-of-bag error   (b) Optimal subspace functionality

(c) ROC curve

Fig. 3. ROC curve and OOB error at sink level

operating characteristics ROC curve obtained at the sink level, using steganalyzer published in [11]. This classifier uses the features extracted by the method called CC-PEV [12], and it divides the collected features into two sets (training set and testing set). This ensemble classifier is indeed composed of many base learners, each base learner is trained on sets $\{X_m, \overline{X}_m\}$ for cover and stego features. Each base learner is implemented as the Fisher Linear Discriminant. It is independently trained on the data composed by cover and stego features. The final decision is obtained by assembling each result produced by these base learners. As it can be observed, the obtained ROC curve is close to the first diagonal, leading to the conclusion that the area observed by both natural and faked sensors would probably appears as natural for the sink. The testing error called *out-of-bag* (OOB) it estimated using equation 1.

$$E_{OOB}^{(n)} = \frac{1}{2N^{trn}} \sum_{m=1}^{N^{trn}} (B^{(n)}(X_m) + 1 - B^{(n)}(\overline{X}_m)) \tag{1}$$

in which X_m and $\overline{X}_m$ are respectively features of original and associated stego features, $m = 1, ..., N^{trn}$, for the cover and stego feature vectors, n is the number of trained base learners, trn is the size of the training set. Figures 3(a), 3(b) show the progression of the error with the number of base learners. As it can be seen, this error does not significantly decrease when the number of base learners increases. It can be deduced from these results that the adversary has achieved to slightly modify some sensors without being detected at sink level.

5 Conclusion

In this article, the usefulness of information hiding technologies for various WSN security concerns has been evoked. It has been described in which contexts steganographiers, steganalyzers, fragile or robust watermarking schemes can be used, and the associated security concern has been detailed. Furthermore, an original application of a well-known steganographier, namely the nsF5 algorithm, has been experimented, while the interest of steganalyzers to detect malfunctioning observed devices has been signaled.

In future work, the authors intention is to investigate more deeply the links evoked between WSN and IH techniques. Cryptographic definitions of security in steganalysis domain will be reformulated in terms of WSN security. A WSN specific malfunctioning detector based on steganalysis literature will be designed and tested, while an attack on a real network already deployed will be executed using the nsF5, to prove the effectiveness of the approach.

References

1. Hiding, I.: Steganography and Watermarking-Attacks and Countermeasures. Kluwer Academic Publishers, Norwell, MA, USA (2001)
2. Bahi, J., Couchot, J.-F., Guyeux, C.: Steganography: a class of secure and robust algorithms. The Computer Journal 55(6), 653–666 (2012)
3. Bahi, J., Guyeux, C., Makhoul, A., Pham, C.: Low cost monitoring and intruders detection using wireless video sensor networks. International Journal of Distributed Sensor Networks, 11 p. (2012)
4. Chanu, Y.J., Singh, K.M., Tuithung, T.: Image steganography and steganalysis: A survey. International Journal of Computer Applications, Published by Foundation of Computer Science 52(2), 1–11 (2012)
5. Chanu, Y.J., Tuithung, T., Singh, K.M.: A short survey on image steganography and steganalysis techniques. In: 2012 3rd National Conference on Emerging Trends and Applications in Computer Science (NCETACS) pp. 52–55 (2012)
6. Farid, H.: Detecting steganographic messages in digital images. Technical report, Hanover, NH, USA (2001)

7. Fridrich, J., Long, M.: Steganalysis of lsb encoding in color images. In: 2000 IEEE International Conference on Multimedia and Expo ICME 2000, 3 pp. 1279–1282 (2000)
8. Fridrich, J., Goljan, M.: Practical steganalysis of digital images - state of the art. In: Proceedings of SPIE pp. 1–13 (2002)
9. Fridrich, J., Pevný, T., Kodovský, J.: Statistically undetectable jpeg steganography: Dead ends challenges, and opportunities. In: Proceedings of the 9th Workshop on Multimedia & Security, MMSec 2007, New York, pp. 3–14 ACM (2007)
10. Gul, G., Kurugollu, F.: A new methodology in steganalysis: breaking highly undetectable steganograpy (hugo). In: Filler, T., Pevný, T., Craver, S., Ker, A. (eds.) IH 2011. LNCS, vol. 6958, pp. 71–84. Springer, Heidelberg (2011)
11. Kodovsky, J., Fridrich, J., Holub, V.: Ensemble classifiers for steganalysis of digital media. IEEE Transactions on Information Forensics and Security 7(2), 432–444 (2012)
12. Kodovský, J., Fridrich, J.: Calibration revisited. In: Proceedings of the 11th ACM Workshop on Multimedia and Security, MMSec 2009, New York, pp. 63–74, ACM (2009)
13. Morkel, T., Eloff, J.H.P., Olivier, M.S.: An overview of image steganography. In: Les Labuschagne Hein S Venter, Jan H P Eloff and Mariki M Eloff, editors, Proceedings of the Fifth Annual Information Security South Africa Conference (ISSA2005), Sandton, South Africa, Published electronically (2005)
14. Provos, N.: Defending against statistical steganalysis. In: Proceedings of the 10th Conference on USENIX Security Symposium - Vol. 10, SSYM 2001, pp. 24–24, Berkeley. USENIX Association (2001)
15. Westfeld, A.: Lecture Notes in Computer Science. In: Moskowitz, I.S. (ed.) F5a steganographic algorithm. Information Hiding, pp. 289–302. Springer, Berlin Heidelberg (2001)
16. Pfitzmann, A. (ed.): IH 1999. LNCS, vol. 1768. Springer, Heidelberg (2000)
17. Zhang, W., Liu, Y., Das, S.K., De, P.: Fast track article: Secure data aggregation in wireless sensor networks: A watermark based authentication supportive approach. Pervasive Mob. Comput. 4(5), 658–680 (2008)

Evaluation of Malware Spreading in Wireless Multihop Networks with Churn

Vasileios Karyotis$^{(\boxtimes)}$ and Symeon Papavassiliou

Institute of Communications and Computer Systems (ICCS),
School of Electrical and Computer Engineering,
National Technical University of Athens, Zografou, 15780 Athens, Greece
vassilis@netmode.ntua.gr, papavass@mail.ntua.gr

Abstract. Modeling malware spreading in wireless networks has attracted significant interest lately, since this will increase the robustness of such networks that constitute the lion's share of Internet access nowadays. However, all of previous works have considered networks with fixed number of devices. In this work, we focus on users that can dynamically join and leave the network (node churn) as a result of the effects of malware, or their own operation, i.e. energy depletion. We adopt and adapt a queuing-based model for malware spreading for the case of wireless distributed networks with churn. The corresponding methodology captures the dynamics of SIS-type malware, where nodes are always prone to receive new or already spreading infections over a long period. The employed framework can be exploited for quantifying network reliability and study network behavior, which can be further used for increasing the robustness of the system against the most severe attacks.

Keywords: SIS malware · Network churn · Wireless multihop networks · Product-form queuing networks · Network robustness

1 Introduction

The wireless communications market has expanded massively in the last decade, constituting nowadays the most preferred way for Internet access by users around the world. Following suit, wireless services and applications, software and wireless devices' technologies have also proliferated, orders of magnitude compared to the ones available ten years ago. Unfortunately, since the emergence of the first computer virus and the corresponding malicious software (malware) targeting mobiles (cabir bluetooth virus in 2004 [1]), malware spreading in wireless networks has exhibited exponential growth (see [2] and references therein).

Modeling accurately the dynamics of malware spreading is of high research and practical importance with numerous associated benefits, especially for wireless networks where the impact of malware can be more severe. In this paper, we focus on exactly this aspect of modeling malware dynamics and in fact, contrary to the majority of other research works, we address this problem in dynamic networks, where nodes join and leave the network (denoted as node churn).

© Institute for Computer Sciences, Social Informatics and Telecommunications Engineering 2014
N. Mitton et al. (Eds.): ADHOCNETS 2014, LNICST 140, pp. 63–74, 2014.
DOI: 10.1007/978-3-319-13329-4_6

Such networks with "node churn" emerge in most of the applications of wireless multihop topologies, e.g. ad hoc, sensor, vehicular, etc., and from this perspective, the contribution of this paper is of great interest for the aforementioned applications of wireless distributed networks.

In the past, various attempts to model malware in general have emerged (see [3] and references therein), each aiming at different objectives. Furthermore, diverse modeling approaches have employed various analytical tools for their purposes. These earliest attempts to model malware spreading in the Internet and wireless networks were based on deterministic methodologies adopted from epidemics [4], while the majority did not consider the possibility of network churn at all. Lately, some notable effort has been devoted to the macroscopic dynamics of malware propagation, especially in wireless decentralized networks [5,6]. Macroscopic modeling refers to the generic study of malware propagation for a long time period, where different types of attacks spread and present recurring behavior, i.e. users become infected repeatedly after their recoveries.

In this paper, we will extend the above direction and study the macroscopic modeling of malware propagation for wireless distributed networks with churn. Based on a closed queuing network model, the transitions of states of legitimate nodes attacked by malicious users are evaluated, while legitimate nodes might enter/leave the network due to exhausting their energy/recharging and/or the impact of malware. We adopt a closed queuing network model, initially developed in [7], based on which a product-form solution is obtained through the Norton equivalent methodology. We use this framework to study and analyze the behavior of wireless distributed networks attacked by a single attacker. The results can be used for assessing the robustness of the network, and can be further exploited in increasing network reliability against the worst possible outbreaks.

The rest of this paper is organized as follows. Section 2 summarizes related works and distinguishes our contribution from them, while Section 3 presents concisely the employed queuing model along with relevant analysis. Section 4, provides quantitative results for the networks of interest and finally, Section 5 concludes the letter.

2   Related Work

Malware can be broadly classified in two main types, i.e. direct and indirect, where threats propagate via physical neighbors only [8], or via multihop infections, e.g. email viruses [9]. In this work, we will focus on the first, since the second can be implicitly analysed as a case of direct malware spreading at a higher protocol layer, e.g. users directly connected at the Application layer.

Furthermore, there are two main infection models[1], denoted by Susceptible - Infected - Removed (SIR) and Susceptible - Infected - Susceptible (SIS), corresponding to the allowed state transition sequence [10]. The SIR is more suitable for the short-term study of independent threats, e.g. CodeRed worm

---

[1] The term 'infection model' characterizes the discipline under which legitimate nodes become infected and recover, if so, due to malware spreading and their operation.

virus, while the SIS is more appropriate for the long-term (macroscopic) study, where nodes oscillate between susceptibility and infection due to recurrent or newly emerging malware. In this paper, we focus on the long-term and steady-state behavior of distributed wireless networks, and thus, we adopt the SIS node infection paradigm for legitimate nodes.

Traditionally, malware propagation modeling has employed epidemics mathematics [4,10], properly adapted to fit communications networks. The problem is cast as a system of ordinary differential equations with respect to the number of infected and the number of removed nodes, if applicable. Epidemics are threat-specific, i.e. more suitable for SIR infection paradigms. However, even in case of advanced epidemic models, e.g. epidemics combined with Kalman estimation [11]), the proposed models cannot describe the evolution of malware propagation in networks with dynamic node churn, such as sensor or ad hoc topologies for example.

As the attack rate increases, in accord with the importance of wireless infrastructures, more generic approaches analyzing malware propagation are required to secure commercial and critical networks. Various models have emerged towards this direction, most of which attempt to analyze malware propagation in more general settings compared to traditional epidemics techniques. Contrary to the differential equations based approach of epidemics, probabilistic tools have been mostly employed for the latest and more generic approaches. In [12], probabilistic models based on Interactive Markov Chains have been proposed, which attempt to partially capture the inherently stochastic nature of attackers over arbitrary topologies. In [13] the impact of topology on the dynamics of the propagation was identified and exploited to design effective countermeasures.

A queuing-based framework has been proposed in [14] for wireless multihop networks, and it was exploited in various capacities, e.g. study of attack strategies. The proposed model describes the macroscopic behavior of malware propagation in wireless multihop networks without churn. The approach presented in this work, adopts the same framework, but extends it in the more general scenario of dynamic networks with node churn.

A stochastic optimization approach was introduced in [15,16], where the concept of varying the transmission power in order to design effective defenses has been jointly considered with epidemic dynamics. Optimal strategies have been developed by exploiting Pontryagin Maximum Principle. However, the proposed framework has been developed for specific energy-depleting attacks and does not consider the possibility of new nodes entering the network (node churn).

Unfortunately, all previous works have not considered the most general behavior of dynamic networks, where legitimate nodes enter/leave the network due to their own operation (e.g. exhausting network energy) and/or the impact of malware. In this work, we will adopt from [7] a closed queuing-network-based methodology that extends the approach of [5] for networks with churn, and exploit it to study the behavior of wireless networks with multihop topology attacked by a single malicious user. Infected nodes can also infect their peers.

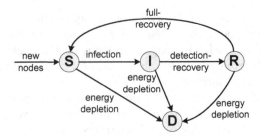

Fig. 1. State transition diagram for legitimate nodes in a network with churn

3 Queuing Based Modeling for Malware Spreading in Wireless Networks with Churn

3.1 System and Malware-Spreading Models

Considering the capabilities of state-of-the-art software and handheld devices that enable recurring malware threats, we focus on the long-term network operation and employ the Susceptible-Infected-Susceptible (SIS) [10] infection model to describe the steady-state behavior of users (legitimate nodes). We consider a static network and also the more general scenario, where users enter and leave the network (node churn [17]), which is often the case in wireless distributed networks, e.g. sensor, vehicular, ad hoc and tactical networks.

In a network with churn, a legitimate node will start susceptible, free of any malware piece, and the corresponding susceptible state is denoted by S (Fig. 1). At some point, a susceptible node will become infected by some spreading threat, e.g. virus, worm, etc., and within a long observation period, the node will eventually return to the susceptible state (by removing the malware). The infected state is denoted by I. In the general case of networks with churn, but also for networks without churn, the short-term behavior of nodes and their corresponding state transition may involve other intermediate states as well, as shown in Fig. 1. These intermediate transitions may involve a recovery state (denoted by R) and a state where nodes are considered dead (denoted by D). The dead state cumulatively represents nodes that cease operation due to exhausted energy or due to malware operation. Nodes that complete their recovery, return to the susceptible state, and without loss of generality, we assume that new nodes entering the network also begin their lifetime in the susceptible state. Dead nodes are completely removed from the network (potentially re-introduced in the network as new susceptibles after a long time). Consequently, the overall system follows the SIS paradigm, where it will be possible for susceptible nodes to become infected and eventually recover again to the susceptible state.

Regarding the communication model, we assume that at each time the network has n legitimate nodes, each with transmission radius R_t. For simplicity, it is also assumed that node pairs are formed only within the transmission range of nodes, as in [5,6]. More general communication models can be incorporated in a straightforward manner.

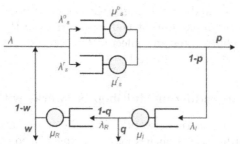

(a) Generic malware propagation queuing model.

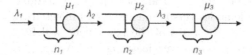

(b) Equivalent product-form serial queuing system.

Fig. 2. Queuing models for malware spreading in networks with churn

With respect to Fig. 1, it can be observed that each user spends an amount of time in each node state that varies stochastically. Furthermore, given the succession of state transitions depicted in Fig. 1, a node entering the network at the susceptible state, might either deplete its energy and become dead with probability p or could become infected by malware and transition to the infected state. From the infected state the node might either deplete its energy as well, cease opearation due to malware and become dead with probability q, or it could transition to the recovery state. Finally, from the recovering state the user either recovers to the susceptible state and the cycle begins again, or the node depletes its energy while recovering and it is removed from the network to the dead state with probability w.

Thus, the behavior of legitimate users can be segregated in two main modes, susceptible and infected-recovering (non-operational). In the first mode, nodes could be operational (some of which might exhaust their energy and leave the network) or recharging. In the infected-recovering mode, nodes become infected and either they move to recovery until they become susceptible again or they are removed from the network. This behavior can be mapped to the operation of a queuing network as shown in Fig. 2(a), where queuing and processing correspond to the time spent by each node in each different state described before. In Fig. 2(a) the upper part corresponds to the normal operation of nodes (susceptible operational - susceptible recharging) and the lower part to the infection-recovery mode. The customers of the queuing network correspond to the nodes of the network as they change states due to malware and node churn. It should be noted that the queuing network is open due to node churn, allowing for new customers to enter (corresponding to new susceptible nodes) and customers to leave (corresponding to nodes depleting their energy or becoming dead due to malware). The depicted input/output and service rates of the queuing network correspond to node churn rates and infection/recovery of the actual legitimate network users under attack, respectively.

3.2 Analysis of Spreading in Multihop Networks with Churn

In order to analyze the generic network of Fig. 2(a), the Norton equivalent [18] of the upper part with parallel queues may be employed, so that a single queue substitutes that part of Fig. 2(a). This does not harm the analysis because in the study of robustness we are not particularly interested in which nodes are susceptible-operational and which are susceptible-recharging. We focus on the number of susceptible nodes versus the number of infected and recovering. From the Norton equivalent, the rates of the new queue will be $\mu_S = \mu_s^o + \mu_s^r$ and $\lambda_S = \lambda_s^o + \lambda_s^r$, where μ regard service rates and λ input rates in general. All μ, λ depicted in Fig. 2(a) correspond to the cumulative queue service rates, which in turn depend on the partial rates of the link infection rate in susceptible state (λ_e), service rate in the infected (μ_i) and recovering (μ_r) queues of each individual node. Without loss of generality these partial rates are considered the same for all users. It should be also noted that all initial input and services are exponential with rates as shown in Fig. 2(a).

The Norton equivalent queuing network obtained from Fig. 2(a) can be analyzed in turn using Jackson's Theorem for product form networks [19]. The latter will have a product form steady-state distribution and it is equivalent to a network of three cascade queues as shown in Fig. 2(b). The service rates of the final cascade network are directly obtained from the Norton equivalent, as $\mu_1 = \mu_S$, $\mu_2 = \mu_I$, $\mu_3 = \mu_R$. The arrival rates in the product-form network (Fig. 2(b)) can be obtained as:

$$\lambda_1 = \frac{1}{1 - (1-p)(1-q)(1-w)}\lambda, \tag{1}$$

$$\lambda_2 = \frac{(1-p)}{1 - (1-p)(1-q)(1-w)}\lambda, \tag{2}$$

$$\lambda_3 = \frac{(1-p)(1-q)}{1 - (1-p)(1-q)(1-w)}\lambda. \tag{3}$$

as functions of the external input of susceptible nodes λ and the probabilities for customers to leave the network p, q, w.

The steady-state distribution of the cascade product-form network will be:

$$p(n_1, n_2, n_3) = p_1(n_1)p_2(n_2)p_3(n_3) \tag{4}$$

where n_1, n_2, n_3 is the number of users in the susceptible, infected and recovering states respectively and at every time instant $n_1 + n_2 + n_3 = n$, where n is the instantaneous total number of network nodes. Even though the combined inputs in Fig. 2(a) are not Poisson, thus nor are the outputs, Jackson's theorem allows to treat each stage (queues in Fig. 2(b)) as independent $M/M/r_i$ queues with input rate λ_i and total service rate μ_i, $i = 1, 2, 3$, where r_i is the number of parallel servers in each stage (here $r_1 = 2, r_2 = r_3 = 1$). An input policy regulating the arrival of new susceptible nodes with respect to the death/removal rates should be employed to ensure $n < \infty$, since all practical networks have finite nodes. Distribution $p_i(n_i)$ provides the number of users in each stage, and since the service rates of the two parallel queues in stage 1 are not the same, we consider the first stage as an $M/M/2$ queue with different service rates for the two servers and obtain its steady-state distribution as:

$$p_1(n_1) = \begin{cases} \left[1 + \frac{C}{\rho_1(1-\rho_1)}\right]^{-1}, & n_1 = 0 \\ \frac{C}{\rho_1 + \frac{C}{1-\rho_1}}, & n_1 = 1 \\ \rho_1^{n-2}\frac{C}{1+\frac{C}{\rho_1(1-\rho_1)}}, & n_1 \geq 2 \end{cases} \tag{5}$$

where $\rho_1 = \lambda_1/\mu_1$, C is a constant depending on λ_1, μ_1, given by:

$$C = \frac{\lambda_1^2}{2\mu_s^o\mu_s^r}, \tag{6}$$

and for the second and third stage, the distributions are respectively:

$$p_2(n_2) = \rho_2^{n_2}\frac{1-\rho_2}{\rho_2} \tag{7}$$

$$p_3(n_3) = \rho_3^{n_3}\frac{1-\rho_3}{\rho_3} \tag{8}$$

where $\rho_2 = \lambda_2/\mu_2$, $\rho_3 = \lambda_3/\mu_3$, $\rho_1, \rho_2, \rho_3 < 1$ and $n_1, n_2, n_3 \geq 0$.

The number of dead nodes is unimportant, since they do not participate in malware dynamics and in addition, it is assumed that new nodes are always available. The service rate of each queue in Fig. 2(b) is the equivalent service rate from Fig. 2(a), which in turn depends on the infection model, malware dynamics and the topology of a network.

The average number of users in the system is given by

$$L = L_1 + \sum_{i=2}^{3} p_{r_i}\frac{\rho_i}{(1-\rho_i)^2} \tag{9}$$

where L_i is the average number of users in each queue and $p_{r_i} = \frac{(\lambda_i/\mu_i)^{r_i}}{r_i!}p_{i,0}$, $i = 2, 3$. In this case, the average number of susceptible (operational) and infected legitimate nodes are respectively:

$$L_1 = \frac{C(1-\rho_1)}{\rho_1(1-\rho_1)+C}\left[1 + \frac{\rho_1(2-\rho_1)}{(1-\rho_1)^2}\right] \tag{10}$$

$$L_2 = \frac{\rho_2}{1-\rho_2}, L_3 = \frac{\rho_3}{1-\rho_3}. \tag{11}$$

Using the customer distributions (5), (7) and (8), other quantities of interest can be computed, e.g. the average throughput of stage 1 provides the average infection rate of the system. Similarly, the average throughput of stage 3 provides the average recovery rate of the system, while the average throughput of stage 2 the average healing rate of infected nodes. Weighting these throughput quantities by the corresponding loss rates p, q, w, the corresponding cumulative node churn loss rate is obtained.

Until this point the analysis is generic and applies to all types of networks with churn. However, the framework developed in Fig. 2, allows more detailed results to be obtained on a per network type case. For instance, apart from n_1, n_2, n_3, one may obtain analytical expressions of the average n_2 with respect to network parameters, such as the infection/recovery rates, node transmission radius and node densities of an ad hoc network. Such task is network type/scenario specific and depends on the topology type and operation. In the following, we will explore from a more practical perspective some of these possible results for multihop networks with churn.

4   Behavior Evaluation in Wireless Distributed Networks

4.1   Simulation Setting

In this section we present numerical and simulation results regarding the operation and behavior of wireless distributed networks with churn, when attacked by a single attacker. Infected nodes are assumed to further propagate the infectious malware they received, while recovering nodes are prevented from doing so. This means that the spreading of malware is mainly due to the network, while the attacker has a smaller role in spreading dynamics, mostly needed to generate new infections in the event that a network manages to recover completely for an instance. Thus, the network spreading dynamics will be studied in the following.

We developed a discrete event simulator in Matlab to study the behavior of the attacked network. At each epoch (slot) of the simulator one event takes place, according to the current state of the system $\{n_1, n_2, n_3\}$, the topology of the network and the corresponding infection (S→I transition), recovering (I→R transition) and full-recovery rates (R→S transition). This is ensured by the nature of the system in Fig. 2.

For the multihop networks we focus on, the link infection rate λ_e of a susceptible node represents the probability that this user will become infected from a malicious neighbor. The multihop topology is considered in our case as a random geometric graph. Combining this with the link infection, a detailed analysis of the system in Fig. 2(a) yields the total infection rate, as the service rate of the single queue of susceptible nodes in the Norton equivalent (which is equal to μ_1 in the product-form equivalent). This infection rate will be $\sum_{i=1}^{n_1} k_i \lambda_e$, where k_i is the number of malicious neighbors of susceptible node i (counting both the attacker and infected legitimate nodes). The total recovering (corresponding to μ_2 in Fig. 2(b)) and full-recovery rates (corresponding to μ_3 in Fig. 2(b)) depend on n_2, n_3, and may be computed as $n_2\mu_i$, $n_3\mu_r$, respectively.

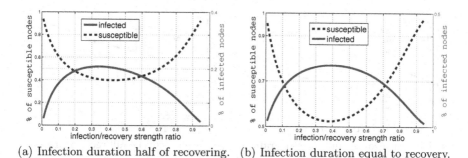

(a) Infection duration half of recovering.   (b) Infection duration equal to recovery.

Fig. 3. Percentages of susceptible-infected nodes as a function of infection to recovery strength (numerical)

Due to space limitations we only provide some indicative results that can be used for the assessment of network reliability and attack potentials. Regarding node churn, we study the behavior of the system for positive churn, i.e. for a $\lambda/(p + q + w) > 1$, which means that the network will be growing on average. This is preferable for the study, as a decreasing network could sometimes lead to degenerate (disconnected) topologies, or even to the extinction of the network.

4.2 Numerical and Simulation Results

Fig. 3 presents some numerical results obtained from the analysis, valid for arbitrary networks, providing intuition on the behavior of the average number of nodes in the states of the system. Churn strength is equal to 1.67, which translates to a growing network. Notice the different scales in the vertical axes in both figures and for both y-axes of each figure, indicating how the expected number of susceptible and infected nodes vary with respect to the time each node is expected to spend in each of the three stages (service rates).

As expected, a decrease in susceptible nodes translates to an increase in the infected nodes. By comparing Fig. 3(a) and Fig. 3(b), it can be also observed that regarding the dependence on the infection/revocery strength, some symmetry (Fig. 3(b)) should be expected when the recovery (μ_i) and full recovery (μ_r) rates are the same. These results, and many similar that can be obtained from the expressions provided before, can be used to assess the robustness of the network. Malware dynamics are represented via the infection and recovery rates, while the full recovery rate represents the countermeasures' efficiency. Thus, given these parameters, the expected state of the system can be evaluated.

The following results have been obtained through simulations, in which a square deployment region with size $L = 1000m$ was employed and all devices used a transmission radius $R_t = 150m$. Fig. 4 presents the expected number of nodes in each state of the system as a function of network density (we fixed the deployment region and increased progressively network nodes). Fig. 4(a) regards a network with uneven recovery-full recovery rates, $\mu_i - \mu_r$ respectively.

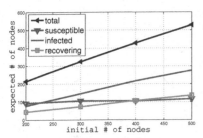
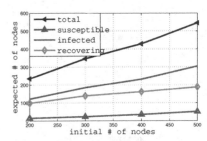

(a) Uneven recovery-full recovery rates.   (b) Even recovery-full recovery rates.

Fig. 4. Expected number of nodes in each state of the network with respect to network density

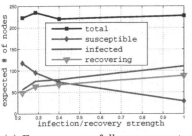
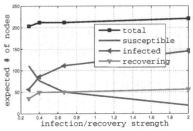

(a) Even recovery-full recovery rates.   (b) Uneven recovery-full recovery rates.

Fig. 5. Expected number of nodes in each state of the network with respect to infection/recovery rates

This means that the mean infection and recovery times will be uneven as well. Fig. 4(b) shows the corresponding results for even rates.

It is observed that as the network density increases, so do the expected number of nodes in each state, and such increase is almost linear. However, the corresponding increase rates are different for uneven recovery-full recovery rates and similar for even rates. In both cases, the infection to full recovery strength is $\lambda_e/\mu_r = 2$. This also explains the fact that the number of infected nodes is the smallest compared to infected and recovering nodes, revealing potential vulnerabilities for the network with respect to the specific malware dynamics and the network structure, as it was also possible to do with the numerical results we presented before.

However, different trends emerge regarding the expected number of nodes in each state with respect to the infection/recovery strength, as shown in Fig. 5. As before, the expected number of susceptible nodes has a complementary behavior to the expected number of infected and recovering nodes. The trend though is not linear. In fact, the number of recovering nodes, especially in Fig. 5(b) seems to saturate for increasing infection/recovery strength. Such results can be again

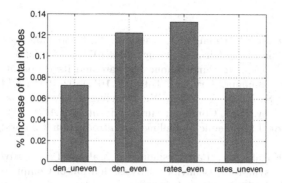

Fig. 6. Expected percentage variation of the total number of nodes with respect to node density and infection/recovery strength

used to evaluate the robustness of the network with respect to the expected behavior under various attack-countermeasure parameters.

Finally, Fig. 6 shows the average percentage difference of network size for equal/unequal infection/recovery strengths and with respect to node density and the intensity of the infection/recovery strength. As expected, this difference is positive (even though small in some cases, since the churn strength was set slightly higher than 1 in all scenarios to ensure a proper topology). The first two bars in Fig. 6 are the average node increase as the density of the network increases, while the last two bars represent the average node count increase for increasing infection/recovery strength. It can be observed that in general even infection-recovery strengths yield higher increase than uneven ones. Equal infection/recovery rates corresponds to strategies providing countermeasures that match the effect of malware at the same time scales, which in turn allow the network to maintain more nodes on average by preventing some I→D transitions (infected nodes becoming dead) due to malware.

5   Conclusions

In this work, we exploited and adapted a queuing framework for modeling malware spreading in wireless multihop networks that exhibit node churn due to malicious attacks and/or energy depletion/recharging. We obtained general expressions for the number of infected nodes in the steady-state of such systems and studied the potentials of the network behavior for possible varying attack profiles. These outcomes can be exploited for enhancing network robustness and security against a broad spectrum of attacks and for various network topologies. Our future work will focus on obtaining spreading optimal controls for malware non-propagative and propagative wireless distributed networks both from the attackers' and network's perspectives.

References

1. Wang, P., Gonzalez, M., Hidalgo, C., Barabasi, A.: Understanding the Spreading Patterns of Mobile Phone Viruses. Science **324**, 1071–1075 (2009)
2. Peng, S., Yu, S., Yang, A.: Smartphone Malware and its Propagation Modeling: A Survey. IEEE Commun. Surv. and Tutorials **16**(2), 925–941 (2014)
3. Wang, Y., Wen, S., Xiang, Y., Zhou, W.: Modeling the Propagation of Worms in Networks: A Survey. IEEE Commun. Surv. and Tutorials **16**(2), 942–960 (2014)
4. Daley, D.J., Gani, J.: Epidemic Modelling: An Introduction. Cambridge University Press (2009)
5. Karyotis, V., Kakalis, A., Papavassiliou, S.: Malware-Propagative Mobile Ad Hoc Networks: Asymptotic Behavior Analysis. Journal of Computer Science and Technology (JCST) **23**(3), 389–399 (2008)
6. Khouzani, M., Sarkar, S., Altman, E.: Maximum Damage Malware Attack in Mobile Wireless Networks. IEEE/ACM Trans Netw. **20**(5), 1347–1360 (2012)
7. Karyotis, V., Papavassiliou, S.: Macroscopic Malware Propagation Dynamics for Wireless Complex Networks with Churn. IEEE Commun. Letters (submitted)
8. Shiu, Y.-S., Chang, S.Y., Wu, H.-C., Huang, S.C.-H., Chen, H.-H.: Physical Layer Security in Wireless Networks: A Tutorial. IEEE Wirel. Commun. Mag. **18**(2), 66–74 (2011)
9. Zou, C.C., Towsley, D., Gong, W.: Email Virus Propagation Modeling and Analysis, Technical Report: TR-CSE-03-04 (April 2004)
10. Pastor-Satorras, R., Vespignani, A.: Epidemic Spreading in Scale-Free Networks. Phys. Rev. Lett. **86**, 3200–3203 (2001)
11. Zou, C.C., Gong, W., Towsley, D., Gao, L.: The Monitoring and Early Detection of Internet Worms. IEEE/ACM Trans. Netw. **13**(5), 961–974 (2005)
12. Garetto, M., Gong, W., Towsley, D.: Modeling Malware Spreading Dynamics. In: Proc. 22nd Annual Joint Conf. IEEE Comp. and Commun. Societies (INFOCOM), vol. 3, pp. 1869–1879 (March-April 2003)
13. Ganesh, A., Massoulie, L., Towsley, D.: The Effect of Network Topology on the Spread of Epidemics. In: Proc. 25th Annual Joint Conf. IEEE Comp. and Commun. Societies (INFOCOM), vol. 2, pp. 1455–1466 (March 2006)
14. Karyotis, V., Papavassiliou, S., Grammatikou, M., Maglaris, V.: A Novel Framework for Mobile Attack Strategy Modeling and Vulnerability Analysis in Wireless Ad-hoc Networks. Int'l Journal of Security and Networks (IJSN) **1**(3/4), 255–265 (2006)
15. Khouzani, M., Sarkar, S.: Dynamic Malware Attack in Energy-Constrained Mobile Wireless Networks. In: Proc. 5th Symp. Inf. Theory and Applications, UCSD (February 2010)
16. Khouzani, M., Sarkar, S., Altman, E.: Maximum Damage Malware Attack in Mobile Wireless Networks. In: Proc. 29th IEEE Conf. on Computer Communications (INFOCOM) (March 2010)
17. Holzer, S., Pinkolet, Y.A., Smula, J., Wattenhofer, R.: Monitoring Churn in Wireless Networks. Elsevier Journal of Theoretical Computer Science **453**, 29–43 (2012)
18. Schwartz, M.: Telecommunications Networks. Addison-Wesley, USA (1987)
19. Bertsekas, D., Gallager, R.: Data Networks, Prentice Hall, 2nd edn., USA (1992)

Security and Privacy-Preserving Mechanism for Aggregator Based Vehicle-to-Grid Network

Binod Vaidya, Dimitrios Makrakis[✉], and Hussein T. Mouftah

School of Electrical Engineering and Computer Science,
University of Ottawa, Ottawa, Canada
{bvaidya,dimitris,mouftah}@eecs.uottawa.ca

Abstract. Electrification is foremost actor in superseding internal combustion engine vehicles with electric vehicles (EV). The EV technology will lead to fundamental shift in existing power grid as well as transportation systems. In Smart grid, EVs play vital roles to reduce dependence on fossil fuel, in turn, minimize green house gas emissions. In Vehicle-to-Grid (V2G) network, EVs communicate with power grid operators to trade demand response services by delivering stored electricity into the electric power grid. Communication between aggregator and EVs is central for such an approach. Viewing security and privacy requirements for V2G communications, privacy-preserving technique is central for efficacious V2G network implementation. In this paper, we have proposed effective security and privacy-preserving mechanism for aggregator based V2G network, which is built on ECC-based restrictive partially blind signature. We have provided security analysis and shown that the proposed mechanism is efficient than existing ones in terms of computational overheads.

1   Introduction

Rising escalations in fossil fuel prices and mounting environmental concerns are fundamental drivers in the growing interest in "green" electric-powered vehicles alternatives to internal combustion engine vehicles. For the emerging Smart grid environment, electric vehicles (EVs) play vital roles to reduce dependence on fossil fuel energy, in turn, minimize green house gas (GHG) emissions. Another noteworthy benefit of EVs is that, with large deployment of such vehicles can be used to store energy and deliver this energy back to the power grid when needed. This concept is typically referred to as Vehicle-to-grid (V2G) [1].

By allowing EVs discharge during peak hours and charge during off-peak hours could bring several benefits to the V2G network such as providing ancillary services (i.e. regulation and spinning reserve) as well as faster response time and optimized schedules for recharging. Thus, the V2G network is vital component of emerging Smart grid, which has capability of providing better ancillary services [2, 3].

However, recharging numerous EVs yields a substantial load for the power grid. In order to tackle this issue, a common monitoring entity, so-called aggregator, is deployed that could communicate directly with each EV to continuously monitor its up-to-date status and to manage charging process. Basically, the status information

© Institute for Computer Sciences, Social Informatics and Telecommunications Engineering 2014
N. Mitton et al. (Eds.): ADHOCNETS 2014, LNICST 140, pp. 75–85, 2014.
DOI: 10.1007/978-3-319-13329-4_7

includes the EV's location, battery's capacity, battery's state-of-charge (SoC), expected time to leave, etc. Furthermore, energy is delivered back from EVs to the power grid in a controlled way such that connected EVs could constitute a distributed grid resource [3]. The aggregator could sell services that support power grid operators with balancing out energy supply and demand [1-3]. EV owners, in turn, could be compensated for providing their energy resource.

It can be perceived that the monitoring process should be continuous due to the fact that not only presence of EVs in the V2G network are dynamic but also EVs' batteries may be damaged with fluctuating SoC. While communicating with the aggregator, the EVs have to provide information such as identity, location, duration of charging etc. to the aggregator, thus, privacy of the EV owners may be at risk [1]. For instance, by scrutinizing the monitoring data of individual EV, such as the location of parking lots it visited and duration of parking, a malicious entity could reveal sensitive details, e.g., a person's habits, social network, and other activities.

Yang *et al.* [10] proposed a privacy-preserving communication and precise reward architecture for V2G networks, in which, two-tier aggregators having single central aggregator (CAG) and multiple local aggregators (LAGs) to lessen communication burden on the CAG. Their protocol is based on identity-based public key cryptography (PKC) and also utilizes the ID-based restrictive partially blind signature for protecting the privacy of EVs. Subsequently, Tseng [11] modified Yang et al.'s protocol and presented a secure and privacy-preserving communication protocol for V2G Networks using certificate-less public key settings. Basic aim of this protocol is to overcome key escrow problem as in ID-based PKC. The problem with these systems is local aggregators have to be fully trustworthy.

Stegelmann and Kesdogan [12] presented design and evaluation of privacy-preserving architecture for V2G interaction, in which Identity Mixer (Idemix) anonymous credential technique is used. And Y. Zhang, *et al.* proposed context-based and role-based authentication mechanisms for V2G communications [14].

In this paper, we have proposed robust and effective security and privacy-preserving mechanism for aggregator based V2G network in Smart grid environment that utilizes ECC-based restrictive partially blind signature (RPBS) [4, 5].

The remainder of this paper is structured as follows. Section 2 discusses design model and security requirements, while Section 3 presents proposed security mechanism for V2G network. And Section 4 describes system analysis. Finally, in Section 5, we provide concluding remarks.

2 Network Architecture

In this section, we have presented network model for an aggregator based V2G network well as security and privacy requirements.

2.1 Network Model

A network model of the V2G network has similar architecture as in [10], hence we follow similar concept of business model for EV energy exchange as mentioned in [10]. Figure 1 shows a network model of the aggregator based V2G network.

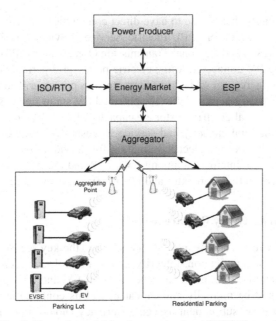

Fig. 1. Network model for Aggregator-based V2G Network

Fundamentally, there are following principal parties, incorporating trusted authority (TA), aggregator (AG), electric vehicle charging station (EVCS), aggregating points (APs) and electric vehicles (EVs). In this network model, a loosely bound two-tier aggregation technique with single AG and multiple APs is deployed. Having direct communication with individual EV, APs provide distributed local authentication and assist AG by collecting information from EVs. The TA is usually an offline authority that executes system initialization including generating system parameters and allotting partial-private-key parameter to all entities in the particular V2G network. The single TA can serve to more than one V2G network.

Electric vehicle charging station, also called electric charging point or electric vehicle supply equipment (EVSE), is an element in an EV infrastructure that supplies electric energy for the charging/recharging of plug-in electric vehicles. EVSEs may belong to a commercial parking lot or a private residence, through which the EV can connect to the electric power grid.

Each parking lot (either private or public) has at least one aggregating point (AP) to serve numerous EVSEs. The AP is particularly being positioned in every local access network such that the entire geographically outsized V2G network is covered. The main objective of the AP is to provide distributed local authentication for the EVs and mediate between the EVs and the AG. Furthermore, the AP collects secured monitoring data from each EV and sends aggregated such data to the AG. In this architecture, even gateway router of the charging station may act as AP.

Communication between the EV and the AP in the local access network is realized with various wired and wireless technologies whereas communication between APs and AG could be possible using various wide-area network (WAN) technologies.

The AG is the entity that is able to have direct communication with the energy market including Power Producer (PP), Electric Service Providers (ESPs), Independent System Operators (ISO) and Regional Transmission Organizations (RTO) [6, 7].

Every partaking EV connected to the electric power grid periodically yields its recent status to the aggregator (AG). Furthermore, the power grid announces service requests in the electricity market. With the obtained EV status updates, the aggregator can evaluate current total electricity storage capacity of each EV in the V2G network. Hence, based on the total capacity and service requests from the power grid, the aggregator can make bids in the electricity market for providing some of the V2G services. In this paper, the interaction among EVs, APs and the AG is considered, while the interaction between the aggregator and other players is neglected.

2.2   Security and Privacy Requirements

In the context of wireless access in the V2G network, the key security considerations may be as follows: authentication, integrity, access control, confidentiality, and non-repudiation. Essentially, communication between an EV and the aggregators in the V2G network should be mutually authenticated, and its confidentiality and integrity protected. Furthermore, subsequent aspects of privacy should be considered in V2G environments: anonymity, context privacy, untraceability and unlinkability.

3   Proposed Security and Privacy-Preserving Mechanism

In this section, we have proposed efficient and robust security and privacy-preserving mechanism for aggregator based V2G system. In this mechanism, we have used ECC-based RPBS along with collective group-oriented signcryption technique to offer efficient V2G-enabled service. Considering above-mentioned requirements, the proposed mechanism is divided into four phases, namely, initialization phase, license generation phase, license verification phase and EV status monitoring phase. A combination of license generation phase and license verification phase is categorized as an ECC-based access control mechanism.

In initialization phase, every entity (EV, AP, AG) in the V2G system needs to contact the trusted authority (TA) to obtain partial-secret parameter in order to construct key pair using ECC-based self-certified public key cryptosystem. Furthermore, the EVs have to open their accounts at the AG.

The key generation phase is grounded on ECC-based self-certified public key cryptosystem (SC-PKC). Initially, an entity (i.e. EV, AP, and AG) submits identification information such as unique identity (ID_A) to the trusted authority (TA). The TA derives a partial-private key using the user's identity and its master key. The entity then combines the partial-private key with a secret value to generate an actual private key. Then it can create its public key as well. It can be seen that the TA in

SC-PKC does not have access to the user's private key. The system is not ID-based, because the public key is no longer computable from a user's identity.

Prior to participating the V2G network, every EV has to undertake the registration at the registration authority (RA) at the AG. Registration phase begins when the EV wants to create user account at the AG, the AG requests the EV to provide his legal identification. The AG stores its real identity (ID_{EV}) of the particular EV along with unique account information ($\Lambda_E = \iota_E.P$) in the database. The AG also sends a group secret $\langle \varpi_S \rangle$ to all the group members (i.e. AP, EV). Figure 2 depicts ECC-based self-certified public key generation process as well as the entity registration process with RA/AG.

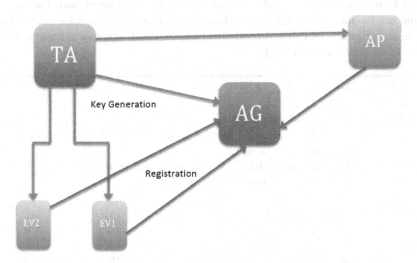

Fig. 2. Key generation and Registration Processes

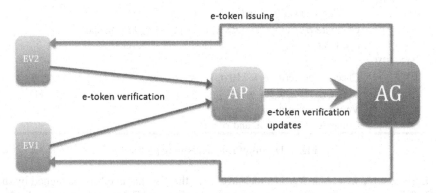

Fig. 3. E-token issuing, e-token verification and updating processes

Figure 3 illustrates e-token issuing process as well as e-token verification process and e-token verification updating process. In order to allow only the authorized EVs to access the V2G network, accredited e-tokens (TOK_{EV}) are issued to the eligible EVs after the legitimate registration. For this purpose, we have proposed ECC-based access control mechanism. This access control mechanism includes e-token issuing phase and e-token verification phase. So the ECC-based restrictive partially blind signature scheme is proposed, which has applied same concept as stated in the scheme mentioned in [10].

In e-token issuing phase, an EV has sent a request with its real-identity to obtain dynamic pseudo-identity (PID_{EV}) and an e-token (TOK_{EV}) from the AG. And ECC-based restrictive partially blind signature technique is deployed such that the AG would not be able to link EV's real identity after this phase. In the e-token issuing phase, the proposed ECC-based restrictive partially blind signature scheme is similar to the scheme mentioned in [10].

EV	Compute $\kappa_i = (\kappa_{1x}, \kappa_{1y}) = \varpi_S.x_{EV}.X_{AG}$; and $e_i = H(m, \Sigma_{EV}, \kappa_{1x}, t_1)$
EV→AG	$\{ID_{EV}, \Sigma_{EV}, m, e_1, t_1\}$
AG	Check t_1 and verify Σ_{EV}
	Compute $\kappa_i = (\kappa_{1x}, \kappa_{1y}) = \varpi_S.x_{AG}.X_{EV}$ and verify $e_1 = ? H(m, \Sigma_{EV}, \kappa_{2x}, t_1)$
	Generate $w, \delta, k_1, k_2 \in Z_n^*$
	Compute $PID_{EV} = H(ID_{EV}, \delta)$; $z = x_{AG}.m$; $a = w.P$; $b = w.m$;
	$u = k_1.P + k_2.X_{AG}$; and $e_2 = H(PID_{EV}, z, a, b, u, \kappa_{1x}, t_2)$
AG→EV	$\{PID_{EV}, z, a, b, u, e_2, t_2\}$
EV	Check t_2 and verify $e_2 = ? H(PID_{EV}, z, a, b, u, \kappa_{1x}, t_2)$
	Generate $\alpha, \beta, \gamma, \lambda, \mu, \xi \in Z_n^*$
	Compute $m' = \alpha.m$; $z' = \alpha.z$; $a' = \gamma.a + \lambda.P$; $b' = \alpha.\gamma.b + \lambda.m'$;
	$B = (\beta + \gamma).P$; $u' = \mu.\xi.X_{AG} + H(\Delta)(\mu.u - X_{TA})$; $c' = H(m', u', z', a', b', B)$;
	$c_1 = \gamma^i(c')$; $c_2 = \mu^i(c') + \xi$; and $e_3 = H(c_1, c_2, \kappa_{1x}, t_3)$
EV→AG	$\{c_1, c_2, s_3, e_3, t_3\}$
AG	Check t_3 and verify $e_3 = ? H(c_1, c_2, \kappa_{1x}, t_3)$
	Compute $\sigma_1 = w + c_1.x_{AG}$; $\sigma_2 = c_2.x_{AG} + (k_1 + k_2.x_{AG}).H(\Delta)$; and
	$e_4 = H(\sigma_1, \sigma_2, \kappa_{1x}, t_4)$
AG→EV	$\{\sigma_1, \sigma_2, e_4, t_4\}$
EV	Check t_4 and verify $e_4 = ? H(\sigma_1, \sigma_2, \kappa_{1x}, t_4)$
	Verify $\sigma_1.P = c_1.X_{AG} + a$ (1)
	Verify $\sigma_1.m = c_1 z + b$ (2)
	Compute $\sigma_1' = \gamma\sigma_1 + \lambda$; and $\sigma_2' = \mu\sigma_2$

Fig. 4. Details of E-token issuing protocol

Let's assume $m = \Lambda_E + X_{EV}$ is a message from the EV that needs to be signed by the AG. Prior to accessing a local access network of the V2G network, a particular EV primarily computes its shared secret key (κ_{1x}, κ_{1y}) with AG. Next, the EV sends a request message including its certificate. After proper confirmation, the AG computes dynamic pseudo-identity (PID_{EV}) as well as commitments and sends to the EV.

The EV chooses some random numbers called blind factors to jumble message such that the signer (i.e. AG) will be blind to the prior message. Upon receiving the blinded message, the AG produces the blind signatures and then sends them to the EV, which in turn, creates a number of e-token (TOK_{EV}). Figure 4 shows the details of e-token issuing protocol.

The proposed ECC-based restrictive partially blind signature on (m', Δ) is (u', z', c', σ_1', σ_2'). And an e-token is given as $TOK_{EV} = \{(m', \Delta) (u', z', c', \sigma_1', \sigma_2'), B\}$.

In e-token verification phase, any legitimate entities (i.e. AP) can verify whether the e-token (TOK_{EV}) is genuine or not. For diverse V2G services, the EV may need to access the V2G network at different locations, thus APs can provide distributed local authentication.

Before validating e-token (TOK_{EV}), the mutual authentication between the EV and the AP takes place. The AP also checks expiration time of the TOK_{EV}. If they are valid, the AP checks legitimacy of the blind signature of the given TOK_{EV} by validating following equations (Eq. 2 & 3). If these equations meet, then the AP temporarily stores information of the particular EV. A detail explanation of the e-token verification protocol is depicted in Figure 5.

EV→AP	$\{PID_{EV}, TOK_{EV}\}$
AP	Derive $\varepsilon = (PID_{EV} \parallel \varpi_S \parallel m' \parallel B)$
	Compute $\kappa_E = (\kappa_{E_x}, \kappa_{E_y}) = x_{AP}, \varpi_S.P$; $d = H(\varepsilon, X_{AP}, spec)$; and
	$AUTH_1 = HMAC\kappa_{E_x}(ID_{AP}, \varepsilon, d)$
AP→EV	$\{ID_{AP}, d, AUTH_1\}$
EV	Derive $\varepsilon = (PID_{EV} \parallel \varpi_S \parallel m' \parallel B)$
	Compute $\kappa_E = (\kappa_{E_x}, \kappa_{E_y}) = \varpi_S.X_{AP}$
	Verify $HMAC\kappa_{E_x}(ID_{AP}, \varepsilon, d) = ? AUTH_1$
	Compute $q_1 = d\alpha_E + \beta\varepsilon$, and $q_2 = d\alpha_{EV} + \gamma\varepsilon$
EV→AP	$\{Resp, q_1, q_2\}$
AP	Compute $a' = (\sigma_1'.P - c'.X_{AG})$; and $b' = (m'.\sigma_1' - c'.z')$
	Verify $c' = ? H(m', u', z', a', b', B)$ (2)
	Verify $\sigma_2'.P = ? u' + c'.X_{AG} + H(\Delta).X_{TA}$ (3)
	Verify $(q_1 + q_2).P = ? d.m' + \varepsilon B$ (4)

Fig. 5. Details of E-token Verification protocol

Then the AP will batch the e-token verification updates for certain time interval and send it to the AG by using Schnorr-like digital signature. The AG verifies such digital signature and stores the e-token information of all received EVs. In case the e-token is used more than once for particular PID_{EV} of the given EV, then the AG can check the exculpability of the e-token for such EV. Figure 6 shows the details of e-token verification updating protocol.

After authentic e-token validation, the AP continuously obtains secured EV status in its neighborhood and sends aggregated data to the AG. Due to space limits, the details of EV status monitoring protocol are excluded in this paper.

AP	Generate $v \in Z_n^*$
	Compute $W = v.P$ and $\kappa_2 = (\kappa_{2x}, \kappa_{2y}) = \varpi_S.x_{AP}.X_{AG}$
	Concatenate $\Theta = \{(PID_{EV_1}, TOK_{EV_1}, q_{1_1}, q_{2_1}, spec_1), ..,$
	$(PID_{EV_i}, TOK_{EV_i}, q_{1_i}, q_{2_i}, spec_i)\}$
	Encrypt $\Theta_{EN} = \Theta \oplus \kappa_{2x}$
	Compute $h_1 = H(\Theta, \kappa_2)$; and $g_1 = v + x_{AP}.h_1$
AP→AG	$\{ID_{AP}, W, \Theta_{EN}, g_1\}$
AG	Compute $\kappa_2 = (\kappa_{2x}, \kappa_{2y}) = \varpi_S.x_{AG}.X_{AP}$
	Decrypt $\Theta = \Theta_{EN} \oplus \kappa_{2x}$
	Verify $g_1.P =? W - H(\Theta, \kappa_2).X_{AP}$ (5)
	Keep $\{(PID_{EV_1}, TOK_{EV_1}, q_{1_1}, q_{2_1}, spec_1), ...,$
	$(PID_{EV_i}, TOK_{EV_i}, q_{1_i}, q_{2_i}, spec_i)\}$

Fig. 6. Details of E-token Verification updating protocol

4   System Analysis

In this section, we provide security analysis, efficiency analysis and performance analysis of the proposed mechanism.

4.1   Security Analysis

We have postulated security analysis of the proposed security and privacy-preserving mechanism.

Proposition 1: The proposed ECC-based restrictive partially blind signature scheme fulfills the property of restrictiveness.

The restrictiveness property of the protocol can be apprehended by the following assumption. The recipient acquires a signature on a message that can only be the form m'. During e-token issuing protocol, α is randomly selected and $m' = \alpha m$ is computed by the EV. Thus the proposed mechanism achieves the restrictiveness.

Proposition 2: If the underlying primitives (i.e. RPBS) are secure, then the proposed mechanism satiates the requirements of anonymity and untraceability.

Since the e-token issuing protocol is based on restrictive partially blind signature technique, the AP cannot deduce the EV's real identity from dynamic pseudonym (PID_{EV}) while verifying the e-token (TOK_{EV}). Anonymity is the distinguishing property of our e-token. The privacy of the EV is guaranteed even against collaboration of the involved parties (i.e., AG and AP), unless the EV tries to use same e-token twice in the process.

Proposition 3: If the underlying primitives (i.e. RPBS) are secure, then the proposed mechanism gratifies the unlinkability.

The EV exploits dynamic pseudonym (PID_{EV}) as well as fresh RPBS-based e-token (TOK_{EV}) for every parking session, hence APs or the AG would not be able to link the specific EV's manifold parking sessions with the same EV and construct its user profile.

4.2   Efficiency Analysis

We have shown efficiency analysis of the proposed mechanism in terms of computational costs. Table 1 show the efficiency comparison for issuing protocols, whereas Table 2 shows the efficiency comparison for verification protocol of the proposed mechanism with those of the existing schemes.

Table 1. Efficiency Comparison for Issuing Protocols

	EV	AG or CAG
Yang et al.'s scheme [10]	$8\,t_p$ (5 offline), $9\,t_{ECM}$, $3\,t_{ECA}$, $9\,t_{EXP}$	$4\,t_p$, $5\,t_{ECM}$, $1\,t_{ECA}$
Tseng's scheme [11]	$8\,t_p$ (5 offline), $7\,t_{ECM}$, $5\,t_{ECA}$, $9\,t_{EXP}$	$4\,t_p$, $3\,t_{ECM}$, $1\,t_{ECA}$
Proposed scheme	$15\,t_{ECM}$, $5\,t_{ECA}$	$6\,t_{ECM}$, $1\,t_{ECA}$

Table 2. Efficiency Comparison for Verification Protocols

	EV	AP or LAG
Yang et al.'s scheme [10]	$1\,t_p$, $1\,t_{ECM}$	$6\,t_p$, $1\,t_{ECM}$, $1\,t_{ECA}$, $6\,t_{EXP}$
Tseng's scheme [11]	$1\,t_p$, $1\,t_{ECM}$	$6\,t_p$, $1\,t_{ECM}$, $1\,t_{ECA}$, $2\,t_{EXP}$
Proposed scheme	$1\,t_{ECM}$	$10\,t_{ECM}$, $5\,t_{ECA}$

In Table 1 and Table 2, notations used are as follows: t_P is time required for computing pairing operation; t_{ECM} is time required for computing Elliptic curve (EC) scalar multiplication operation; t_{ECA} is time required for computing EC addition operation; and t_{EXP} is time required for computing exponentiation operation. For sake of convenience, we have omitted computational overheads of hash functions and HMAC since their contribution to overall computational cost will be insignificant.

It can be seen that the existing representative schemes [10,11] use pairing operations, whereas the proposed mechanism uses EC scalar multiplication operations, which is much more efficient than pairing operation and consumes much less time. According to [13], time to perform EC scalar multiplication (t_{ECM}) and pairing operation (t_P) are 0.6 ms and 4.5 ms respectively, thus our protocols are more effectual than the existing protocols [10, 11].

4.3   Security Proof

In this sub-section, we have shown security proof of the proposed mechanism.

Lemma 1. If the prover is honest (i.e. he knows a representation and follows a protocol), the verifier will accept it such that the protocol will satisfy the property of completeness.

Proof. The legitimacy of the blind signature of the given TOK_{EV} can be proved by validating Equations 2 and 3.

$$
\begin{aligned}
c' &= H(m', u', z', a', b', B) \\
&= H(m', u', z', (\sigma_1'.P - c'.X_{AG}), (m'.\sigma_1' - c'.z'), B)
\end{aligned}
$$

$$
\begin{aligned}
\sigma_2'.P &= u' + c'.X_{AG} + H(\Delta).X_{TA} \\
&= \mu\xi X_{AG} + H(\Delta)(\mu.u - X_{TA}) + c'.X_{AG} + H(\Delta).X_{TA} \\
&= \mu\xi X_{AG} + \mu H(\Delta)(k_1.P + k_2.X_{AG}) - H(\Delta).X_{TA} + c'.X_{AG} + H(\Delta).X_{TA} \\
&= \mu\xi X_{AG} + \mu H(\Delta)(k_1.P + k_2.X_{AG}) + c'.X_{AG} \\
&= c'x_{AG}.P + \mu\xi x_{AG}.P + \mu H(\Delta)(k_1.P + k_2.X_{AG}) \\
&= \mu x_{AG}(\mu^1 c' + \xi).P + \mu H(\Delta)(k_1.P + k_2 x_{AG}.P) \\
&= \mu(x_{AG}c_2 + (k_1 + k_2.x_{AG})H(\Delta)).P \\
&= \mu\sigma_2.P \\
&= \sigma_2'.P
\end{aligned}
$$

5   Conclusions and Future Works

In this paper, we have proposed security and privacy preserving mechanism for aggregator based V2G network that utilizes ECC-based RPBS. For this purpose, we have proposed ECC-based access control mechanism. We have provided security analysis, efficiency analysis and security proof of the proposed mechanism. The proposed mechanism provides privacy aspects such as anonymity, privacy, untraceability, and unlinkability that would be desirable for V2G communication. Furthermore, it can be seen that our proposed mechanism is superior to the existing ones while conducting the efficiency analysis of respective issuing and verification protocols.

In future, we will incorporate EV status monitoring process and investigate the performance of the proposed mechanism. And other future works will be secure financial transaction and other services involved in the aggregator based V2G networks.

Acknowledgement. This work was supported by the Government of Ontario under the ORF-RE WISENSE project.

References

1. Guille, C., Gross, G.: A conceptual framework for the vehicle-to-grid (V2G) implementation. Energy Policy **37**(11), 4379–4390 (2009)
2. Kempton, W., Tomic, J.: Vehicle-to-grid power implementation: From stabilizing the grid to supporting large-scale renewable energy. Journal of Power Sources **144**(1), 280–294 (2005)
3. Brooks, A.N.: Vehicle-to-Grid Demonstration Project: Grid Regulation Ancillary Service with a Battery Electric Vehicle Tech. Rep. Contract no. 01-313, AC Propulsion, Inc. (December 2002)
4. Chaum, D.: Blind signatures for untraceable payments. In: Proc. of CRYPTO 1982, pp. 199–203 (1982)
5. Maitl, G., Boyd, C.: A Provably Secure Restrictive Partially Blind Signature Scheme. In: Naccache, D., Paillier, P. (eds.) PKC 2002. LNCS, vol. 2274, p. 99. Springer, Heidelberg (2002)
6. Jansen, B., et al.: Architecture and Communication of an Electric Vehicle Virtual Power Plant. Proc. of IEEE SmartGridComm 2010, 149–154 (2010)
7. Marra, F., et al.: Electric vehicle requirements for operation in smart grids. In: Proc. of IEEE PES ISGT Europe (2011)
8. Tuttle, D.P., Baldick, R.: The Evolution of Plug-In Electric Vehicle-Grid Interactions. IEEE Transactions on Smart Grid **3**(1), 500–505 (2012)
9. Markel, T., et al.: Communication and control of electric drive vehicles supporting renewables. Proc. of IEEE VPPC 2009, 27–34 (2009)
10. Yang, Z., et al.: P2: Privacy-Preserving Communication and Precise Reward Architecture for V2G Networks in Smart Grid. IEEE Transactions on Smart Grid **2**(4), 697–706 (2011)
11. Tseng, H.R.: A Secure and Privacy-Preserving Communication Protocol for V2G Networks. In: Proc. of 2012 IEEE WCNC, pp. 2706–2711 (2012)
12. Stegelmann, M., Kesdogan, D.: Design and Evaluation of a Privacy-Preserving Architecture for Vehicle-to-Grid Interaction. In: Petkova-Nikova, S., Pashalidis, A., Pernul, G. (eds.) EuroPKI 2011. LNCS, vol. 7163, pp. 75–90. Springer, Heidelberg (2012)
13. Zhang, C., et al.: On batch verification with group testing for vehicular communications. Wireless Network **17**(8), 1851–1865 (2011)
14. Zhang, Y., et al.: Securing Vehicle-to-Grid Communications in the Smart Grid, In: IEEE Wireless Communications (2013)

An Improved TCP for Reduced Packet Delay in IEEE 802.11s-Based Smart Grid AMI Networks

Nico Saputro[✉] and Kemal Akkaya

Department of Computer Science, Southern Illinois University,
Carbondale, IL 62901, USA
nico@siu.edu, kemal@cs.siu.edu

Abstract. Transmission Control Protocol (TCP) can handle packet
losses by retransmitting them when the corresponding acknowledgement
(ACK) packets are not received within a certain time interval. This time
interval is referred to as *retransmission timeout* (RTO) and setting its
value is critical to reduce the packet delay in Smart Grid Advanced Metering Infrastructure (AMI) networks. In this paper, we propose a novel
mechanism to set the RTO of each smart meter (SM) to improve the performance of TCP in IEEE 802.11s-based AMI networks in terms of packet
delay. The idea is based on using the location of the SMs in the network
topology and assign an RTO based on its distance from the gateway. In
addition, we propose eliminating the doubling of RTO value when ACK
packets are not received. The simulation results under ns-3 simulator indicate that the delay performance can be improved at least 40% with the
use of these mechanisms.

Keywords: IEEE 802.11s · Advanced Metering Infrastructure ·
Transmission Control Protocol · Retransmission Timeout

1 Introduction

Advanced Metering Infrastructure (AMI) is one of Smart Grid (SG) applications which is used specifically for the collection of periodic power consumption
readings from the customers. Typically, these fine-grained power readings are
sent to the utility companies at some pre-defined intervals. In addition to billing
purposes, this huge amount of data can be used for leakage detection, demand
response, state estimation [1] and various statistical analysis [2].

Recently, there has been several proposals for forming the communication
infrastructure to be used in AMI applications [3,4]. Among these alternatives,
wireless mesh networking has been one of the viable options exploited by several
utility companies. In this architecture, the smart meters (SMs) form a wireless mesh network (WMN) among them and forward their readings to a single
gateway for relaying to the utility company. This WMN is operated in a neighborhood area network (NAN) and can be implemented using proprietary or open
standards. Our focus is on WMN that based on standard IEEE 802.11s [5] and
we refer this WMN as SG AMI networks hereafter.

© Institute for Computer Sciences, Social Informatics and Telecommunications Engineering 2014
N. Mitton et al. (Eds.): ADHOCNETS 2014, LNICST 140, pp. 86–97, 2014.
DOI: 10.1007/978-3-319-13329-4_8

SG AMI networks are expected to carry different types of traffic due to availability of various other SG applications that need to communicate with SMs. For instance, in addition to sending regular power readings, the network will carry traffic for demand response applications where the utility will need to access the SM and the SM needs to collaborate with the neighbors for reducing the power usage in the neighborhood [6]. Similarly, plug-in hybrid electric vehicle (PHEV) power stations may need to communicate with each other through this NAN in order to share the load for PHEV charging [7]. For such cases, the end-to-end delay of the sent packets is crucial for real-time state estimation of the grid to prevent power outages as well as reducing the stress on the grid in a timely fashion. Thus, in any case the end-to-end delay of the packets sent/received on the NANs is a critical issue to be tackled.

To address this issue one of the options is to use user datagram protocol (UDP) so that the overhead of the protocols can be avoided and thus end-to-end delay can be reduced. However, this is not a strong option due to the characteristics of SG applications. Reliable delivery of the packets in SG AMI application is of utmost concern since the data are used for crucial issues such as billing. Therefore, in most cases TCP becomes the only option for guaranteeing reliable delivery of the readings to be received at the utility company. This is done through congestion control and retransmission mechanisms. With these mechanisms, TCP is showing high end-to-end (ETE) data delivery ratio. However, this performance is at the expense of high ETE delay.

We tackle the problem of increased delays because of the use of TCP and propose two mechanisms to reduce the delay so that TCP can be used in SG AMI networks. The first mechanism is based on the idea of proper setting of RTO values for the SMs. Rather than using a single RTO value for all the nodes as done in traditional networks, we propose to set the RTO value for each SM based on its location in the mesh topology given that SG AMI networks are large-scale multi-hop networks. In this way, closer SMs will have smaller RTO values compared to distant SMs. As a result, distant nodes from the gateway will have more time to respond and thus less retransmissions will occur. The assignment is done using a spanning tree of the topology so that the nodes at similar distances from the gateway will have same RTOs. The second mechanism we propose is based on the idea of limiting the number of doubling when the RTO timer expires. This is motivated from the fact that doubling the RTO increases the RTO value too much that negatively affects the packet delay. The simulation results indicate that both approaches contribute to reduction of ETE delay under a variety of network conditions without any impact on other metrics such as packet delivery ratio and throughput.

This paper is organized as follows. The next section summarizes the related work. Section 3 provides preliminaries on SG AMI, TCP retransmission timeout and description of the problem. Section 4 includes the description of the proposed approaches. In Section 5, we assess the performance of the proposed approaches. Finally, the paper is concluded in Section 6.

2   Related Work

The use of TCP in wireless networks has been a major area of research in the past. The main issue was the triggering of slow start algorithm employed by TCP when congestion occurs in wired networks. However, wireless networks have four major characteristics that distinguish them from wired networks [8]: (1) channel contention; (2) signal fading; (3) mobility; and (4) limited power and energy. These characteristics induce non-congestion events which cause packet loss. Hence, the traditional TCP congestion control mechanisms may react inappropriately due to the misinterpretation of the caused of the packet loss in wireless networks. Therefore, a lot of approaches have been proposed to improve the performance of TCP in terms of various metrics. A good summary of these efforts can be found in [8].

Among these metrics, throughput has been widely studied. A number of approaches have been proposed for the reduction of channel contention to improve the TCP throughput such as multichannel assignment for forming WMNs without hidden node problem [9] and decreasing the number of transmitted ACKs. To this end, instead of sending an ACK for every segment (e.g., TCP layer packet), an ACK is delayed until after two segments are received or after a specific time limit (typically 0.2s) is reached (i.e., if two segments are not received within this limit) [10]. The delayed ACK can also be based on certain criteria, such as the number of segment [11], channel condition [12], and the path length [13]. Note that all of these approaches focus on TCP throughput improvement and thus may bring additional delay which is contradicting with our goal of improving the ETE delay.

The works which dealt with RTOs were proposed in [14,15]. In [14], the main motivation was to handle the spurious RTO timeouts due to the delayed ACKs used in various previous works. The authors proposed an adaptive minimum RTO to identify the data segments whose ACKs will possibly be delayed. A fixed extended Minimum RTO is assigned for those identified segments. In [15], the authors presented a heuristic mechanism for mobile ad hoc network, called Fixed RTO, that assumes a route failure occurs when there are two consecutive RTOs. The un-ACKed segment is retransmitted without doubling the RTO timer anymore (i.e. the RTO timer is kept fixed) until an ACK has been received for that segment. These approaches also adjust RTOs as ours but the goals are very different and the process is done on a need basis. In our case, we do it for every node in advance based on their location in the network topology.

With the deployment of SMs and several other SG devices, TCP is started to be revisited for tuning its performance for SG domain. The main focus of these efforts is on reliability since this is one of the most important metrics for SG applications. Very recently, two revisions had been proposed for TCP [16,17]. The work in [16] focuses on the reliability and throughput performance of TCP in a large-scale setting. The main goal is to aggregate the TCP traffic from SMs at certain regional aggregators. The domain of the work in [17] is not AMI. It focuses on the monitoring aspect of the SG. Phasor Measurement Units (PMUs) which are sent real-time are considered as the data traffic sources. The work addresses issues regarding reliability along with security.

3   Preliminaries

3.1   SG AMI Networks

In a SG AMI network, SMs will send their readings to the data collector using mesh path selection and forwarding mechanisms of IEEE 802.11s called Hybrid Wireless Routing Protocol (HWMP) [5]. Mesh path selection enables path discovery within the mesh network using layer-2 (MAC) addresses rather than IP addresses. The frequency of readings (or reports) from SMs may change from one utility to another and type of the consumers. For instance, residential homes' data can be collected in minutes while industrial building's data can be collected in seconds. However, it is not uncommon to collect meter data from 5 to 30 seconds [18,19].

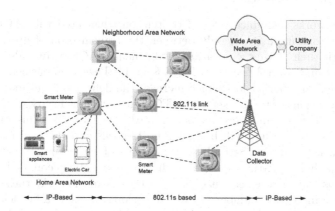

Fig. 1. A sample of SG AMI Network

While SG AMI network uses IEEE 802.11s, it still communicates with other networks that are part of the SG network. For instance, as depicted in Fig. 1, home appliances may communicate with the SMs, or electric stations for PHEVs can talk to each other via this SG AMI network. Similarly, sensors and utility company will be communicating with this SG AMI network. Therefore, IP based protocols are still used. At the transport layer, TCP or UDP can be used. However since reliability is an important metric in collecting power readings, TCP is the most widely used option at the transport layer for the utilities.

3.2   Overview TCP Retransmission Timeout

TCP uses retransmission timeout (RTO) timer to identify segment loss. Whenever a sender sends a data segment to a destination, an RTO timer is activated. TCP assumes segment loss when RTO timer expires before receiving the ACK. For this case, TCP retransmits the segment and a new RTO timer is assigned for it. The value of an RTO timer is defined in RFC-6298 [20]. At the beginning when there is no measured samples, 1sec is recommended as the initial RTO timer. The RTO timer for the next transmitted segment is the maximum between the minimum RTO and the value computed in Eq. 1. The recommended minimum RTO is 1sec. In case of retransmission, the new RTO timer is doubled from the previous RTO timer.

$$RTO = SRTT + 4 \times RTTVAR \qquad (1)$$

where, SRTT represents smoothed Round Trip Transmission (RTT) delay of the measured samples, and RTTVAR represents the RTT variation. Note that the RTT samples must not be taken from packets that were retransmitted.

3.3   Problem Motivation

SG AMI networks introduce a lot of contention when used with TCP. This is because the contention is not only between the transmission of upstream data packets with their downstream acknowledgements (ACKs), but also from the management and control frames of IEEE 802.11s. These contentions eventually cause collision and packet loss which increase the delay. Another major issue is the retransmissions of the packets. The TCP data streams in SG AMI networks are performed in a multi-hop manner towards the gateway. This may create several issues. First, there will be traffic bottlenecks and this will increase the chance of packet collisions. Second, the probability of packet drops due to wireless environment characteristics will increase due to increased hop counts. Finally, the TCP streams may be received out-of order at the destinations. All these problems contribute to increasing number of retransmissions and thus ETE delay.

The problem of retransmissions can introduce additional delays in SG AMI Networks because of the increased frequency of data collections. Recall that the data collection frequency in some AMI applications can vary from 5secs to 30 secs. In such a case, it is important to collect all the required SM readings for each round so that this data can be used for real-time objectives such as state estimation. However, there is a risk for some of the segments not to be received by the destinations before the next round of data collection begins. This is mainly due to retransmissions as detailed below.

The recommended values in RFC 6298 may not be suitable for periodic data reporting in SG AMI networks. Typically, all SMs will send their reading at the same predefined time schedule. Initially, when there is no measured RTT samples, such as after the network restart, all SMs will have the same initial RTO timer (e.g 1sec). When all SMs send their readings, the network contention for media access are high and heavy congestion may occur. Some SMs may not receive ACKs for their readings either due to packet loss or the RTO timer expires. These SMs will retransmit their data at the same time again and will have the same new RTO timer (i.e. doubled from the previous one). As a consequence, when some of the SMs still do not receive any ACKs, the similar problem persists: these SMs will retransmit again at the same time and have the same new RTO timer and so on. Doubling the RTO timer may also pose additional delay, especially when its value exceeds the next power reading reporting time. To assess the seriousness of the problem, we conducted some experiments to measure the number of segments which cannot be transmitted until the next round. The results depicted in Fig. 2 indicate that there are indeed a good number of segments which could not be transmitted.

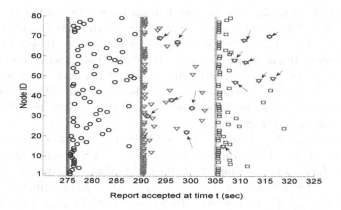

Fig. 2. Arrival time for some of the readings exceed the next reading schedule. These are shown by arrows in the figure. The reporting is done every 15 secs (i.e., 275, 290 and 305s).

In such a case, the next data reporting action at the SMs must wait for the previous reading to be acknowledged first. In case of waiting too much, the RTO timer may expire before the SM can send its reading to the gateway. In case the timer expires, this next reading can be sent together with the previous reading, either partially or in a whole, depending on the window size. However, since TCP sends data in byte streams, there is no definite boundary between the previous and the next data readings. Hence, the receiver must know exactly the data size in order to recover both readings individually. The receiver also needs a temporary storage when the next reading is partially sent due to the window size limitation. This partial reading must be stored until the next segment arrives and the whole reading can be recovered. These results suggest that retransmissions not only will increase the delay but also complicate things in order to handle failed readings. Therefore, it is important to address this problem for SG AMI networks.

3.4   Problem Definition

Given the issues regarding the retransmissions in SG AMI networks, our problem focuses on reduction of ETE packet delay. The problem can be defined as follows: "Given a SG AMI network with a certain number of SMs, their locations, topology and data collection frequency, our goal is to propose a mechanism to reduce the number of retransmissions and thus the ETE delay when TCP is employed."

4 Improved TCP for SG AMI Networks

We propose two mechanisms for SG AMI networks in order to reduce the delay when TCP is used: (1) spanning tree-based minimum RTO setting, and (2) freezing RTO mechanism. The first mechanism takes into account the location of SM and the IEEE 802.11s proactive tree-based path selection. Typically, the location of a SM is attached to a certain household location. Hence, its location is known a priori. IEEE 802.11s proactive tree-based path selection on the other hand, builds a tree topology rooted at the gateway. Hence, each SM has an associate node's position in the network tree topology and different hop count to the gateway. It takes longer time to send to and receive data from the gateway as the SM's hop count increases.

To identify the unique location of each SM in the network, we propose building a spanning tree (ST) for the SG AMI network. An ST of a connected graph G can be defined as a maximal set of edges of G that contains no cycle, or as a minimal set of edges that connect all vertices. Determining the minimum ST (MST) of a network has been widely studied in the literature (e.g., Prim's MST Algorithm [21]) and this can be done by the gateway node after collecting the MAC addresses of the SMs in the SG AMI network.

Our goal is to assign different minimum RTO for each SM based on its position in the ST. Specifically, the SMs at the same ST depth level will have a similar minimum RTO while the nodes that are further away from the gateway (i.e., has a higher network tree depth level) will be assigned a higher minimum RTO. We use the following formula for setting the RTO for a particular node i at level d_i:

$$minRTO_d^i = 0.1 \times d_i + r_i \tag{2}$$

where r_i represents a random value introduced for each dept level so that the nodes at the same depth level will have different RTO values.

The second mechanism is proposed due to the fact that RFC 6298 does not specifically define the upper bound of the doubling mechanism when the RTO timer expires. We also follow an idea for stopping the doubling of RTO timer when the ACK is not received. Basically, if an ACK is not received after first doubling of RTO timer, then the timer is not re-doubled but frozen until the ACK is arrived. In this way, whenever RTO timer expires again after that, the retransmission intervals for the corresponding packet is constant.

5 Performance Evaluation

5.1 Experiment Setup

We evaluated the performance of our proposed approaches in ns-3 [22]. We created SG AMI networks that consist of **N** by **N** mesh nodes. One mesh node acts as a data collector while the rest act as SMs. The transmission range of each node is assumed to be 120m. The underlying MAC is assume to be 802.11g. HWMP proactive modes is used to determine the paths among the SMs and gateway. The power readings are put in a packet size of 512 bytes and these packets are transmitted every 15secs which is consistent with some of the real SMs on the market [19]. The packets are assumed to be sent at the same times by all the SMs since this data will be used by the utility to do real-time state estimation. We measure at the application layer, the average End-to-end (ETE) delay of all the packets sent from SMs to the gateway. We also looked at the packet delivery ratio (PDR) which indicates the ratio of the total number of packets sent by SMs and successfully received by the gateway. A final metric is throughput which is the total number of bits received at the gateway in a second. We conducted experiments to assess these three metrics and compared them to the baseline. The baseline is the basic operations of HWMP and TCP/IP protocol stacks in ns3.18, and uses the recommended initial RTO and minimum RTO values in RFC 6298 (i.e 1sec).

5.2   ETE Delay Performance

We first conducted experiments to assess the ETE delay of the tree-based minimum RTO allocation. The results are depicted in Fig. 3. On average, tree-based approach improves the ETE delay around 18% compared to the baseline. However, there are fluctuations in the results and the improvement is not very significant. Therefore, we decided to do more investigation through additional experiments.

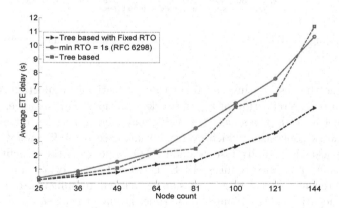

Fig. 3. The ETE delay performance results

Firstly, the ETE delay is less than that of the baseline approach except for 144 nodes. When we looked at the situation in more details, we figured out that there is one node that is not able to establish a TCP connection with the gateway due to Address Resolution Protocol (ARP) issues. Basically, ARP requests could be lost and some of the nodes may not establish a TCP connection as shown in previous study [23]. This may result in less traffic and thus less contention in the network, reducing the ETE delay for the baseline. In the tree-based approach however, all the nodes were able to send their readings.

Secondly, we picked the topology with 81 nodes and investigated the behavior of RTO setting and timeouts. The maximum depth level for this topology is 16 and hence the highest minimum RTO based on Eq. 2 would be around 2s. Fig. 4 shows a snapshot of arriving packets and RTO expiration times. The results indicate that the variation of RTO timer is very high. In fact, some of the RTO values are higher than 2s. This indicates that the network was previously having high contention and collision that make the RTTs of previous sending reports are high. It is also estimated by the RTT estimator that the current report will having the same issue.

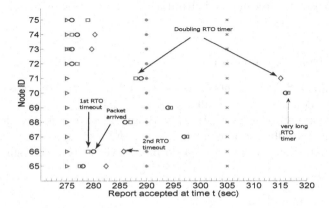

Fig. 4. Doubling the RTO timer exceeds the next reading schedule, we only show for packets sent at 275s

We argue that estimating the RTO value is critically important since it is expected to be the reflection of the network conditions. For instance, when the actual packet is not lost, a small RTO value may trigger a packet retransmission due to network congestion which eventually increase the ETE delay. However, when the packet is actually lost, a small RTO value gives the benefit of a fast retransmission and hence reduces the ETE delay. On the other hand, a longer RTO may prevent a packet retransmission since it will be sufficient to receive the ACK. The negative side of a longer RTO timer is when the packet is actually lost and the sender need to wait long enough before it can retransmit the packet. This situation increases the ETE delay. These situations can be observed in Fig. 4. Five packet retransmissions have occurred (e.g., node ID 65, 66, 71, 73, and 74) and the gateway receives those packets not long after the RTO expires. The node ID 73 and 74 have a smaller RTO timer compared to the others and thus they have lower ETE delay. Recall that doubling the RTO value when the RTO expires poses a problem when the value encompasses the next data reading scheduled. For instance, the node with the ID 71 has the second highest RTO value that exceeds the next two data reading scheduled. Fortunately, the data reading has been received by the gateway and its acknowledgement also has been received by the sender before the next scheduled so that the node can send its next scheduled report as planned. On the other hand, node with ID 70 has a very long RTO value that exceeds the next two scheduled. Hence, the next two packets are held until the previous packet has been received and acknowledged. These increase the ETE delay significantly. As a result, we decided that freezing RTO value at the SMs may reduce ETE delay as will be discussed next.

We repeated the same experiments by applying the idea of RTO freezing. Basically, for each SM, after the RTO is doubled, it stops there and no more doubling is performed. The results which are shown in Fig. 3 indicate that freezing the RTO significantly help reducing the ETE delay. Overall, this approach reduces the ETE delay around 48% (on average of all node count) and 41% compared to baseline and tree-based approach respectively. This is attributed to the fact that retransmissions are forced and thus a sender does not have to wait too long for the congested packets which really need for retransmission. Eventually, the ETE delay is reduced. We confirmed the effectiveness of this improvement by checking the arrival times of readings compared to the snaphot in Fig. 2. In our proposed approaches, the gateway was able to receive all the packets before the next reading scheduled starts.

5.3 PDR and Throughput Performance

We also looked at the two other performance metrics to verify that the proposed approaches do not impose any adverse effect on them. However, due to limited space, we can not show the results in a table or graphs. The results indicate that the PDRs for the proposed approaches are as better as the baseline. The PDR stays 100% for smaller network sizes. For larger network sizes, the PDR is still close to 100% and our tree-based approach along with freezing performs even slightly better which is promising. For the throughput, we observe a similar situation. The proposed approaches do not impact the throughput. On the contrary, in large-scales the throughput is even slightly higher.

6 Conclusion

In this paper, we proposed an improved TCP that can be used for SG AMI networks that can support a varity of applications. The idea of the approach was to set the RTOs of each SM in order to reduce the end-to-end packet delay. The setting was done by considering the distance of each SM from the gateway in the network. Specifically, distant SMs are provided with longer RTOs so that their RTO will not expire quickly and thus retranmission of data segments will be prevented. We also proposed a mechanism for freezing the RTO in order to further reduce the ETE delay. The proposed approaches are implemented and compared with the existing TCP in terms of packet delay, throughput and PDR.

The results indicate that significants reductions in the delay can be achieved regardless of the network size. In addition, the proposed approaches do not negtively impact the PDR and throughput performances. In the future, we plan to investigate whether the QoS-based EDCA (i.e., MAC protocol for QoS support in IEEE 802.11s) can be utilized to further accelerate the transmission of ACK packets and thus reduce the delay further.

Acknowledgments. This work is supported by US National Science Foundation under the grant number 1318872.

References

1. Baran, M., McDermott, T.: Distribution system state estimation using ami data. In: Power Systems Conference and Exposition PSCE 2009, pp. 1–3. IEEE/PES (March 2009)
2. Fang, X., Misra, S., Xue, G., Yang, D.: Smart grid - the new and improved power grid: A survey. IEEE Communications Surveys Tutorials (2011)
3. Saputro, N., Akkaya, K., Uludag, S.: A survey of routing protocols for smart grid communications. Comput. Netw. **56**(11), 2742–2771 (2012)
4. Gao, J., Xiao, Y., Liu, J., Liang, W., Chen, C.P.: A survey of communication/networking in smart grids. Future Gener. Comput. Syst. **28**, 391–404 (2012). http://dx.doi.org/10.1016/j.future.2011.04.014
5. Ieee standard for information technology-telecommunications and information exchange between systems-local and metropolitan area networks-specific requirements part 11: Wireless lan medium access control (mac) and physical layer (phy) specifications amendment 10: Mesh networking. IEEE Std 802.11s-2011, 1–372 (October 2011)
6. Maharjan, S., Zhu, Q., Zhang, Y., Gjessing, S., Basar, T.: Dependable demand response management in the smart grid: A stackelberg game approach. IEEE Transactions on Smart Grid **4**(1), 120–132 (2013)
7. Erol-Kantarci, M., Sarker, J., Mouftah, H.: Communication-based plug-in hybrid electrical vehicle load management in the smart grid. In: 2011 IEEE Symposium on Computers and Communications (ISCC), pp. 404–409 (June 2011)
8. Leung, K.-C., Li, V.O.: Transmission control protocol (tcp) in wireless networks: issues, approaches, and challenges. IEEE Communications Surveys & Tutorials **8**(4), 64–79 (2006)
9. Tung, L.-P., Shih, W.-K., Cho, T.-C., Sun, Y., Chen, M.C.: Tcp throughput enhancement over wireless mesh networks. IEEE Communications Magazine **45**(11), 64–70 (2007)
10. Braden, R.: Rfc 1122 - requirements for internet hosts - communication layers (October 1989). http://tools.ietf.org/rfc/rfc1122.txt
11. Altman, E., Jiménez, T.: Novel Delayed ACK Techniques for Improving TCP Performance in Multihop Wireless Networks. In: Conti, M., Giordano, S., Gregori, E., Olariu, S. (eds.) PWC 2003. LNCS, vol. 2775, pp. 237–250. Springer, Heidelberg (2003)
12. de Oliveira, R., Braun, T.: A dynamic adaptive acknowledgment strategy for tcp over multihop wireless networks. In: Proceedings of the IEEE INFOCOM 2005 24th Annual Joint Conference of the IEEE Computer and Communications Societies, vol. 3, pp. 1863–1874 (March 2005)

13. Chen, J., Gerla, M., Lee, Y.Z., Sanadidi, M.Y.: Tcp with delayed ack for wireless networks. Ad Hoc Netw. **6**(7), 1098–1116 (2008). http://dx.doi.org/10.1016/j.adhoc.2007.10.004
14. Psaras, I., Tsaoussidis, V.: On the properties of an adaptive TCP minimum RTO. Computer Communications **32**(5), 888–895 (2009). http://www.sciencedirect.com/science/article/pii/S0140366408006610
15. Dyer T.D., Boppana, R.V.: A comparison of tcp performance over three routing protocols for mobile ad hoc networks. In: Proceedings of the 2nd ACM International Symposium on Mobile Ad Hoc Networking & Computing. ACM, pp. 56–66 (2001)
16. Khalifa, T., Abdrabou, A., Naik, K., Alsabaan, M., Nayak, A., Goel, N.: Split- and aggregated-transmission control protocol (sa-tcp) for smart power grid. IEEE Transactions on Smart Grid **5**(1), 381–391 (2014)
17. Kim, Y.-J., Thottan, M.: Sgtp: Smart grid transport protocol for secure reliable delivery of periodic real time data. Bell Labs Technical Journal **16**(3), 83–99 (2011). http://dx.doi.org/10.1002/bltj.20523
18. Pressley, L.: Austin smart meters (July 2013), http://www.austinsmartmeters.com
19. Korean electric power research institute (2013), http://www.kepri.re.kr/
20. Paxson, V., Allman, M., Chu, J., Sargent, M.: Rfc 2988 - computing tcp's retransmission timer (June 2011), http://www.rfc-editor.org/rfc/rfc6298.txt
21. Cormen, T.H., Stein, C., Rivest, R.L., Leiserson, C.E.: Introduction to Algorithms, 2nd edn. McGraw-Hill Higher Education (2001)
22. Andreev, K., Boyko, P.: Ieee 802.11 s mesh networking ns-3 model, IITP, WNS3 (March 2011)
23. Saputro, N., Akkaya, K.: An Efficient and Secure ARP for Large-scale IEEE 802.11s-based Smart Grid Networks. In: Mellouk, A., Sherif, M.H., Bellavista, P., Li, J. (eds.) ADHOCNETS 2013. LNICST, vol. 129, pp. 203–217. Springer, Heidelberg (2013)

A Cluster-Based and On-Demand Routing Algorithm for Large-Scale Multi-hop Wireless Sensor Networks

Natale Guzzo[1,2]($\boxtimes$), Nathalie Mitton[2], Pascal Daragon[1], and Arulnambi Nandagoban[1]

[1] TRAXENS SAS, Marseille, France
[2] Inria, Villeneuve d'Ascq, France
natale.guzzo@inria.fr

Abstract. Reducing the energy consumption and improving the robustness of a Wireless Sensor Network (WSN) are the main requirements for many industrial and research applications. The sensors usually use a routing protocol in order to deliver the sensing data to a Base Station (BS) which may be far away from the monitoring area. Many algorithms proposed in the literature compute the routing process by clustering the network and by designing new election mechanisms in which the cluster-heads are chosen taking account of the remaining energy, the communication cost and the density of nodes. However, they do not consider the connectivity to the BS, and assume that all the nodes or only few pre-fixed nodes are able to directly communicate with it. We believe that this assumption is not suitable for many applications of WSN and to tackle this problem we propose CESAR, a multi-hop and energy-efficient routing protocol for large-scale WSN which includes a new cluster-head selection mechanism aware of the battery level and the connectivity to the BS. Furthermore, our solution employs an innovative hybrid approach to combine both clustering and on-demand techniques in order to provide an adaptive behavior for different dynamic topologies. Simulation results show that our solution outperforms in terms of energy consumption and data delivery other known routing algorithms in the literature.

Keywords: Wireless Sensor Networks (WSN) · Distributed clustering · Multi-hop routing protocol · On-demand scheme · Base Station (BS) connectivity · Energy-efficiency

1 Introduction

The Wireless Sensor Networks (WSN) are often composed of a large number of sensors that collaborate in order to transmit the sensing data to the Base Station (BS) by satisfying some requirements such as coverage, robustness, scalability and lifetime. Several solutions concerning the physical, MAC and network layers have been proposed in the literature. Regarding the routing protocols, the clustering techniques are employed to reduce the message overhead, the overhearing

© Institute for Computer Sciences, Social Informatics and Telecommunications Engineering 2014
N. Mitton et al. (Eds.): ADHOCNETS 2014, LNICST 140, pp. 98–109, 2014.
DOI: 10.1007/978-3-319-13329-4_9

and the interferences between the nodes in the network. The benefits introduced by this approach lead to a high scalability, simple routing decisions, and low energy dissipation by reducing the data traffic and the overhead caused by the flow of routing information.

In this paper we present the Cluster-based Energy Saving Affiliation Routing protocol (CESAR) which is a new multi-hop and energy-efficient algorithm that aims to reduce the energy consumption in WSN by introducing a scheme with innovative features. The main aspects considered in the design of the routing scheme are the energy consumed by the nodes and the data delivery, since our objectives are to create a robust and scalable network and extend its lifetime as long as possible, while fulfilling application requirements. We will show in the next sections that our clustering scheme outperforms the other simulated algorithms.

We survey the related work in Section II. The main features of CESAR are presented in Section III. In Section IV CESAR is employed in different simulated scenarios inspired by industrial use case applications and we analyze the results in comparison with other routing algorithms. Finally, Section V gives the concluding remarks and reports the direction for future works.

2   Background and Related Work

Several cluster-based protocols have been proposed in the literature in the last few years to reduce the energy consumption and prolong the network lifetime in WSNs. They can be classified according to the goals and the approaches employed for cluster formation and cluster-head selection. The main distinction is related to the cluster formation mechanism. In this sense, we can distinguish centralized algorithms such as PEGASIS [1] and CDC [2], and distributed algorithms like LEACH [3], HEED [4], and DSBCV [5]. Other schemes are based on Geographical clustering as RCHR [6] and TTDD [7], on the concentric clustering such as CCS [8], or on the use of specific cluster-head election techniques like BLAC [9]. The algorithm named SECC selects the nodes to add to the clusters according to their energy or distance from the cluster-head [10]. In this section we describe in brief some distributed clustering schemes by listing their features and limitations.

Nevertheless, the most of the algorithms studied in the literature suppose that all the nodes can always directly communicate with the BS. We believe that this assumption is quite restrictive and not suitable for many applications of WSNs in which the sensors may not be able to connect to the BS because of the excessive distance or the bad radio environment. Moreover, some schemes such as LEACH and HEED need the synchronization between the nodes in order to start the clustering process at the same time. If the nodes are not synchronized the performances of the two algorithms in terms of energy consumption and data delivery are significantly degraded, since the cluster-head selection cannot be well performed. The solution presented in this paper does not adopt such an assumption, since it considers the connectivity to the BS as one parameter to use in the cluster-head selection scheme.

3   CESAR Algorithm

Our solution is addressed to specific applications where the sensors are equipped with a long-range radio module to communicate on the link towards the BS (BS-link) and a short-range radio module for the communication peer-to-peer with the other sensor nodes (P2P-link). The nodes do not know the position of the BS and they are supposed to communicate directly with it only whether the received signal strength on the BS-link is high enough. Moreover, depending on the radio environment and the distance from the BS, the nodes do not detect the same quality on the BS-link. As a result, only some of them may be able to connect to the BS and they may need to use different transmission powers in order to deliver their data. Such nodes may also change over time depending on the variations of the BS-link quality. In terms of energy consumption, the transmission of data on the BS-link is much more expensive than the transmission of the same amount of data on the P2P-link. In fact, we suppose that the communication on the BS-link requires a transmission power 10 to 20 times higher than the communication on the P2P-link and introduces a connection delay lasting approximately one minute.

We focus on sensor networks where the nodes are positioned at the edges of a 3-dimensional grid. We believe that this model well describes different kinds of scenarios such as the monitoring of goods in storage areas. We believe that CESAR is also suitable in applications where the nodes move within the sensing area. Vehicle tracking in a town, surveillance in an airport, and fauna monitoring are some examples in which CESAR can be employed.

The most significant features of CESAR are the following:

- CESAR is a hybrid algorithm that combines clustering and on-demand approaches in order to dynamically adapt the behavior of the nodes to the topology changes. For this purpose, it does not involve every node in a cluster without preventing it to send data to the BS.
- The proposed cluster-head selection mechanism is aware of the connectivity to the BS and the battery level: only the nodes that have the signal strength on the BS-link and the battery level greater than prefixed thresholds can become cluster-heads.
- A recovery scheme is employed to keep alive the routes between the nodes and the cluster-heads with low cost operations.
- A data aggregation scheme can be employed by the members of the clusters before to send data packet to the cluster-head

In the next paragraphs we explain in more details the cluster-head selection mechanism and the cluster formation scheme. Before that, we need to introduce the types of nodes and routing messages used in different processes. We defined four types of nodes:

- HEAD: nodes which are able to communicate with the BS and are in charge of creating and managing a cluster by sending announcement messages.

- MEMBER: nodes which have joined a cluster after receiving an announcement transmitted by a HEAD node.
- LOOSE: nodes which have not joined any cluster and are not able to transmit data to the BS.

The routing messages were defined as follows:

- RANN: hop-bounded broadcast messages used by HEAD nodes to build their clusters.
- REQR: hop-bounded broadcast messages used by LOOSE nodes to discover a nearby cluster.
- REP: unicast messages used to reply to REQR messages.
- ROFF: broadcast messages used by HEAD nodes to destroy their clusters.
- DATA: unicast messages used by MEMBER nodes to deliver their data.
- ACK: unicast messages used by HEAD nodes to acknowledge DATA packets.

3.1   The Cluster-Head Selection Mechanism

Every node in the network periodically executes the cluster-head selection process to check whether they have the requirements to become HEAD nodes. As already explained, a node can become a cluster-head only if both the battery level and the signal strength on the BS-link are greater than a prefixed threshold. However, these are not the only conditions to become HEAD. There may be other cluster-heads nearby that have better conditions than the considered node. In this case, the latter should become member of one of such clusters, rather than becoming HEAD itself.

This decision process is made by calculating the HEAD metric defined as cost and it takes account of the battery level and the quality of the BS-link. Therefore, the higher the metric, the less likely a node to be elected as cluster-head. As we can see from Algorithm 1, if node u is MEMBER and has the requirements to become HEAD, it checks whether the metric of its cluster-head is 1.5 times greater than its own metric, as shown at line 5. In that case, u becomes HEAD, otherwise it remains a MEMBER. Such an approach is introduced in order to avoid the election of several HEAD nodes close to each other, and reduce the overall number of connections to the BS and, thus the global energy consumption.

We defined a second threshold for the signal strength on the BS-link to avoid frequent cluster-head elections and resignations when such a parameter continuously varies around the main threshold. Regarding the resignation of a HEAD node, it may occur in two cases. In the first case, the node has no longer the requirements to be a cluster-head, since it has not enough energy or it is no longer able to directly communicate with the BS. The second case occurs when the considered node receives an announcement from a new HEAD in the neighborhood that has a metric lower than its, as we explain in the next paragraph. When a node resigns as HEAD, it destroys its cluster and, in the second case, it becomes MEMBER of another cluster.

Algorithm 1. CESAR (Cluster-head selection algorithm run on node u)

Parameters:

- connectivity: signal strength measured on the BS-link
- battery: remaining energy
- conn_thr1, conn_thr2: thresholds for the connectivity parameter
- batt_thr: threshold for the battery parameter

1: **if** (connectivity(u) ¿ conn_thr1 AND battery(u) ¿ batt_thr) **then**
2:    **if** (u is HEAD) **then**
3:       Send RANN;
4:    **else if** (u is MEMBER) **then**
5:       **if** (metric(head of u) ¿ 1.5 * metric(u) **then**
6:          Become HEAD;
7:          Send RANN;
8:       **end if**
9:    **else if** (u is LOOSE) **then**
10:       Become HEAD;
11:       Send RANN;
12:    **end if**
13: **else if** (connectivity(u) ¿ conn_thr2 AND battery(u) ¿ batt_thr) **then**
14:    **if** (u is HEAD) **then**
15:       Send RANN;
16:    **end if**
17: **else if** (connectivity(u) ¡ conn_thr2 OR battery(u) ¡ batt_thr) **then**
18:    **if** (u is HEAD) **then**
19:       Become LOOSE;
20:       Send ROFF to destroy the cluster;
21:    **end if**
22: **end if**

3.2   Cluster Formation and Destruction

The cluster-heads form the clusters in the network and periodically connect to the BS to deliver the sensing data received from other nodes. The clusters are built by broadcasting a bounded-hop RANN in which the header field named Time To Live (TTL) is set to the number of hops that can be traversed by the message before to be discarded. In this way, only the nodes that are at a limited hop-distance from the considered HEAD are recruited into the cluster.

The RANN messages are periodically broadcast by the HEAD nodes in their cluster in order to keep the MEMBER nodes up-to-date about their metric.

If a non-clustered node receives a RANN message from a HEAD node, it immediately becomes MEMBER of the announced cluster. However, if the considered node receives multiple RANN messages from different cluster-heads, it then compares their metrics and joins the cluster with the lowest one. In the case a HEAD node receives a RANN message, it checks whether its metric is 1.5 times lower than the metric of the announced HEAD. If the latter condition holds, the considered node resigns as HEAD, destroys its cluster and joins the cluster of

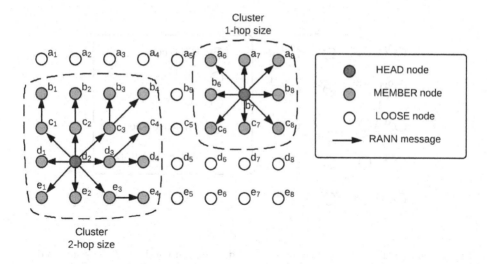

Fig. 1. Cluster formation. The RANN are broadcast by the HEAD nodes to form clusters of different sizes.

the HEAD announced in the RANN message. Such a condition has been defined in order to avoid frequent cluster destruction when the HEAD nodes are close to each other. After joining a cluster, the MEMBER nodes store in the routing table the last hop traversed by the received RANN in order to have a route to the HEAD. As a result, a routing tree is formed into the clusters between the MEMBER nodes and the cluster-head.

The size of the clusters is decided by the HEAD nodes according to their operating parameters. In this way, CESAR aims to concentrate the collection of the sensing data in the HEAD nodes with better conditions in order to smartly balance the energy consumption between them.

When a HEAD node resigns, it destroys its cluster by sending a ROFF message to all the members that leave the cluster and become LOOSE nodes upon the message reception.

3.3 The On-demand Scheme

As already explained, the LOOSE nodes do not have any routes to any cluster-head, so they are not able to transmit data to the BS. Thus, when one of them has some data to deliver to the server, it starts a special procedure that aims to discover a cluster nearby.The discovering procedure consists of broadcasting a hop-bounded REQR message that will be received by the nodes in the neighborhood. When a MEMBER node receives such a message, it replies with a REP message containing information about the status of the HEAD of its cluster. The discovery process continues until a cluster is found or the max hop distance is reached. In the latter case, the process is reinitialized and restarted after a certain time interval.

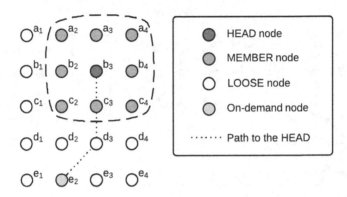

Fig. 2. On-demand scheme. The non-clustered nodes employ REQR messages to discover a cluster in the neighborhood and find a route a HEAD node.

For instance, let's assume that the node e_2 in Figure 2 needs to send the sensing data to the BS. It broadcasts a REQR message in which the TTL is set to TTL_MAX. The nodes d_1, d_2, d_3, e_1 and e_3 are not MEMBER nodes, so they do not reply to the request. Nodes c_1, c_2, c_3, members of the cluster created by the node b_3 receive the REQR and reply with a REP message that reports the metric of their cluster-head. Such a message passes through the nodes traversed by the latest REQR message. In the figure, we suppose that the REP messages are received by the node d_3 and forwards the message to the requesting node e_2. The latter stores in the routing table the next hop on the path towards to the reported cluster and records the metric of its HEAD. After that, it can deliver the collected data to the HEAD node b_3 by passing through the nodes d_3 and c_3.

If there are more than one cluster in the nearby, the considered node may receive more than one REP message, and then it should evaluate to which cluster to deliver its data by comparing the metrics of the respective cluster-heads.

3.4   Data Aggregation

The aggregation of the sensing data allows the reduction of the time needed for transmissions and receptions decrease, and thus, the energy consumption and the risks of collisions decrease as well. The data aggregation in CESAR can be performed in three different ways. The least strong approach is the aggregation of data only at the cluster-heads before deliver it to the BS. A stronger approach is to aggregate data also at the member nodes at the borders of the clusters. In this case, such nodes collect the data coming from the LOOSE nodes and aggregate it before transmitting to the cluster-head. Finally, the strongest way is to perform the data aggregation at the cluster-heads and at every member of the clusters. However, in this paper we evaluate CESAR without performing any aggregation of data.

3.5 Routing Maintenance and Recovery

The CESAR algorithm uses ACK messages to acknowledge every data packet. Thus, all the nodes expect to receive an ACK message as confirmation that the transmission succeeded and the data was received by the cluster-head. If no ACK messages are received after a prefixed timeout, then the sender node considers the packet lost and transmits it again to the same HEAD. If the transmission fails 3 times, then the considered node becomes LOOSE and restarts the on-demand scheme to find another route to the same HEAD or to another cluster. Thus, we set a specific timeout in the MEMBER nodes to check if the RANN messages are periodically received. Such a timer is restarted at every reception of RANN messages from the cluster-head and if the timeout occurs, then the node leaves the cluster and becomes LOOSE.

4 Performance Evaluation

In this section we simulate the CESAR algorithm in WSNET [11] and we analyze the obtained results in order to compare its performances with two of the most popular clustering protocols studied in the literature: LEACH [3] and HEED [4]. We consider a network in which the nodes are positioned in a 3d grid with dimensions 160x160x110 m^3 and for each experiment we vary the number of sensors in the same area. Thus, the density and the distance between the nodes change at each scenario. In such a way, we analyze the behavior of the algorithm in low-density and high-density networks.

Table 1. Critical parameters of CESAR

Connectivity threshold 1	40%
Connectivity threshold 2	30%
Battery threshold	20%
Status update frequency	every 2 min
RANN frequency	every 1 min
Maximum cluster size	5 hops
Data delivery frequency	every 10 min

Since we want to use a realistic model for the energy consumption, we consider the transmission and the reception powers reported in the datasheets of XBee and XBee-PRO DigiMesh 2.4 provided by Digi International [12]. We considered two different devices since CESAR uses a multi-hop approach and,

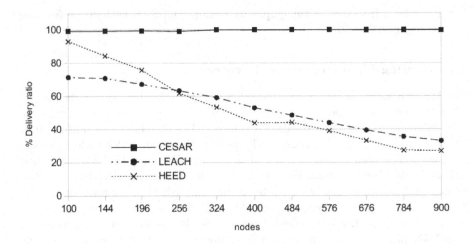

Fig. 3. Data delivery

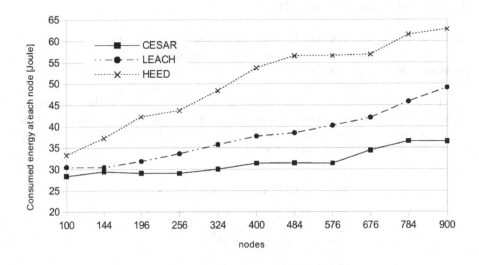

Fig. 4. Energy consumption at each node

therefore it needs a lower transmission power than LEACH and HEED which are single-hop routing protocols.

CESAR has some critical parameters that should be configured in order to evaluate its performances. Such parameters are set to optimized values obtained from long series of simulation as reported in Table 1.

Regarding the other simulation parameters we set to 6 hours the virtual duration for each experiment and we suppose to receive from the application layer 4096 Bytes of sensing data every 10 minutes. The energy available at each sensor at the beginning of the simulations is 100 Joules. We believe that the latter values are fair enough to simulate a generic application running on sensors with a generic hardware.

4.1   Data Delivery

In many applications in which the sensor networks are employed, the robustness is a primary requirement to ensure the delivery of the sensing data to the BS. In this section, we measure the percentage of data generated by the sensors that is successfully delivered to the BS, with different experiments in which we change the number of nodes in the sensing area.

As we can observe in Figure 3, the LEACH and HEED algorithms are less robust than CESAR, which uses dedicated mechanisms to recover and maintain the routes between the nodes as explained in Section III. The losses experienced by the first two algorithms are mainly caused by the interferences between the cluster-heads in the set-up phase, in which some messages related to the cluster formation may be lost and ,thus, some nodes are not able to join any cluster. Moreover the LEACH algorithm experiences more data losses because of its cluster-head selection mechanism which, unlike HEED and CESAR, does not take account of the distribution of the cluster-heads into the network.

4.2   Energy Consumption

The energy consumed by each node is measured by performing different tests in which we increase the number of the nodes in the sensing area.

As we can see from the results shown in Figure 4, CESAR is less expensive in terms of energy and more scalable than LEACH and HEED, thanks to the mechanisms described in Section III.

The graphs show that CESAR is also more scalable than LEACH and HEED which suffer of interferences and high overhead for the assignation of the time-slots by the cluster-heads to the members of the cluster.

5   Conclusions

The algorithm described in this paper combines the clustering and the on-demand approaches in order to reduce the energy consumption in the whole network. A new cluster-head selection mechanism is proposed in order to consider the situations in which the nodes have limited battery capacity and not all of them are capable to communicate with the BS to which deliver the own sensing data. The further mechanisms employed for the reduction of the energy consumption and improvement of the robustness make CESAR suitable for many low data rate applications of WSNs. The simulations described in Section IV show that CESAR performs better than some popular algorithms such as LEACH and HEED, and the experiments performed on the FIT-IoT-lab [13] platform show that our solution well perform also in real sensor networks. Thanks to the on-demand mechanism and the adaptability of the cluster size, we believe that CESAR is also suitable for networks composed of mobile sensors. A new metric can be investigated to take account of the mobility of the nodes and adapt the above-mentioned features to the dynamic of the network topology. Regarding future developments, CESAR will be tested in combination with some Low Power Listening (LPL) protocols , such as X-MAC [14] and LA-MAC [15], in order to figure out which one is the best choice to minimize the energy consumption and ensure the robustness of the network.

Acknowledgments. This work was partially supported by a grant from CPER Nord-Pas-de-Calais /FEDER Campus Intelligence Ambiante.

References

1. Lindsey, S., Raghavendra, C.: Pegasis: Power-efficient gathering in sensor information systems. In: IEEE Aerospace Conference Proceedings. vol. 3, pp. 3–1125-3–1130 (2002)
2. Bajaber, F., Awan, I.: Centralized dynamic clustering for wireless sensor network. In: International Conference on Advanced Information Networking and Applications Workshops : WAINA 2009, pp. 193–198 (2009)
3. Radu, V.: Application. In: Radu, V. (ed.) Stochastic Modeling of Thermal Fatigue Crack Growth. ACM, vol. 1, pp. 63–70. Springer, Heidelberg (2015)
4. Younis, O., Fahmy, S.: Distributed clustering in ad-hoc sensor networks: a hybrid, energy-efficient approach. In: Twenty-third AnnualJoint Conference of the IEEE Computer and Communications Societies, INFOCOM 2004, vol. 1, p. 640 (2004)
5. Liao, Y., Qi, H., Li, W.: Load-balanced clustering algorithm with distributed self-organization for wireless sensor networks. Sensors Journal, IEEE **13**(5), 1498–1506 (2013)
6. Gao, T., Jin, R.: A regional centralized-clustering routing algorithm for wireless sensor networks. In: 4th International Conference on Wireless Communications, Networking and Mobile Computing, WiCOM 2008, pp. 1–4 (2008)
7. Luo, H., Ye, F., Cheng, J., Lu, S., Zhang, L.: Ttdd: two-tier data dissemination in large-scale wireless sensor networks. Wirel. Netw. **11**(1–2), 161–175 (2005)
8. Jung, S.-M., Han, Y.-J., Chung, T.-M.: The concentric clustering scheme for efficient energy consumption in the pegasis. In: The 9th International Conference on Advanced Communication Technology, vol. 1, pp. 260–265 (2007)
9. Ducrocq, T., Mitton, N., Hauspie, M.: Energy-based Clustering for Wireless Sensor Network Lifetime Optimization, in WCNC - Wireless Communications and Networking Conference - 2013. Shanghai, Chine (2013)
10. Bala Krishna, M., Doja, M.N.: Self-organized energy conscious clustering protocol for wireless sensor networks. In: 14th International Conference on Advanced Communication Technology (ICACT) (2012)
11. http://wsnet.gforge.inria.fr/
12. http://www.digi.com/xbee/

13. Burin des Roziers, C., Chelius, G., Ducrocq, T., Fleury, E., Fraboulet, A., Gallais, A., Mitton, N., Noël, T., Vandaele, J.: Using senslab as a first class scientific tool for large scale wireless sensor network experiments. In: Domingo-Pascual, J., Manzoni, P., Palazzo, S., Pont, A., Scoglio, C. (eds.) NETWORKING 2011, Part I. LNCS, vol. 6640, pp. 147–159. Springer, Heidelberg (2011)
14. Buettner, M., Yee, G.V., Anderson, E., Han, R.: X-mac: A short preamble mac protocol for duty-cycled wireless sensor networks. In: Proceedings of the 4th International Conference on Embedded Networked Sensor Systems, ser. SenSys 2006, pp. 307–320 (2006)
15. Corbellini, G., Strinati, E., Duda, A.: La-mac: Low-latency asynchronous mac for wireless sensor networks. In: IEEE 23rd International Symposium on Personal Indoor and Mobile Radio Communications (PIMRC), pp. 380–386 (2012)

Social OLSR:

A Social Based Routing Algorithm for Mobile Ad Hoc Networks

Leïla Harfouche[✉]

Institut National de la Poste et des Technologies de l'Information
et de la communication INPTIC, Alger, Algeria
l_harfouche@inptic.edu.dz

Abstract. In our area of *Mobile Multimedia*, the expansion of wireless networks is dazzling and mobility has become a major issue exacerbated by the significant increase in the number of mobile users. A node operating in a *basic mobile network* behaves the same way a blind person moving in our universe by developing his own representation with his stick, a mechanism known in the literature as *terminal mobility*. To reduce this blindness, several methods have been developed that are based on community behavior. One of the facets of the use of community behavior is the integration of the faculty of "perception" of groups in social communities at the heart of a routing protocol for mobile networks.

We propose a routing protocol based on the original *Optimized Link State Routing* protocol (*OLSR*) to which we add the component of social perception of groupings of individuals. We attache our proposal to tests in simulated environment which shows that indeed the stability of wireless network is more sustainable when the perception exists that in its absence.

Keywords: Ad Hoc networks · Social networks · Routing protocols · OLSR

1 Introduction

In this paper, we discuss the routing protocols themselves as new prospective space alternative to the use of community behavior in mobile networks. After a state of the art, we propose to revisit the *Optimized Link State Routing (OLSR)* protocol. Then we move to the heart of this paper which is a social approach of *OLSR* protocol (*OLSR-S*). We test this approach by simulating a mobile network which implements the resulting protocol. We report the results of measurements on the different organs of our simulated mobile network and conclude on the benefits of this approach.

2 State of the Art: Social Routing Protocols

"The routing of a message in a mobile network is made difficult because the graph of the network is rarely (or ever) connected. Under these conditions where

© Institute for Computer Sciences, Social Informatics and Telecommunications Engineering 2014
N. Mitton et al. (Eds.): ADHOCNETS 2014, LNICST 140, pp. 110–120, 2014.
DOI: 10.1007/978-3-319-13329-4_10

the nodes are free in their movement, finding a path that offers good end to end delivery performance in a short time is a challenge " wrote [1] in an article that presents a multidisciplinary solution based on the consideration of the *small world dynamics.* It was initially proposed as a lever to facilitate economic and social studies. Recently, it is successfully applied to the dissemination of information in wireless networks. To this end, some bridge nodes are identified by their ability to be central (in the sense *PBX*), that is to say, according to their ability to act as a broker of information exchange between nodes that would otherwise be disconnected. Given the difficulty of measuring the centrality in a populated network, the notion of *ego networks* is exploited: nodes are not required to exchange global information on the network topology, but only local. *SimBet* routing protocol is then proposed [2], it operates the *betweenness* and the social *similarity* of destination node which is determined locally. The paper presents simulations using real data traces and shows that *SimBet* gives results, in terms of routing messages, that are close to the *epidemic* routing [3], but for a greatly reduced cost. In addition, the paper shows that *SimBet* surpasses the *PROPHET* routing protocol [4], especially when transmitting and receiving nodes have low connectivities. *SocialCast* [5] is a routing framework in *publish-and-subscribe* mode. It uses predictions based on the social interactions (such as modes of travel within a community) to identify the best carriers of information. The paper highlights the underlying principles of this protocol, illustrates its operation and evaluate its performance using a mobility model based on a social network validated using real traces. Analysis of the results shows that the prediction of collocation and mobility of nodes can publish for them, events steadily, keeping the control traffic and latency as low as possible, regardless of fluctuations in the density, the number of replicated messages and speeds. A sensitive to social relationships routing protocol, designed for sharing content on mobile applications, is proposed by [6]. It describes the design and implementation of a social relationship sensitive routing protocol. The social relationship is given a central role in the routing evaluation system *metrics.* Simulation results show that the proposed routing protocol has a higher flow rate and a lower control flow than the dynamic *Destination-Sequenced Distance-Vector, DSDV* routing protocol proposed by [7].

3   *Optimized Link State Routing, OLSR*

3.1   Why *OLSR?*

In [8], [9] and [10] we perform many simulations and shown that *OLSR* is more sensitive to social behavior than *AODV* and by the way it's more suitable for networks having social behavior especially when we use an adequate mobility model. Theses results make us thinking to try to ameliorate the existing *OLSR* protocol.

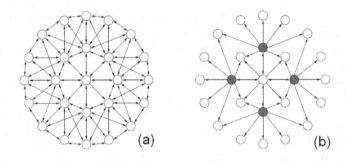

Fig. 1. Retransmission Gain 50 % : (a) without MPR, (b) with MPR

3.2 *OLSR* Protocol

The *Optimized Link State Routing (OLSR)* protocol can be described as an adaptation of *Open Shortest Path First (OSPF), RFC 2328*, for mobile networks. The optimization is the introduction of the notion of *MultiPoint Relay (MPR)*. The idea is to reduce the number of control packets avoiding their *flooding*, that is to say that all nodes always broadcast all control packets. In *OLSR*, a node n choses its *MPR* set, V_{n_m}, among its *one hop neighbors*, V_{n_1}. These *MPR* will disseminate its control packets. Its other neighbors, $V_{n_1} - V_{n_m}$, receive and process its packets without any broadcast. In addition, n holds another subset of its neighbors, V_{n_s}, including those who have designated it as their *MPR*. The elements of V_{n_s} are called the *MPR Selectors* of n. Any broadcast message from $s \in V_{n_s}$ received by n is broadcasted. V_{n_m} and V_{n_s} are defined and evolve with the emission of *Hello* messages every two seconds, *Hello Interval*.

A *Hello* message contains, besides the *Willingness* that indicates the propensity of a node to assume the role of *MPR*, a_n, the sending node's n address and $\forall v \in V_{n_1}$, a_v, the address of v and l_v, the type of link (n, v) which takes it values in $T_L =$ {symmetric, asymmetric, lost, unknown, symmetric neighbor, *MPR*, ... }. Any new link (n, v) is declared by n as *asymmetric*. It becomes *symmetric* when n receives the same link from v. Thus v becomes eligible as an *MPR* of n and vice versa. V_{n_1} is then made up of v such that (n, v) is *symmetric*. V_{n_2}, the *two hop neighbors* of n consists of v_2 nodes such as v_2 is a neighbor of $v \in V_{n_1}$ and $v_2 \notin V_{n_1}$.

Fig. 1 shows the gain obtained by the use of *MPR*: 12 retransmissions are sufficient to broadcast a message to 3 hops nodes from the transmitting node, i.e. the central node in Fig. 1a. Without this concept, it needs 24 transmission, Fig. 1b. This is the *first optimization* of OLSR. The *second optimization* is that in a *Topology Control, TC* message, only the vicinity of the nodes is transmitted and not the entire network as in the *Link State Advertissement, LSA*, message of the *OSPF* protocol. Finally, the *third optimization* is that these *TC* messages (and other control messages *MID* and *HNA* that are outside of our discussion) are never relayed by the non *MPR* nodes.

4   A Social Approach of *OLSR*: OLSR-S

As the movement of mobile devices is mainly based on the decisions and behavior of people carrying them, it is important to consider the social behavior of humans in the modeling of the mobility of these devices. One can notice that the movements of a man can be represented as a compromise between the strong need of people to socialize with others and their habits and/or interests. So, human social behavior can be characterized by:

- Attraction Points: some places considered important for the group and should be visited by its members,
- Community of travelers: people in a given community and who visit the same places.

We choose to consider the heart of the *OLSR* protocol, that is to say his *MPR* selection algorithm, as the ideal place to introduce the consideration of social groupings of users in a mobile network, and create our *Social OLSR, OLSR-S*.

The concept of grouping criterion can be implemented in different ways. A mechanism of *publish-and-subscribe* can allow a node to issue an offer and the others to accept for a period determined by a date, a start time and an end time. During this time, our *Social OLSR (OLSR-S)* protocol will adapt to be local to this group. Another mechanism closer to our works is to consider that a node will take the "color" of the first Attraction Point that it visits, in the sense that it assigns a group identifier of its own for a specified period. Note that a group is often formed at an event and do not discard on rapidly. Finally, nothing prevents the nodes to assign an arbitrarily group identifier chosen before starting the simulation tests. The group aspect is a specialty going far beyond this paper, we choose for our test the latter option.

The question is then: how to cheaply add the "perception" of community groups in *OLSR*? Inspired by [11] who proposes an original and simple approach for an energy aware OLSR, the answer we give is as follows: give to the nodes of the same community the same propensity to be *MPR*. Indeed, as mentioned above, the *Willingness* parameter of the *Hello message* indicates the propensity of a node to assume the role of *MPR*. This parameter can take any value between 0 (*Will_Never*) and 7 (*Will_Always*) with a default value of 3. Nothing prevents us to define, a priori, a particular value for each community group and assign it to the *Willingness* of all its stations.

5   Application

We add new values for the *Willingness* parameter: *Will_Social_Group_a*, where $a = A, B, C, D$, that defines a community group identifier. For our tests we need four groups, but there is no reason to not create more if needed.

In addition, we add the following condition to the *MPR* selection algorithm (written in pseudo-code) :

```
// Place the following code in the branch where you can choose
// between several MPR candidates and the criterion of choice
//is to take the larger Willingness

// Initialize the selected MPR,m ,to null
m = null

// n is social ?
IF n.Willingness > Will_Always THEN

    // n is social

    // Browse MPR candidates, search of that which
    // would have the same Willingness as n

    FOR every MPR candidate c DO
        IF  c.Willingness = n.Willingness THEN
            m = c
            EXITFOR
        ENDSI
    ENDFOR
ENDSI

// Place the basic OLSR algorithm
IF m = null THEN
    m = c[0]
    FOR every MPR candidate c DO
        IF  c.Willingness > m.Willingness THEN
            m = c
        ENDSI
    ENDFOR
ENDSI
```

Note that the "EXITFOR" is optional: in the version *with* "EXITFOR", we choose the first suitable candidate *MPR*; in the version *without* "EXITFOR", we choose the first suitable candidate *MPR*. In our algorithm, we choose the first one.

6   *AMN* Mobility Model

Assuming that mobile divices are carried by people, *Ant Mobility Model, AMN* [10] is a social mobility model which tries to mimic the realistic motion of people in a network. This model is based on *Ant Colony Systems (ACS)*.

We all notice for example, in sales period, there are some stores more crowded then others and the more a store is crowded, the more people enter it; the same goes when choosing destination of ones vacancy, the more a place is crowded, the more people choose it; when shoping upon the Internet too: if a item appears in the most-bought product list, more people will rush to buy it. This is because people do think if it is so crowded or chosen, its because its a good bargain or an interesting place. In the literature, attraction points model such centers of interest.

AMN uses this notion of attraction points and introduce some social behavior shows interresting results when used to simulate a network. We choose this model for the evaluation of the performances of our new algorithm.

7   Implmentation

We compare our approach with the basic *OLSR* protocol using our *Ant Manhattan Mobility Model (AMN)* mobility model.

For our performance studies, we use the following statistic:

- *Node statistics, OLSR, MPR Status* which relates the *"is MPR"* attributes of the considered node.

The network will consist of:

- 4 Attraction Points: AP_a where $a = A, B, C, D$;
- 4 mobile nodes "Station An" where $n = 1, 2, 3, 4$ for group A;
- 4 mobile nodes "Station Bn" where $n = 1, 2, 3, 4$ for group B.

The resulting network is shown in Fig. 2.

To implement our OLSR-S, we add our new values of *Willingness* to allow node to recognize the group as an eventual *MPR*.

The corresponding code allows us to establish the corresponding control flow :

```
Initializes the process;
Sleep mode;
Wake up if: Packet arrival or Timeout.
```

Each neighborhood or [1] topology changes [2] , the computation [3] of the *MPR* set is done.

Assuming that the nodes *"Station Ai"* and the nodes *"Station Bi"* belong respectively to the same groups, the nodes of a group will, as we can notice in real life, have the same behavior and move towards the same places (i.e. the same Attraction Points, AP).

---

[1]   appearance/disappearance of a one or two hops neighbor, or new asymmetric link. Appearance $\Longleftrightarrow$ link becomes symmetric. Disappearance $\Longleftrightarrow$ not a link at all. Asymmetric link $\Longleftrightarrow$ potential one hop neighbor.

[2]   create/delete/end interfaces of node, resulting from the arrival of a *Topology Control Message, TC* or a timeout for a validity of en interface.

[3]   it is rather an update.

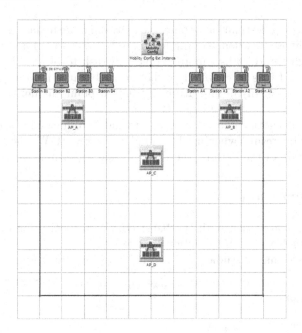

Fig. 2. Simulated Network

The trajectories of the nodes of A and B groups are described in Fig. 3.

This configuration will allow us to see the impact of our *OLSR-S* algorithm on the selection of *MPR*.

Places where a node has a high probability to change its *MPR* are represented by two circles.

To force the groups to follow these trajectories, we simply select the Attraction Points to visit.

To compare our new approach with basic *OLSR* algorithm we realize two scenarios:

- "Without Social OLSR" : *Willingness* is set to *Will_default*;
- "With Social OLSR" : initializes *Willingness* to:
    - → *Willingness_grpA* for group A;
    - → *Willingness_grpB* for group B.

Our choice is to have a uniform stations (iso-functional stations). So we set the traffic generator uniformly over all stations. Finally, the statistic *OLSR Status* of *Opnet Modeler* is chosen.

OLSR Status is set to 1 when a node is *MPR*, 0 otherwise.

In our results, we display the average value of this statistic. Do not be surprised to see different values from 0 and 1.

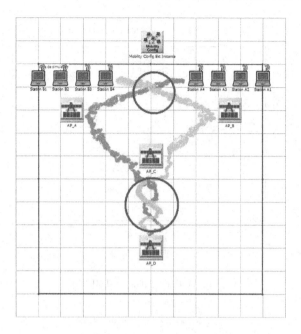

Fig. 3. Trajectories

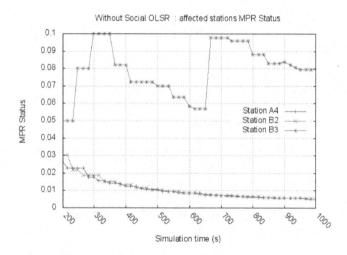

Fig. 4. MPR Status (OLSR)

8   Results

The first scenario does not use *Social OLSR (OLSR-S)* and gives the results shown in Fig. 4. This represents the three stations that played a role of *MPR*. These stations are *A*4, *B*2 and *B*3. *B*3 is, from the start, well positioned to

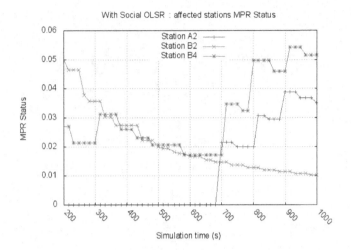

Fig. 5. MPR Status (OLSR-S)

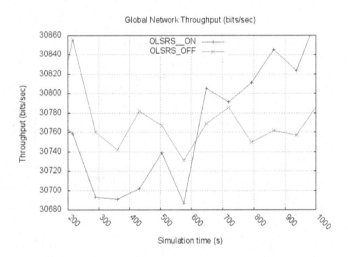

Fig. 6. Throughput (OLSR vs OLSR-S)

be the unique *MPR*. After about 4 minutes, we see that *A*4 and *B*2 bow and surrender their *MPR* position for *B*3. The group *A* has taken as *MPR* a station from group *B*.

The second scenario uses *Social OLSR (OLSR-S)* and gives the results shown in Fig. 5. This represents the three stations that played a role of *MPR*. These stations are *A*4, *B*2 and *B*3. *B*3 is, from the start, well positioned to be the unique *MPR*. But after about 10 minutes, we find instead that *B*2 tilts and sold its *MPR* position for *A4* and not *B2*. The stations of the group *A* have always an *MPR* of their group and it's the same for group *B*.

One can ask what it changes for the network as a whole to have less change of *MPR*. We compare the *Throughput* of both scenarios and the answer is given by the curves of Fig. 6.

These shows that the overall amount of received data, on average, on all stations of the mobile network is higher when we use *Social OLSR (OLSR-S)* than when we do not use it where it stagnates.

9   Conclusion

In this paper, we introduced one of the aspects of the use of community behavior in mobile networks: the integration of a "perception" of social aspects into the hearts of routing protocols for mobile networks. We first gave a brief overview of what is being done in this area. Then, we proposed a routing protocol based on the *Optimized Link State Routing* protocol and which adds the social component of perceiving groupings of individuals. We have attached to our proposal a simulation test environment which shows that the stability of a wireless network is more sustainable when this perception exists. However, a drawback should be mentioned and it is the energy management of social *MPR*, being more stable, they are likely to consume more energy and become the weak link of the whole network (in term of energy). Hence the interest of a hybrid *e-OSLR + OSLR-S*.

References

1. Daly, E.M., Haahr, M.: Social network analysis for routing in disconnected delay-tolerant manets. In: Proceedings of the 8th ACM International Symposium on Mobile Ad Hoc Networking and Computing, MobiHoc 2007, pp. 32–40. ACM, New York, USA (2007b)
2. Daly, E.M., Haahr, M.: Social network analysis for routing in disconnected delay-tolerant manets. In: Proceedings of the 8th ACM International Symposium on Mobile Ad Hoc Networking and Computing, MobiHoc 2007, pp. 32–40. ACM, New York, USA (2007a)
3. Yoneki, E., Hui, P., Crowcroft, J.: Bio-inspired computing and communication. Chapter Wireless Epidemic Spread in Dynamic Human Networks, pp. 116–132. Springer-Verlag, Berlin, Heidelberg (2008)
4. Lindgren, A., Doria, A., Schelén, O.: Probabilistic routing in intermittently connected networks. SIGMOBILE Mob. Comput. Commun. Rev. **7**, 19–20 (2003)
5. Costa, P., Mascolo, C., Musolesi, M., Picco, G.P.: Socially-aware routing for publish-subscribe in delay-tolerant mobile ad hoc networks. IEEE Journal on Selected Areas in Communications **26**(5), 748–760 (2008)
6. An, J., Ko, Y., Lee, D.: A social relation aware routing protocol for mobile ad hoc networks. In: IEEE International Conference on Pervasive Computing and Communications, PerCom 2009, pp. 1–6 (March 2009)
7. Perkins, C.E., Bhagwat, P.: Highly dynamic destination-sequenced distance-vector routing (dsdv) for mobile computers. In: Proceedings of the conference on Communications architectures, protocols and applications, SIGCOMM 1994, pp. 234–244. ACM, New York, USA (1994)

8. Harfouche, L., Boumerdassi, S., Renault, E.: Towards a Social Mobility Model. In: Proceedings of the 20th International Symposium on Personal, Indoor and Mobile Radio Communications, PIMRC 2009, pp. 2876–2880. IEEE Publisher, Sao Paulo (2009)

9. Harfouche, L., Boumerdassi, S., Renault, E.: Weighted Social Manhattan: Modeling and performance analysis of a mobility model. In: Proceedings of the 21th International Symposium on Personal, Indoor and Mobile Radio Communications, PIMRC 2010, pp. 2019–2023. IEEE Publisher, Istanbul (2010)

10. Harfouche, L., Costantini, H., Boumerdassi, S.: Social Mobility Models using Ant Colony Systems. In: Proceedings of the 22th International Symposium on Personal, Indoor and Mobile Radio Communications, PIMRC 2011. IEEE Publisher, Toronto (2010)

11. Ghanem, N., Boumerdassi, S., Renault, E.: New energy saving mechanisms for mobile ad-hoc networks using olsr. In: Proceedings of the 2nd ACM International Workshop on Performance Evaluation of Wireless Ad Hoc, Sensor, and Ubiquitous Networks, PE-WASUN 2005, pp. 273–274. ACM, New York, USA (2005)

Improving Stability in QoS Routing
for Ad-Hoc Networks

Tiago Coelho[✉], António Costa, Joaquim Macedo,
and Maria João Nicolau

Centro ALGORITMI, Universidade do Minho, Braga, Portugal
a44048@alunos.uminho.pt, {costa,macedo}@di.uminho.pt, joao@dsi.uminho.pt

Abstract. Routing in mobile Ad-Hoc networks is normally a difficult task, but even more challenging if the network is expected to provide support for audio and video streaming between human-carried devices. Besides normal movement and signal impairment difficulties, those multimedia applications may impose extra end-to-end requirements. The computation of optimized and/or constrained network paths using one or more metric restrictions is called QoS (Quality-of-Service) routing. This paper presents QMRS, a QoS routing protocol for Ad-Hoc networks which aims to support applications with QoS requirements including requirements for the end-to-end delay. This protocol proposes a on-demand multiple routes discovery mechanism that is able to find up to three node-disjoint paths that meet the QoS requirement. Additionally, and for the purpose of guarantee the stability of the routing process, it uses the signal strength of the links between neighbouring nodes to elect the most stable route. Such route will be used as the primary choice to forward traffic. The other discovered routes will be maintained as backup in order to eventually replace the primary route, in case of disruption or degradation of required QoS.

QMRS was implemented in NS-3 and evaluated in comparison with AODV and AMR (an AOMDV-like protocol). Simulation results show significant improvements, with respect to the average end-to-end delay, packet delivery ratio and throughput.

1 Introduction

A mobile Ad-Hoc network is a self-configuring network composed by mobile nodes that communicate directly, while within the appropriate signal range. The nodes have the ability to autonomously create a communications network between them, without assistance from a network infrastructure. All network nodes behave simultaneously like end-systems and routers. They participate in the packets routing process and also host several applications.

The increased diversity and capacity of wireless mobile devices and the simultaneous evolution of multimedia applications has created the need to propose and evaluate strategies to provide QoS guarantees for end-to-end traffic, in order to comply with requirements requested by such applications (bandwidth, end-to-end delay, jitter, etc). Due to the nodes mobility, the network topology is highly

© Institute for Computer Sciences, Social Informatics and Telecommunications Engineering 2014
N. Mitton et al. (Eds.): ADHOCNETS 2014, LNICST 140, pp. 121–133, 2014.
DOI: 10.1007/978-3-319-13329-4_11

dynamic and unpredictable failures may occur in established paths. Moreover, the wireless communications medium is shared between the neighbouring nodes. These factors mean that routing traffic with QoS requirements constitutes an even greater challenge in Ad-Hoc networks than doing it in fixed networks.

In this work, a proposal is made for an on-demand routing protocol that is able to find multiple disjoint paths in Ad-Hoc networks, that can meet end-to-end QoS requirements. The end-to-end delay was chosen as an example. The protocol, called QMRS (Ad hoc QoS On-Demand Multipath Routing with Route Stability) determines route stability based on signal strengths observed along the path and uses it as the main criteria to choose the best route. By keeping more than one alternative feasible path, stability is also preserved in case of failures. QMRS was implemented and tested using the NS-3 simulator.

The rest of the paper is structured in five more sections. Section 2 presents related work, namely some routing protocols for mobile adhoc networks. Section 3 describes the proposed protocol, detailing its most important mechanisms. Section 4 describes the implementation of the proposed protocol in the NS-3 simulator. Section 5 shows the obtained results and Section 6 the conclusions and further work.

2   Related Work

Routing protocols are usually classified into two main categories: proactive (table-driven) or reactive (on-demand). Proactive routing protocols (eg, Optimized Link State Routing Protocol - OLSR [1]) aim to keep all routing tables always updated. They provide low latency for packet forwarding since routes are always available, but they need to constantly exchange control messages even without any traffic. With expected high mobility and energy limitations of nodes, such control information overload is seen as a possible limitation.

Reactive routing protocols (eg, Ad hoc on demand Distance Vector - AODV [2]) only compute routes at the request of a node. The route discovery process is initiated only when a source node wants to transmit to a given destination, and there is no valid route in its routing table. In this way, there are less control messages on the network, thus allowing the devices to save processing resources and, above all, energy. Among reactive routing protocols, AODV is usually one of the most cited. However, during the route discovery phase, AODV only finds a single route to the destination. This means that if the existing route breaks, the route discovery process must be restarted.

To overcome this problem, and reduce the need for frequent discovery of routes from the same source to the same destination, some protocols were proposed that are able to find multiple paths within the same request (eg, Ad hoc On-demand Multipath Distance Vector - AOMDV [3]). AODMV is a variant of the protocol AODV that discovers various alternative routes but without any specific quality of service concerns. However, many other routing protocols exists that aim to provide such QoS guarantees in mobile Ad-Hoc networks.

Y. Hwang and P. Varshney proposed a protocol (An Adaptive QoS Routing Protocol with Dispersity for Adhoc Networks - ADQR [4]) that can discover multiple disjoint paths per route request. Based on the bandwidth information collected during the discover phase, resource reservations must then be requested on all routes found. Data is transmitted on all reserved paths. The protocol monitors the network to detect topology changes and update routes before they become unavailable. With the discovery and maintenance procedures, ADQR aims to significantly improve the network performance and to provide end-to-end QoS in mobile Ad-Hoc networks. Nevertheless, ADQR doesn't solve the packet reordering problem inherent to load balancing traffic between multiple paths. Furthermore, to process route requests it needs to store topology state information in each node. Finally, the proactive monitoring that is required for normal operation originates an overhead of control packets.

Qi Xue and Aura Ganz proposed a QoS routing protocol (Ad hoc QoS on-demand routing - AQOR [5]) based on AODV with resource reservation. The protocol is able to estimate the available bandwidth and measure the end-to-end delay, in order to provide QoS. It includes also bandwidth reservation and route recovery mechanisms. To avoid having to deal with the release of reserved resources in each node, in case of connection failure, the resource reservation is performed only temporarily. The route recovery procedure includes the detection of broken links, the verification of the required QoS and a destination-initiated recovery process.

Nityananda Sarma and Sukumar Nandi proposed the SMQR (Route Stability based Multipath QoS Routing) [6] protocol for ad-hoc networks. This protocol is able to discover multiple disjoint routes with higher stability. The discovered routes meet the requirements of a maximum end-to-end delay and a minimum effective transfer rate, in order to support real-time applications. Based in simulation results, the authors claimed improvements when compared with AODV protocol in terms of packet delivery ratio, average end-to-end delay, maximum delay variation and effective throughput.

Shun Liu and Jian Liu proposed a QoS routing protocol (Delay-aware multipath source routing protocol)- DMSR [7]) to support real time applications in Ad-Hoc networks. These applications are throughput and delay sensitive. DMSR is a multipath routing protocol that uses end-to-end delay as a metric. At each node, local information is collected and the delay experienced in the node is computed. This metric is used to select the best path. It combines the number of neighbour nodes, the contention time, and the number of packets in queue.

3   A Proposal for QoS Routing in Ad-Hoc Networks

This section presents the proposed protocol called QoS Multipath Routing with Route Stability (QMRS), a reactive protocol based on AODV. The new features introduced enable the discovery of multiple paths, reach QoS requirements and optimize the stability of the routing process. The QMRS protocol enables the discovery of up to three node-disjoint paths that meet an end-to-end delay requirement. Among the paths found, the most stable one is selected as the active path, while the others are maintained as alternatives. If the paths found have the same stability, the one with the lowest end-to-end delay is selected.

The discovery of multiple node-disjoint alternative paths allows a faster reaction when a fault occurs on the active path. In this case, the source node will react to the fault notification by changing the active path to one of the alternatives. The probability for existence of a valid alternative is high due to the algorithm used for finding paths. This algorithm only considers as alternative paths those without any nodes in common between the source and the destination. If the paths found contained disjoint links instead of disjoint nodes, the movement of only one node could break all alternative routes between source and destination. In that case the source node would need to restart the route discovery process again. Thus, the discovery of multiple node-disjoint alternative paths decreases the amount of control traffic on the network and consequently the end-to-end delay for data flow transmission. Figure 1 illustrates the concept of node-disjoint paths. With such topology gathered during the route discovery process, it would be possible to discover three node-disjoint paths: *source-A-D-destination, source-B-destination, source-C-E-destination*. As can be verified, the same intermediate node can only belong to one of the paths found between the source and destination, and can never belong to other alternative paths found and stored in the routing table.

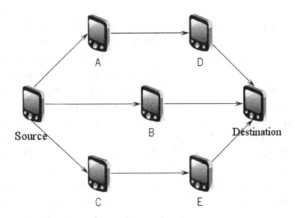

Fig. 1. Multiple node-disjoint alternative paths

As described, QMRS begins by discovering multiple node-disjoint paths between source and destination that meet the QoS requirement. Then, and to improve stability, QMRS uses the received signal strength to select the best route for transmission. If two or more discovered paths present similar values for received signal strength metric, end-to-end delay is used to select the best route.

A route maintenance mechanism is applied on all paths found between the source and destination nodes, in order to periodically check if the QoS guarantees are maintained. The values of the used metrics (end-to-end delay and received signal strength) are updated. Then, a route change may occur, to one of the valid alternative routes stored in the routing table. With these mechanisms, the proposed protocol enables an efficient data transmission providing QoS guarantees.

3.1 Maintaining State Information Between Neighbours

Periodic exchanges of *Hello* messages occur between the nodes within the transmission range. The reception of these *Hello* messages indicates that the neighbours are available and accessible, information that is required for the route discovery and maintenance procedures. Through the *Hello* messages, the received signal strength and the delay for each neighbour are also updated. The signal strength on reception is directly taken from the physical layer via a cross-layer interaction. The delay for each neighbour is the time since the packet is queued until it reaches the neighbour. This time includes the queue time, contention and media access time, transmission time and propagation time. The periodic exchange of *Hello* messages is necessary to maintain the values of these metrics updated and enable intermediate nodes to answer route requests for its neighbours. When a neighbour misses *Hello* messages during a given time interval, a route recovery process must be initiated.

3.2 Route Discovery

The route discovery process is based on AODV protocol. Significant changes were done in order to introduce additional mechanisms to enable the discovery of multiple node-disjoint paths that meet an end-to-end delay requirement. *End-to-end delay* is an additive metric that results from the sum of all the delays obtained in the nodes that constitute the path. For each path found, QMRS algorithm also computes the *signal strength*, a concave metric that is computed as the minimum value of the received signal strength in all links that make up the path.

When a node wishes to transmit data to some destination node, and doesn't have a valid route for that destination in its routing table, it has to start the process of route discovery. This process consists on a broadcast of a *Route Request (RREQ)* packet to all neighbouring nodes. The *RREQ* packet contains information about the source node (*Originator IP Address* and *Originator Sequence Number*) and the destination node (*Destination IP Address* and *Destination Sequence Number*). The sequence numbers are increased by the source node, every time a *RREQ* packet is sent. Upon receiving a *RREQ* packet, each intermediate node can verify if the information it contains on its routing table is still updated or already obsoleted, in relation to the information hold by the request originator. The mentioned fields, along with the *ID* field and advertised *hop count* are essential to distinguish between successive requests and avoid routing cycles. Table 1 shows the structure of *Route Request (RREQ)* and *Route Reply (RREP)* packets.

Table 1. RREQ and RREP Packet Fields

RREQ ID
Destination IP Address
Destination Sequence Number
Originator IP Address
Originator Sequence Number
hopCount
firstHop
RxSignalStPath
delayAcc
delayPath
delayReq

(a) RREQ Packet

Destination IP Address
Destination Sequence Number
Originator IP Address
hopCount
firstHop
RxSignalStPath
RxSignalStPathToDst
delayPath
delayReq

(b) RREP Packet

When receiving the *RREQ* packet, neighbouring nodes increment the *hopCount* field and introduce their own address in the *firstHop* field. This field is used to verify if the path found is a node-disjoint path. When a node receives the *RREQ* packet for the first time (verifiable by the *RREQ ID* and *Originator IPAddress* fields, that uniquely identify the request) and doesn't have a valid route to the requested destination, it broadcasts the *RREQ* again through the network in order to find the destination node or an intermediate node that has a valid route to the destination node. The route is considered valid only if the intermediate node contains in its routing table a route to destination node with a sequence number (*Destination Sequence Number*) greater than or equal to the one contained in the *RREQ* packet received. When an intermediate node responds to a request, made by a source node, it must also send a packet called *Gratuitous Route Reply* to inform the destination node of the route to the source node. After retransmitting the *RREQ* packet, the intermediate node waits a period of time for a valid response. The reception of a *Route Reply (RREP)* packet validates the route to destination.

When receiving the *RREQ* packet, the intermediate nodes must also update the routing entries relative to the source node. The intermediate node begins to check if the sequence number of the source node contained in the packet is greater than or equal to the one in the routing table. In case of being equal, and if it is a node-disjoint path, then it is also checked whether the number of routes contained in the routing table is less than three (the protocol stored up to three node-disjoint paths). After these checks performed, the routing table entry to the source node is updated. If the sequence number is greater than the one in the routing table, the routes to the source node are removed and replaced by the new one found.

During the route discovery, a mechanism for admission control is used. Whenever there is non compliance with maximum end-to-end delay required by the application (*delayReq*), the *RREQ* packet is discarded. To verify that the QoS requirement is being met during the route discovery, a node calculates the delay that occurs in the node and adds it to the one contained in the *RREQ* packet (*delayAcc*). A comparison is then performed between the calculated value and the maximum end-to-end delay required. If the accumulated end-to-end delay isn't less than the requested one (*delayAcc* < *delayReq*) the packet is discarded.

When the path already traversed meets the QoS requirement contained in *RREQ* packet (*delayReq*), the accumulated end-to-end delay (*delayAcc*) and the minimum received signal strength (*RxSignalStPath*) from the path so far is updated on the *RREQ* packet. The signal strength is obtained directly from the physical layer, through a cross-layer interaction. The value obtained on receiving node (*RSSRead*) is compared with the value stored in the *RREQ* packet. If the value read is less than the value stored in packet, it is a new minimum, and must replace the value stored in the packet. Otherwise the value remains unchanged (equation 1). With the metrics updated, the *RREQ* packet is retransmitted by broadcast, to continue the search for a route to the destination.

$$RREQ.RxSignalStPath = min(RREQ.RxSignalStPath, RSSRead) \qquad (1)$$

The reply to the route request, whether made by the destination node or by an intermediate node that has a valid route to the destination, is performed by sending a *Route Reply (RREP)* packet. The information in the *RREQ* packet, updated during its retransmission by intermediate nodes along the path, contains the final end-to-end delay (*delayPath*) and the minimum received signal strength (*RxSignalStPath*) of the path found. This information will be placed in the response *RREP* packet, and this packet will be sent in unicast directly to the source node using the reverse of the route traversed by the *RREQ* packet. In this way, the intermediate nodes validate the routing table entries to the destination node, while retransmitting the RREP packet to the source node. The information on end-to-end delay and the minimum received signal strength, is also inserted into the respective routing table entry and validated by the intermediate nodes. Thus if a node receives a request from another source node to that destination, it can check if the end-to-end delay can be met, as well as inform on the stability of this path.

3.3   Path Selection

Among all node-disjoint paths found that meet the end-to-end delay requirement, the most stable one is chosen for transmission. The stability of a path is based on the minimum received signal strength observed on all its links (*RxSignalStPath*). This is the primary criteria for route selection. The best route is the one with higher *RxSignalStPath* value. Only in case of more than one route have the highest stability, the preference is given to the path with the lowest end-to-end delay.

3.4 Route Maintenance

As a consequence of a route discovery operation, nodes in discovered paths store routes to the destination node and to the source node on their routing tables. Topology changes can however occur due to, for instance, node mobility. Therefore routes can became unavailable and information stored on the routing table obsolete. Whenever a node in a path verifies that the the next hop node is not in transmission range, it must send a *Route Error (RERR)* packet to notify the source node of a link failure. This *RERR* packet is forwarded by all nodes on the path back to the source. Before forwarding the packet, each node must remove the invalid route from its routing table. After receiving a *RERR* packet, the source node checks if the broken route is the active one in use for the destination, and changes the active route to the best stable alternative available on its routing table. When no alternatives exist, a new discovery procedure must be initiated. If the broken route is an alternative route not currently in use, it is simply removed from the routing table without any further action.

A QoS verification procedure must also be carried on all paths discovered and stored in the routing tables. When the end-to-end delay restriction is violated, routes are also removed. Two new packets are used to check for metric changes in the path: *InspectPath* and *ReplyInpectPath*. The verification process is similar to the one used in the discovery phase. The *InspectPath* is forwarded along the path accumulating the new values of delay and signal strength. All nodes in the path use the information carried in the *InspectPath* to update the routing table with the new metric. If the restriction is not met, an *RERR* packet is sent back to the source, notifying all intermediate nodes that the route is no longer usable. Each node that receives the *RERR* packet removes the invalid entry.

4 Implementation

The Network simulator NS-3 [8] was chosen as the implementation tool, among other well known open source alternatives, like NS-2 [9] and OMNeT++ [10]. While NS-2 is still under heavy usage, NS-3 is currently presented as its future replacement, eventually with better performance [11] and more efficient resource usage. In current NS-3 modules we can find some Ad-Hoc routing protocol implementations (like AODV, for instance) but none related to multipath and/or QoS routing proposals. This drawback was in fact faced as a challenge towards an effective move to NS-3. A previous implementation of Ad Hoc On-Demand Multipath Distance Vector (AOMDV) [3], available for NS-2, was used as inspiration and a reference for our implementation on NS-3.

4.1 Data Structures

The routing table structure is based on the structure used in AODV implementation, carefully modified to include multiple entries for the same destination.

Routing entries are stored in a map ($std::map < Ipv4Address, RoutingTableEntry >$ $m\_ipv4AddressEntry$) that uses the IP Address as key. Values associated with the key are of type $RoutingTableEntry$, that contain the data fields and methods associated with a route entry. For each entry, the end-to-end delay and the minimum signal strength measured are also stored. The following fields are used: *destination, sequence number, advertised hop count, next hop, last hop, hop count, rxSSPath, delay, lifetime* and a *list of alternative routes*. The list of alternative routes is a vector ($std::vector < QmrsRoute > m\_routeList$) that stores, for each alternative route, the following fields: *next hop, last hop, hop count,*
rxSSPath, delay and *lifetime*.

4.2   Neighbour State Information

Neighbour nodes must exchange *Hello* messages between them, stating that they are available and accessible. This information is very useful for the route discovery and maintenance procedures. *Hello* messages are in fact special $RREQ$ sent from the node address to the node address and with $TTL = 1$. For each received message, nodes must get the received signal strength from physical layer, through a cross-layer call. The method $GetRxPowerDbmPhy(receiver)$ available on class $RoutingProtocol$, initiates that call that will invoke the $GetRxPowerDbm$ on the *yans-wifi-phy* module. This file was changed to provide the required value.

All methods that process messages must also keep a $delayNode$ value updated. The value is used to update the end-to-end cumulative delay of route requests. The value is computed using the NS-3 packet "tags" feature that allows for the sharing of 20 bytes between layers. The tag is created with the simulation time obtained by calling $tag.Set(Simulator::Now().GetMicroSeconds()$ and $packet-> AddPacketTag(tag)$ in sequence. When the tagged packet arrives at the physical layer for transmission, the time delay is computed and added to the physical transmission delay that can be obtained by calling the method $txDuration.GetMicroSeconds()$. The $delayNode$ value is therefore very accurate.

4.3   Route Discovery

Route discovery functions are implemented with the exchange of *route request messages (RREQ)*(see table) 2a) and *route reply messages (RREP)*(see table 2b). A few details on $RREQ$ send and receive methods are therefore provided here.

The *sendRequest()* method is called to broadcast a $RREQ$ message on the network. The request must include the delay restriction $delayReq$ that is set using the $SetDelayReq()$ method. In order to get the correct end-to-end delay, the $delayNode$ value must be obtained from the node by calling $GetAverageDelayPhy()$ and set in the $RREQ$ message using $SetDelayAcc()$. Before the transmission, packet is tagged with current simulation time as previously described. Each node receives the $RREQ$ message with the method $recvRequest()$. The path delay value must be updated in the message using $rreqHeader.SetDelayAcc(rreqHeader.GetDelay$ $Acc() + delayNode)$.

4.4 Route Maintenance

A source node can proceed with data transmission on an alternative route after receiving a route error notification. But alternate routes can only be fast effective replacements in case they are kept up to date. The end-to-end delay and the minimum receive signal strength metrics must be updated regularly, and the end-to-end delay restriction must be verified. For this maintenance procedure, two new messages were created: *InspectPath* and *ReplyInspectPath*. A periodic call to a method *SendInspectPath()* must be issued by the on every node-disjoint path kept in table. Nodes in the path, receive the message using the method *RecvInspectPath()* to accumulate the new delay and signal strength values. A reply message is sent using *SendReplyInspectPath()* only when the delay restriction stay valid. The *ReplyInspectPath* message is received by all nodes in the path from the destination to the source, using the method *RecvReplyInspectPath()*, and is also used to update the metric values in the routing table entries for the destination.

5 Results

The Network Simulator 3 (NS-3) [8] was used to evaluate QMRS. As a starting point, a multipath routing protocol, called AMR (AdHoc Multipath Routing-protocol) was implemented and used in result analysis. The implementation of AODV already included in NS-3 was also used as a comparative reference.

5.1 Simulation Scenario

A total of 60 simulations were run for each protocol in all scenarios. Therefore, results presented in figures 2, 3 and 4, for each node speed, show the average of the obtained 60 values and the correspondent 95% confidence interval. At simulation start, all 80 nodes are placed randomly in an area of 600mx1500m. Nodes then move at a maximum speed of 0 to 10 m/s, randomly in that area, according to the random waypoint mobility model. All nodes have a transmission range of 160m. Table 2 shows all parameters used in simulations.

During simulation time (200s) a total of 15 CBR (Constant Bit Rate) flows were generated, between randomly selected pairs of source and destination nodes. The UDP protocol carried CBR packets of a 64 *bytes* in size, at transfer rate of 2Kbps. Three metrics were calculated and used in results analysis: the observed end-to-end delay (in miliseconds), the packet delivery ratio (in percentage) and effective transmission rate (in *kbps*).

Parameter	Value
Area	$600m \times 1500m$
Number of nodes	80
Mobility model	Random Waypoint
Node position	Random
Transmission range	$160m$
Traffic type	Constant Bit Rate
Packet size	64 bytes
Number of flows	15
Transmission rate	$2Kbps$
Wifi specifications	IEEE 802.11b, freq. 2.4Ghz Transfer rate up to 2Mbps
Simulation time (s)	200

Table 2. Parameters used in simulations

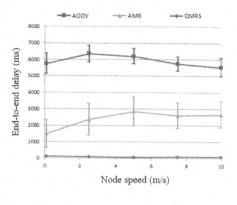

Fig. 2. Results: end-to-end delay

5.2   End-to-end Delay

Figure 2 shows the results obtained for the end-to-end delay metric. QMRS presents and average end-to-end delay value between 0 and 150 ms, while AODV exhibits much higher values. AODV has no concerns regarding delay and it only discovers one route per request, having no way to deal with failures except by restarting the discovery process. On the other hand, AMR computes multiple paths, and is therefore more stable when disruptions occur. It selects routes based on stability without considering delay. It shows less average end-to-end delay than AODV, but higher than QMRS. QMRS is the only protocol in this set that uses delay as a metric.

5.3   Delivery Ratio and Transmission Rate

Figure 3 shows the results obtained for the packet delivery ratio metric. The average delivery ratio for QMRS, measured at the destination node, is in the 70% to 80% range. Values for AODV are placed between 10% and 20% and for AMR between 45% and 60%. Figure 4 shows the exact same tendency for the effective transmission rate observed. QMRS presents values around the 2$kbps$, while AODV remains under 1$Kpbs$. AMR exhibits intermediate values, above 1.5$kbps$ and below 2$kbps$.

QMRS goal is to ensure path stability in the first place, while respecting the end-to-end delay requirements. Nodes that belong to its route paths are therefore less congested. AODV however, considers no delay restrictions and may choose paths that are more congested. Since it only discovers one route per request it has to deal with failures. AMR shows intermediate values because it uses multiple node-disjoint paths, but it doesn't consider any delay metric.

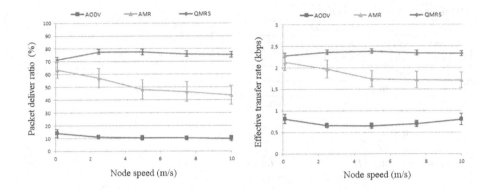

Fig. 3. Results: packet delivery ratio   **Fig. 4.** Results: effective transfer rate

6   Conclusion

In this paper a new protocol called Ad hoc QoS On-Demand Multipath Routing with Route Stability (QMRS) was proposed. QMRS provides mechanisms to discover, in a single discovery attempt, multiple node-disjoint paths between source and destination nodes that can satisfy the specified end-to-end delay restriction. The source node chooses the most stable path for transmission, in order to maintain the route feasible for longer periods of time, without the need to change to an alternate path or re-initiate the route discover procedure. Only in presence of multiple routes with equal stability, the lower end-to-end delay is used as a second criteria of choice. The discovery of multiple alternative node-disjoint paths allows the source node to use an alternative route in case of a failure in the main route eventually caused by node movements. Route stability is based on measured signal strength, which is computed as the minimum value observed in all links that constitute the path. The path with the higher value is the most stable.

The proposed protocol was implemented in Network Simulator 3 (NS-3). Simulation results were obtained and compared with the standard implementation of AODV included in NS-3, and also with a variant of the AODV capable of discovering multipath node-disjoint routes, implemented from scratch on NS-3. Results show that QMRS, with its discovery/maintenance/recovery and delay verification mechanisms, provided lower end-to-end delay in all data transmissions and higher packet delivery ratio and effective transmission rate.

Future work includes further simulation analysis. New traffic models, besides simple CBR traffic, and new simulation scenarios, should also be considered. Alternative metrics may also be used. Another goal is to evaluate the usage of QMRS within a class-of-service model.

Acknowledgments. This work has been suported by FCT - Fundação para a Ciência e Tecnologia in the scope of the project: PEst-OE/EEI/UI0319/2014.

References

1. Clausen, T., Jacquet, P.: RFC 3626 - Optimized Link State Routing Protocol (OLSR) (2003)
2. Perkins, C., Belding-Royer, E., Das, S.: Ad hoc on demand distance vector (AODV) routing (RFC 3561). IETF MANET Working Group (August 2003)
3. Marina, Mahesh K., Das, Samir R.: Ad hoc on-demand multipath distance vector routing. Wireless Communications and Mobile Computing 6(7), 969–988 (2006)
4. Youngki Hwang, Y.H., Varshney, P.: An adaptive QoS routing protocol with dispersity for ad-hoc networks. In: Proceedings of the 36th Annual Hawaii International Conference on System Sciences (2003)
5. Xue, Q., Ganz, A.: Ad hoc QoS on-demand routing (AQOR) in mobile ad hoc networks (2003)
6. Sarma, N., Nandi, S.: A Route Stability Based Multipath QoS Routing (SMQR) in MANETs. In: 2008 First International Conference on Emerging Trends in Engineering and Technology (2008)
7. Liu, S., Liu, J.: Delay-aware multipath source routing protocol to providing QoS support for wireless ad hoc networks. In: 2010 IEEE 12th International Conference on Communication Technology, pp. 1340–1343. IEEE (November 2010)
8. Henderson, T.R., Roy, S., Floyd, S., Riley, G.F.: Ns-3 Project Goals. In: Proceeding from the 2006 Workshop on ns-2: the IP Network Simulator - WNS2 '06, p. 13 (2006)
9. Fall, K. Varadhan, K.: The network simulator (ns-2). http://www.isi.edu/nsnam/ns (2007)
10. Varga, A.: Microsoft Visual, Remote Omnet, and Statistical Synchronization Method. The OMNeT++ discrete event simulation system. In: Proceedings of the European Simulation Multiconference ESM'2001, vol. 42, pp. 319–324 (2001)
11. Weingartner, E., Vom Lehn, H., Wehrle, K.: A performance comparison of recent network simulators, pp. 1–5. IEEE (2009)

Content Centricity in Constrained Cellular-Assisted D2D Communications

Salah-Eddine Belouanas[1](✉), Kim-Loan Thai[1], Prométhée Spathis[1],
Marcelo Dias de Amorim[1], Franck Rousseau[2], and Andrzej Duda[2]

[1] LIP6/CNRS – UPMC Sorbonne Universités, Paris, France
{salah-eddine.belouanas,kim.thai,promethee.spathis,
marcelo.amorim}@lip6.fr
[2] Grenoble Institute of Technology,
Grenoble Informatics Laboratory, Grenoble, France
{franck.rousseau,andrzej.duda}@imag.fr

Abstract. The huge increase of mobile traffic in the latest years has put cellular networks under pressure. To face this situation, operators propose to adopt data offloading techniques based on device-to-device communications to alleviate their infrastructure. In this paper, we consider a specific scenario in which the cellular channel has severe capacity limitations. Existing offloading techniques focus on the underlying communication mechanisms and fail to properly manage the interest users have in *content*. The straightforward approach to tackle this issue is to rely on the content-centric networking (CCN) paradigm. Nevertheless, the hybrid nature of our scenario makes this vision challenging—what should circulate through the cellular channel and what should remain within the opportunistic network? In this paper, we investigate our target scenario and identify a number of challenges therein. We finally define a high-level architecture that we intend to instantiate in the case of a public infrastructure scenario.

Keywords: Opportunistic device-to-device communications · Infrastructure wireless networks · Content-centric networking · Data offloading

1 Introduction

The advent of device-to-device (D2D) communication technologies has extended the traditional use of wireless networks, giving rise to new application opportunities. As co-located nodes may share common interests, an important communication functionality is *data dissemination*, in which a content must reach multiple destinations. Target nodes are said to be "interested" in the content while other nodes may play the role of relays to serve the target nodes. The bridge between those who generate the content and potential destinations falls within the scope of *publish/subscribe* systems that, when combined with a proper retrieval strategy, determine how efficiently content flows between publishers and subscribers.

© Institute for Computer Sciences, Social Informatics and Telecommunications Engineering 2014
N. Mitton et al. (Eds.): ADHOCNETS 2014, LNICST 140, pp. 134–145, 2014.
DOI: 10.1007/978-3-319-13329-4_12

A challenge operators have to face in this context is the evergrowing increase of mobile data (mobile traffic is likely to grow about ten times by 2018, compared with 2013) [1]. Similar observations may also exist in Wi-Fi hotspots handling a large number of users [2]. Generally speaking, the main problem arises when *data transfer volumes go beyond the capacity of the infrastructure access.* Therefore, operators must either increase the capacity of their networks (and reduce their CAPEX/OPEX) or find some alternative ways to handle exceeding data traffic. At this stage, *data offloading* is foreseen as a promising solution to alleviate the burden on the wireless access infrastructure [3–7].

While existing data offloading solutions provide interesting strategies for routing and forwarding mechanisms, they neither consider how users access content nor what they are interested in. In this paper, we tackle this problem from the point of view of *content-centric networking* (CCN) [8,9]. The main idea behind CCN is to shift the network from the traditional, host-centric paradigm to content-centric operation. A content provider in CCN tags its content with a set of attributes and then disseminates it throughout the network. Subscribers interested in that content (or, more specifically, that share similar interests with regard to the content attributes) retrieve the content from the nearest node that has a copy.

The CCN architecture depends on information stored at nodes in the path between the sources of the content and the subscribers. For this reason, adapting the CCN principles to a case where nodes are potentially mobile is challenging. In our target scenario, where subscribers may either retrieve content from the infrastructure using cellular or Wi-Fi access or from other nodes using D2D communications, there is also the risk of overstressing the system with duplicated content and extra signaling traffic.

To achieve a good balance between functionality and efficiency, we focus in this paper on the possibility of designing a *lightweight CCN-based system for D2D communications under infrastructure assistance.* In our idea, since the infrastructure has a capacity-constraint channel, mobile devices have to explore that channel in a moderated manner. We take advantage of specific CCN features (e.g., naming and caching) to leverage the use of the infrastructure as a control support and keep, whenever possible, data in the opportunistic domain. To the best of our knowledge, there are no equivalent approaches specifically designed to the case of mobile opportunistic traffic offloading.

The remainder of this paper is organized as follows. In Section 2, we describe our target scenario where device-to-device communications are supported by a (capacity-constrained) cellular network. In Section 3, we highlight the main architectural features of CCN that seem to be relevant to the context of offloaded D2D content delivery. In Section 4, we investigate how to adapt those features to address the challenges arising in the context of D2D communications. We identify a candidate high-level architecture for our framework in Section 5 and conclude the paper in Section 6.

2   Constrained Cellular-Assisted D2D Communications

The area of traffic offloading has recently generated intensive research activity. Yung et al. classify offloading mechanisms in three categories [10]: (i) broadcast offloading [11], where the infrastructure uses broadcast to reach all users within a cell, (ii) Wi-Fi offloading [5,12,13] that leverages the availability of Wi-Fi access points to mitigate traffic on cellular networks, and (iii) opportunistic offloading [3–7], which exploits device-to-device opportunities to reduce the traffic in the cellular network. In this paper, we are particularly interested in opportunistic traffic offloading.

We consider a system where nodes are, at all times, covered by some sort of wireless infrastructure (e.g., cellular, Wi-Fi). This means that they have permanent access to the Internet. We assume that nodes may bypass the infrastructure and communicate directly in a device-to-device way. In our target scenario, the access channel of the infrastructure is likely to be *highly constrained* with regard to its capacity. The limitations may be due to contention for resources (e.g., due to data avalanche or poor wireless conditions) or to some operational rules. This latter case is of particular interest to our work, as it corresponds to our case study (see Section 5). In a nutshell, this case study is a public service where cellular or Wi-Fi hotspot operators reserve a thin share of their capacity to provide a low-rate, open channel for citizens. These latter have then a minimal possibility of connectivity, even when they are covered by a different operator than her/his (in an equivalent way to emergency numbers that citizens can call even if she/he roams or has no credits available).

We illustrate our system in Figure 1. As we can see, the infrastructure must push the content to at least one of the users that can then rely on device-to-device communications to retrieve the content. As a design principle, we assume that one bit transferred in device-to-device mode costs much less than one bit downloaded from the infrastructure. Although there are some adversaries to this assumption (e.g., battery consumption at devices), it seems to be a good approximation for the purposes of overall capacity improvements [14].

Since interactions between mobile users and their content providers (e.g., through the cellular infrastructure) increase as much as users ask for the content, deciding what and when to offload is an objective of a paramount importance. In other words, we need to find new ways to satisfy users' needs while respecting the constraints of the cellular infrastructure. We believe that the CCN paradigm brings a number of features that fit well our context, which does not come at free, as adapting the CCN architecture to the case of mobile nodes is not straightforward[1].

---

[1] Although several papers in the literature have considered this problem in the case of pure ad hoc or opportunistic networks, little attention, if any, has been paid to the case of cellular-assisted mobile networks.

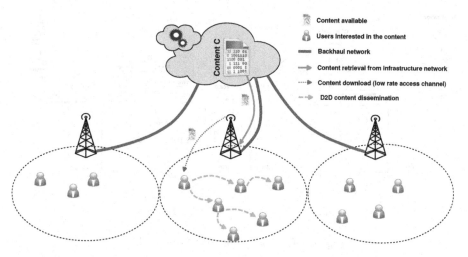

Fig. 1. Offloading scheme. Note the bottleneck due to the limited capacity of the access channel.

3 Accessing Content in Constrained Cellular-Assisted D2D Communications

Common offloading policies that can be found in the literature are mainly based on the analysis of users' mobility patterns [15]. We propose to extend these policies by considering the content itself. The idea is to provide the ability for users to benefit from the availability of content in their vicinity to avoid consuming unnecessary infrastructure resources.

To this end, we investigate the paradigm of content-centric networking (CCN) as a way to leverage on content availability resulting from replication or caching. Content-centric networks have attracted huge interest from the research community leading to the proposal of several architectures following popular designs [16–18]. Motivated by the ability to access content in a location-independent manner, the common underlying paradigm to these architectures calls for a shift in the way communication takes place among network entities since the emphasis is on the content rather than the location. According to this paradigm, a piece of content can be retrieved without relying on the binding of the corresponding data object to its host location. The practical purpose shared in the design of content-centric networks is to meet the data-intensive application needs by improving content delivery performance and reducing traffic overhead. In the following, we choose CCN as a reference architecture [9] and present its main features that, we believe, are the most relevant toward efficient D2D offloading.

3.1 Content-Centric Networking Background

The CCN proposal has gained much attention from the research community [9]. Instead of replacing IP with a clean-state approach, the CCN design follows a

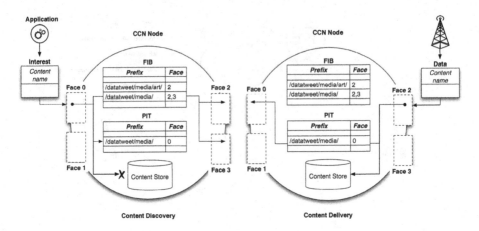

Fig. 2. CCN communication framework

more conventional approach—it aims at showing that removing IP addresses from the Internet does not call for revisiting IP engineering principles. The key objective is to investigate whether the Internet can evolve from a design that has been exclusively host-centric to a content-centric paradigm. As a result, the key choices that have driven the design of CCN were taken to enable the reuse of well-tried mechanisms and techniques borrowed from IP.

As depicted in Figure 2, a CCN communication consists of two phases: content discovery and content delivery. Content discovery uses Interest messages that contain the CCN content name. They are handled in a way that depends on a strategy layer. A strategy defines on which interfaces, also called "faces", a CCN node will forward an Interest. Broadcast is one obvious strategy that can help foster content availability. Carefully designed strategies may be relevant in the context of D2D communications as the list of faces can be seen as the multiple contemporaneous connectivity opportunities. In response to the Interest message, every node that holds a copy of the requested content returns a Data message. Multiple Interest-Data exchanges may be required to complete a request for a content divided in chunks (as the requester may receive each chunk from different sources in parallel).

The CCN node model includes three key data structures depicted in Figure 2, namely the FIB (Forwarding Information Base), the PIT (Pending Interest Table), and the Content Store (buffer memory). The first two structures specify how to process Interest and Data messages, respectively. A FIB entry is defined for a given content and indicates the list of faces pointing towards the content source(s).

PIT contains the list of interfaces on which Interest messages for the same content are received before forwarded upstream, towards the content source(s). Unlike the Interests that are routed according to the FIB, Data messages are returned to the requester by simply following the chain of PIT entries left by the Interest(s) back to the requester. The advantages of PIT is two-fold: PITs avoid loops by propagating multiple instances of the same Interest messages. PITs also allow aggregation of multiple similar Data messages since only one is expected to flow back to the content requester.

The Content Store is used as a cache memory where Data messages are stored on their way back to the content requester. Since content can be accessed in an application-independent way, in-network caching allows every node to be turned into potential content sources by intercepting Interests on their way to the original upstream content source. As so, the content store increases the access efficiency by minimizing the retrieval time and maximizing the upstream bandwidth demand.

4   CCN-Based System for D2D Communications Under Infrastructure Assistance

In the previous section, we have highlighted the main architectural features of CCN that are relevant in the context of D2D traffic offloading. We now investigate how to adapt those features to address the challenges that arise in the context of D2D communications offloaded from a cellular-based infrastructure network. We conclude that some of the CCN key design choices are well suited for enabling resilience to episodic content availability due to hosting node mobility or network failures.

4.1   Naming

The CCN name syntax is inspired by the naming scheme of DNS. Whereas DNS specifies rules for delegating assignment authority over global names, CCN is interested in the support of prefix aggregation enabled by the hierarchical structure of domain names. CCN applies the concept of aggregation introduced by CIDR to the context of URL-based content names. From the use of aggregation as an already well-tried technique, it is expected that routing and forwarding for CCN can achieve scalability.

Instead of DNS-based names, flat namespaces appear to be a better candidate in the context of an opportunistic network. A flat namespace consists of unstructured, location-independent, and human-unreadable identifiers. Flat names are said to be semantic-free since they provide the ability to refer to content and services independently of the hosting endpoint, regardless of its administrative domain, location, or network topology. In contrast to the DNS-based names, content can be replicated or move with their hosts while avoiding broken links or using HTTP redirection, which requires excessive control overhead and increases latency.

A flat name might be a long sequence of bits chosen randomly (typically 128-bit long). It can be derived from the cryptographic hash of the public key of the content owner (for authentication) and of the content itself (for integrity). The granularity of naming is flexible since a name can refer to a host, to a content, or, at finer granularity, to any content item with no reference to the hosting endpoint. At the user-level, it is assumed that a mapping service provides applications with the names corresponding to human readable descriptors such as search keywords.

It might be also relevant to consider the hierarchical structure of cellular networks, especially if the content depends on location and time information, which is also true for contextual content generated by applications with high spatial significance. Content names may include information regarding the location where content is generated or has relevant meaning. Location information allows the use of geographic routing for contextual content discovery.

4.2   Content Discovery and Delivery

In CCN, content discovery uses Interest messages. CCN Interest forwarding relies on FIBs that contain the list of interfaces pointing towards the content sources. FIBs should result from a routing protocol. Routing is and remains, however, a critical area of investigation for CCN as none of the existing proposals has prevailed yet. Proposals exist for the Internet and connected MANETs as they assume end-to-end connectivity [19–21]. Moreover, the paradigm of store-carry-and-forward cannot be directly borrowed from DTNs and applied as is to CCN since the location of the requester is not exposed in the Interest messages during content discovery.

Adapting CCN to the context of opportunistic networks can benefit from the strategy layer that specifies how Interest messages should be handled. As stated previously, a strategy defines on which interfaces a CCN node will forward an Interest. In the context of our reference architecture, the interfaces of a node refer to its connectivity opportunities such as 4G or Wi-Fi. Broadcasting an incoming Interest on all of the interfaces listed by the corresponding FIB entry, is one obvious strategy, but too costly to be adopted. Instead, a CCN node can use more efficient alternatives—we advocate for an implementation of the strategy layer where decisions are taken based on users' preferences and content properties.

The analysis of users preferences can help to detect communities as a way to efficiently deliver content to users using opportunistic contacts [15]. If users interested in the same piece of content show strong spatial locality, CCN Interests can be rerouted from the base station to the neighboring nodes who already retrieved the content earlier. To maximize the benefit of D2D communications, the base station keeps track of the users in its coverage area and decides to broadcast the requested content with respect to the content time constraint. Users can take on the responsibility of transmitting the content to other users in the same community located outside the coverage range of the base station. It may also be worth applying social-based forwarding by ranking community members according to social metrics such as centrality that measures the importance of a node in a network [22]. Interest messages are forwarded through the most popular nodes within the community until the messages reaches a content source.

The characterization of content includes the analysis of popularity distribution and the spatial significance and temporal availability of each piece of content. Content identified as popular is likely to be available in the content store of devices close to the user. Redirecting Interest messages from the infrastructure network toward neighboring nodes makes it much cheaper and faster to access popular content locally. To maximize the benefits of cooperative caching among nodes, heuristics need to be defined so as to select content items to be cached based on the distribution of content popularity. The CCN content store may be used for carry-store-and-forward scheduling by assisting nodes as they can make content available for users on the move while avoiding those users from overloading the infrastructure network. By increasing the availability of less popular content, caching strategies can help nodes bring content in a closeby neighborhood to the interested users for eventual delivery. Content replication strategies driven by the base stations can also be used to further increase less popular content availability to the interested users.

5   High-Level Architecture and Target Use Case

We propose a high-level architecture that covers the requirements and issues discussed in this paper. We do not intend to design the ultimate solution, but only to identify the best possible directions to exploit in a future implementation of the system.

5.1   Architectural Elements and Modules

As depicted in Figure 3, the architecture includes four main modules that we detail in the following. Each module is in charge of several tasks shared among sub-blocks that focus on specific functionalities.

1. **CCN Engine.** This module is responsible for managing the data crossing a mobile node. It is composed of three sub-modules. The *content store* block plays the role of a cache for incoming data messages on both "local" and "public" caches. The PIT manager keeps track of pending interests that have not yet been satisfied, while the FIB manager keeps track of the outgoing traffic on the different faces (as detailed in the CCN main functionalities).
2. **Network Controller.** It defines the interactions with the other entities in the network and encompasses three sub-modules: *interest manager* and *content dissemination* are respectively in charge of controlling the outgoing interest list and incoming data messages, as well as for checking whether they respect the proposed strategy. The last sub-module, namely *neighborhood monitoring*, manages the direct device-to-device communication opportunities.
3. **Surety Module.** This module is in charge of security operations to ensure content integrity and avoid any falsification during the data exchanging process among mobile nodes. The *interface switching* sub-module reports to

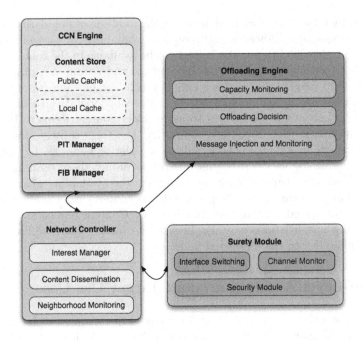

Fig. 3. High-level architecture for the CCN-based data offloading scheme

the node when the infrastructure has performed a vertical handover; in this way, the node can receive the content from the second interface. The *security module* that deals with privacy concerns supervises this latter process. Finally, since the infrastructure is capacity-constrained, monitoring the channel evolution is mandatory to avoid any wireless link congestion or saturation between nodes and base stations—this is performed thanks to *channel monitor* sub-module.

4. **Offloading Engine.** Last but not least, we need a module to focus specifically on the offloading process. One of core functionalities of our system is the decision of whether a given content must be exchanged in an opportunistic way or not; indeed, the overhead generated by offloading signalling messages must be compensated by a reduction of data messages traversing the cellular channel. The offloading module comprises a *capacity monitoring* tool, an *offloading decision* sub-module, in charge of determining whether the offloading is worth triggering, and a *message injection and monitoring* functionality that checks whether the offloading procedure evolves or not.

5.2   Target use Case: DataTweet Public Open Service

DataTweet is a recent French-funded project that proposes to explore the idea of an ubiquitous public data service for transmitting short messages in a similar way to Twitter [23]. Any user or source of the service will be able to send a short message at a very low rate to some destination address over various access networks: open 802.11 hotspots, base stations of LTE, car-to-infrastructure stations of 802.11p, to cite a few. Moreover, it defines a free public channel that could be used by crowds of devices to send their data towards their destination. Devices in DataTweet are supposed to be connected either via an infrastructure (i.e., access points) or together in an opportunistic way, where devices could leverage their contacts opportunities to mitigate the infrastructure load.

In a similar way to the water cycle, crowds of devices and mobile users may generate data sent to the cloud through nearest access points like water evaporating to the sky to form clouds. Collected data become useful information in the cloud, because of all the meaning and interpretation that we can attach to raw data. Then, the cloud can shower the users and devices with the information transmitted in short messages in target areas.

Our work perfectly fits the requirements of the DataTweet project. In fact, the cloud must be careful when deciding to whom content should be sent, as the system may easily diverge from a reasonable operation point. The CCN approach we advocate is expected to address the multiple issues that arise in our target scenario.

6 Summary and Outlook

The main contribution of this paper is to identify and discuss the challenges and promising solutions to address content management in capacity-constrained cellular networks. This is a particular scenario that requires specific solutions that cannot be directly adapted from the well-established, recognized content-centric networking (CCN) paradigm. Achieving efficient data offloading in such a hybrid context requires adapting some functionalities (e.g., naming and caching) to the case where nodes are potentially mobile. As the first solution to this problem, we have proposed a high-level architecture to cope with the unbalanced nature of the network while keeping the main principles of CCN.

Good understanding the new network architecture is the key function that opens several research tracks and a lot of directions to explore. What we consider very important is the development of a real system based on the proposed architecture. To this end, we propose to consider the ANR DataTweet scenario as our substrate case study. As the project has just started, we expect to obtain motivating results in the near future.

Acknowledgments. This work was partially supported by the French National Research Agency (ANR) DataTweet project under contract ANR-13-INFR-0008.

References

1. Cisco, Cisco visual networking index: Forecast and methodology, 2013–2018 (2014)
2. Gupta, A., Min, J., Rhee, I.: WiFox: Scaling wifi performance for large audience environments. In: ACM CoNEXT, Nice, France (December 2012)
3. Han, B., Hui, P., Kumar, V.S.A., Marathe, V.M., Peig, G., Srinivasan, A.: Cellular trafficc offloading through opportunistic communications: a case study. In: ACM CHANTS, NY, USA, New York (2010)
4. Han, B., Hui, P., Kumar, V.S.A., Marathe, M.V., Shao, J., Srinivasan, A.: Mobile data offloading through opportunistic communications and social participation. IEEE Transactions on Mobile Computing 11, 821–834 (2012)
5. Lee, K., Rhee, I., Lee, J., Yi, Y., Chong, S.: Mobile data offloading: how much can wifi deliver? ACM SIGCOMM Computer Communication Review 40(4), 425–426 (2010)
6. Whitbeck, J., Lopez, Y., Leguay, J., Conan, V., de Amorim, M.D.: Push-and-track: Saving infrastructure bandwidth through opportunistic forwarding. Pervasive and Mobile Computing 8, 682–697 (2012)
7. Rebecchi, F., de Amorim, M.D., Conan, V.: DROiD: Adapting to individual mobility pays off in mobile data offloading. In: IFIP Networking, Trondheim, Norway (June 2014)
8. Jacobson, V.; A new way to look at networking. Google Tech Talk (2006)
9. Jacobson, V., Smetters, D.K., Thorntona, J.D., Plass, M.F., Briggs, N.H., Braynard, R.L.: Networking named content. In: ACM CoNEXT, NY, USA, New York (2009)
10. Chuang, Y., Lin, K.C.: Cellular traffic offloading through community-based opportunistic dissemination. In: WCNC 2012. IEEE, Shanghai (April 2012)
11. Bhatia, R., Narlikar, G., Rimac, I., Beck, A.: Unap: User-centric network-aware push for mobile content delivery. In: INFOCOM 2009, IEEE, Rio De Janeiro (2009)
12. Balasubramanian, A., Mahajan, R., Venkataramani, A.: Augmenting mobile 3G using WiFi. In: ACM Mobisys, CA, USA, San Francisco (June 2010)
13. Higgins, B., Reda, A., Alperovich, T., Flinn, J., Giuli, T., Noble, B., Watson, D.: Intentional networking: opportunistic exploitation of mobile network diversity. In: MobiCom 2010. ACM, New York (2010)
14. Moto project. https://fp7-moto.eu/
15. Newman, M.E.J.: Detecting community structure in networks. The European Physical Journal B - Condensed Matter and Complex Systems 38, 321–330 (2004)
16. Caesar, M., Condie, T., Kannan, J., Lakshminarayanan, K., Stoica, I.: Rofl: routing on flat labels. In: SIGCOMM 2006, Pisa, Italy (October 2006)
17. Cheriton, D., Gritter, M.: An architecture for content routing support in the internet. In: USITS 2001, CA, USA, San Francisco (March2001)
18. Koponen, T., Chawla, M., Chun, B.-G., Ermolinskiy, A., Kim, S.K.H., Stoica, I.: A data-oriented (and beyond) network architecture. In: SIGCOMM 2007, NY, USA, New York (2007)
19. Zhang, L., Estrin, D., Burke, J., Jacobson, V., Thornton, J.D., Smetters, D.K., Zhang, B., Tsudik, G., Claffy, K., Krioukov, D., Massey, D., Papadopoulos, C., Abdelzaher, T., Wang, L., Crowley, P., Yeh, E.: Named data networking (ndn) project, tech. rep, ndn-0001 (October 2010)

20. Oh, S., Lau, D., Gerla, M.: Content centric networking in tactical and emergency manets. In: IEEE Wireless Days (WD), NY, USA, New York (October 2010)
21. Wang, L., Afanasyev, Kuntz, R., Vuyyuru, R., Wakikawa, R., Zhang, L.: Rapid traffic information dissemination using named data. In: The 1st ACM Workshop on Emerging Name-Oriented Mobile Networking Design - Architecture, Algorithms, and Applications, New York, NY, USA (2012)
22. Hui, P., Chaintreau, A., Scott, J., Gass, R., Crowcroft, J., Diot, C.: Bubblerap:social-based forwarding in delay tolerant networks. In: ACM Mobihoc, NY, USA, New York (2008)
23. Datatweet project. https://datatweet.imag.fr/

Adaptive Transmit Power Adjustment Technique for ZigBee Network Under Wi-Fi Interference

Tianyu Du, Zhipeng Wang[✉], Dimitrios Makrakis, and Hussein T. Mouftah

Broadband Wireless and Internetworking Research Laboratory,
School of Electrical Engineering and Computer Science University of Ottawa,
Ottawa, Ontario, K1N 6N5 Canada
tdu049@uottawa.ca, {zhipwang,dimitris,mouftah}@eecs.uottawa.ca

Abstract. Energy consumption is one of the most fundamental constraints in wireless sensor network (WSN) design. While data transmission is usually the most energy consuming event, minimizing the transmit power under the condition of satisfying the required packet transmission quality would be an important and effective strategy for reducing energy consumption. In this paper, a novel Adaptive Transmit Power Adjustment technique (ATPA) for ZigBee network under Wi-Fi interference is proposed and implemented in the Crossbow MICAz motes of our testbed. The proposed ATPA technique dynamically and rapidly adapts to the varying interference from the collocated wireless local area network (WLAN) and selects optimal transmit power level that not only decreases the energy consumption of packet transmissions, but also maintains the required packet loss rate (PLR). The effectiveness of ATPA has been validated through the comprehensive performance evaluation experiments conducted on our testbed.

Keywords: Wireless sensor network · Energy consumption · Coexistence · Transmit power control

1 Introduction

Most sensor nodes in wireless sensor networks (WSNs) are powered by batteries, which could be difficult or impossible to replace (e.g. military applications in battlefield environment). Hence, it is very important to use energy in an efficient way so as to extend the lifetime of sensor nodes and WSN as a whole. Since data transmission is one of the most significant factors of energy consumption in sensor nodes, it is advisable to seek effective strategies to minimize the transmit power of sensor nodes on condition that satisfactory quality of communication between sensor nodes can be maintained. Studies (e.g. [1]-[3]) have shown that the low-power ZigBee based WSN are particularly vulnerable to the interference of collocated Wi-Fi wireless local area networks (WLAN) due to the considerably higher transmit power of Wi-Fi devices and their pervasive deployment. With such time varying coexistence interference, it is crucial for sensor nodes to adaptively select appropriate transmit power level, which affects the signal to interference and noise ratio (SINR) of the received packets, thus

© Institute for Computer Sciences, Social Informatics and Telecommunications Engineering 2014
N. Mitton et al. (Eds.): ADHOCNETS 2014, LNICST 140, pp. 146–157, 2014.
DOI: 10.1007/978-3-319-13329-4_13

the communication link's quality. Furthermore, the choice of transmit power for each node in a mesh based WSN determines its set of neighbors. Based on these two facts, the transmit power adjustment schemes in WSN can be mainly classified into two categories: transmission range based topology control and link quality control.

The target for transmission range based topology control is to choose the optimal transmit power for each node, so that the global network connectivity can be maintained and energy metrics (e.g. network lifetime) can be optimized. Several topology control algorithms [4-8] have been developed that select the optimal power for each node in WSN to maintain the network connectivity, i.e. each node is able to communicate to any other node in the WSN via single hop or multi-hop. These solutions derive the static optimal transmit powers at the stage of initial deployment based on the network graph or node density. However, due to the background noise (e.g. thermal noise or environmental noise) and the interference from other wireless networks, the quality of WSN communication links varies with time and environment. The optimal transmit power calculated for fixed or initial channel conditions and a fixed network topology cannot guarantee the communication links' quality.

In recent years, some transmit power control schemes were designed for adapting to the external interference/noise level and adjusting the transmit power to the minimal level that can satisfy the required link quality. Some dynamic transmit power control mechanisms [9-13] adjust the power based on the RSSI readings of the received ZigBee packets. However, these RSSI readings may be the superposition of ZigBee signal and interference. In the case of strong interference, the RSSI reading does not reflect reliably the link's quality. In [14], two power control schemes, named as MIAD PC and PER PC, are proposed. In MIAD PC, the transmit power is increased after a packet loss and decreased after a successful packet reception. When frequent packet loss occurs, this method may lead to unstable operation. PER PC determines the background noise level with periodical measurements of RSSI and then derives the SINR based on the applied channel models (AWGN model or Rayleigh model). With the derived SINR, optimal transmit power is obtained. This approach requires complicated operations and calculation, and is not easy to implement at the resource limited ZigBee motes.

In this paper, a novel and efficient Adaptive Transmit Power Adjustment (ATPA) technique, capable of responding promptly to the changing external interference conditions, is proposed. The ATPA technique estimates the link quality based on the periodically calculated packet loss rate (PLR), and adjusts the transmit power accordingly to meet the PLR requirement. The proposed ATPA was implemented in the Crossbow MICAz motes of our testbed, and evaluated experimentally using the results collected through extensive experimentation. The results show that the ATPA technique improves the energy efficiency of the ZigBee packet transmission while maintaining the predefined maximum tolerable PLR of the application.

The remaining part of this paper is structured as follows. In Section 2, the testbed and system parameters are introduced. Section 3 provides a detailed description of the proposed ATPA technique. In Section 4, a series of comprehensive experiments are performed to evaluate the performance of ATAP technique under Wi-Fi interference and the acquired results are presented. Finally, conclusions are drawn in Section 5.

2   Testbed and Experiment Setup

In this study, we established a testbed using off-the-shelf computing and communication devices and carried out extensive experiments to assess the effectiveness of the proposed technique. By implementing our proposed technique as firmware running on commercially available devices, we ensure the proposed technique is easily implementable and fast deployable. And by performing experimental studies, we get more realistic performance evaluation results without leaving the impact of certain hidden factors on the performance unaccounted or adopting any simplified mathematical models or assumptions, which are often inevitable in theoretical analysis and computer simulations.

The experimental network is formed by ZigBee motes and Wi-Fi nodes. The collocated interfering WLAN consists of an IEEE 802.11 b/g/n wireless router (WR) (ASUS RT-N16), a Dell Inspiron 1545 laptop with Dell Wireless 1515 (IEEE 802.11 a/g/n) WLAN half mini-Card installed, and a Toshiba Satellite 2450 laptop connected to one of the Ethernet ports of the WR. WR is used as Wi-Fi traffic source in our testbed because it provides stable transmit power. The Toshiba laptop runs the Distributed Internet Traffic Generator (D-ITG) [15] and generates traffic with different packet payload, packet rate and inter-departure time (IDT) distribution, which are then fed into the WR for generating various interfering 802.11g Wi-Fi traffic that is having the Dell laptop as destination node. One Crossbow MICAz mote equipped with IEEE 802.15.4-compliant CC2420 transceiver is used as ZigBee client, transmitting IEEE 802.15.4 traffic to the ZigBee coordinator. Another MICAz mote installed on a Crossbow MIB600 programming board is functioning as coordinator, receiving data from the client. A PC is connected to the MIB600 board, collecting the received data from the ZigBee coordinator.

Custom ZigBee client and coordinator software programs were developed and run on the MICAz motes. The client software generates ZigBee traffic with different packet size, generation rate and IDT distribution, and responds to feedbacks from the coordinator (e.g. packet retransmission or transmit power adjustment). The coordinator software collects the received data packets, calculates the PLR, and sends acknowledgements (ACKs) or other feedback messages (e.g. transmit power adjustment commands). The client and coordinator software also perform statistic tasks such as calculating the number of transmitted or retransmitted packets, received packets, cancellation packets, and so on.

Fig. 1 illustrates the testbed setup used for studying the performance of ATPA under Wi-Fi interference. The distance between the WR and the ZigBee source mote is 1m and the distance between the Dell laptop and the ZigBee coordinator is 2m. There is a strong line-of-sight path between the ZigBee source mote and coordinator, with a distance of 1.5m. The Wi-Fi router uses 50 mW transmitting and generates IEEE 802.11g traffic; the transmitting mote can flexibly adjust its transmit power.

By scanning all the Wi-Fi channels, we determine that ZigBee channel 20 (2.449-2.451GHz) is not "contaminated" by interference from any other Wi-Fi access points in the building. To minimize the interference from other coexisting WLANs, ZigBee channel 20 is used as our ZigBee operating channel. In addition, since ZigBee channel 20 is located within the range of Wi-Fi's channel 9 (2.441-2.463GHz) where the power spectral density is the strongest, Wi-Fi channel 9 is used with the WR of our testbed to investigate the ZigBee packet transmission performance in the worst case scenario.

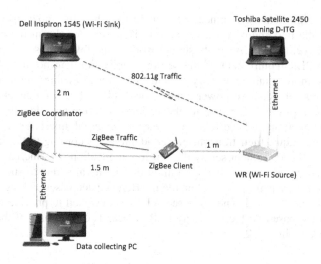

Fig. 1. Testbed setup for studying Zigbee packet transmission under collocated Wi-Fi interference

3   Adaptive Power Adjustment Technique

The MICAz motes can be programmed to operate at different levels of RF power, which enables the implementation of adaptive transmit power adjustment technique, i.e., dynamically adjusting the transmit power according to the strength of the time varying external interference. Table 1 shows the different programmable power levels supported by the CC2420 transceiver in MICAz motes and their corresponding current consumptions [16].

Table 1. Output power settings and current consumptions [16]

Power Level Index	Output Power [dBm]	Current Consumption [mA]
8	0	17.4
7	-1	16.5
6	-3	15.2
5	-5	13.9
4	-7	12.5
3	-10	11.2
2	-15	9.9
1	-25	8.5

As shown in Table 1, MICAz offers a considerable wide range for adjusting the transmit power. It is evident that the SINR decreases when the ZigBee mote transmits with lower power, which consequently leads to more packet losses. Our experimental performance evaluation results, which will be presented in the next section, also show that there is a significant difference between PLRs when the mote operates at the minimum and the maximum power under Wi-Fi interference. From the energy efficiency perspective, the MICAz mote should work at the lowest possible power level as long as the PLR requirement of the sensing application can be met. As external interference is unpredictable and varying with time, for a sensing application with a PLR requirement, an adaptive power control mechanism should be developed to adjust the transmit power according to the external interference. Ideally, when the ZigBee communication link suffers from varying external interference, the motes should be able to adjust their transmit power adaptively according to the interference level and the PLR requirement set by the sensing application, i.e., increase the transmit power when the PLR exceeds the required threshold value due to strong interference, or reduce the transmit power when the interference decreases as long as the PLR requirement can be satisfied. The proposed ATPA is designed to provide such timely power adjustment based on the changing PLR values. The flowchart of the proposed ATPA is illustrated in Fig. 2.

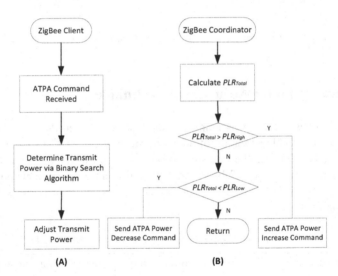

Fig. 2. Flowchart of ATPA: (A) ZigBee Client (B) ZigBee Coordinator

In the proposed ATPA scheme, the required PLR of a specific sensing application is set at the ZigBee coordinator's firmware. To avoid frequent change of transmit power, two PLR threshold values are introduced, denoted as PLR_{High} and PLR_{Low}, respectively. PLR_{High} has the value of the required PLR, while PLR_{Low} is set to a lower value for indicating that the external interference or noise has decreased to a point that the transmit power can be reduced to improve energy efficiency. The motes maintain the transmit power when the measured PLR falls between PLR_{High} and PLR_{Low}. T_{update} is the time interval for calculating and updating the PLR value. The value of T_{update} depends on the needs of dealing with the changing Wi-Fi interference and the sensing application's tolerance of PLR that exceeds limit occasionally. For example, in an environment with very stable WLAN traffic profile, T_{update} can be assigned a large value so as to reduce the frequency of power adjustment. After every T_{update} (e.g. 10 seconds), the coordinator calculates the number of packet losses, denoted as PLR_{Total}:

$$PLR_{Total} = 1 - \frac{N_R}{DSN_{Last} - DSN_{First}} , \qquad (1)$$

where N_R is the number of received packets within T_{update}, DSN_{First} and DSN_{Last} are the data sequence numbers (DSN) for the first and last received packets during T_{update}, respectively. If PLR_{Total} is higher than PLR_{High}, an ATPA command packet is sent to the ZigBee client to increase its transmit power level. Otherwise, if PLR_{Total} is lower than PLR_{Low}, an ATPA command packet with a message to reduce the transmit power is sent. It is noted that ATPA command packets are sent at the maximum transmit power so as to ensure higher delivery rate.

The ZigBee client mote first selects the maximum power level (0 dBm) as the initial transmit power. During the running time, it adjusts its transmit power level based on the received ATPA commands. Considering the power level adjustment happens in every T_{update} seconds, a binary search algorithm is applied to speed up the adjustment mechanism in finding the lowest transmit power that satisfies the PLR requirement. The pseudo code of ATPA binary search scheme is depicted in Fig. 3. As shown in Table 1, each output power level is represented with an integer index. We denote L_{High} and L_{Low} as the two search index limits; $Index_{Max}$, $Index_{Min}$, and $Index_{Cur}$ as the maximum, minimum and current power level index, respectively.

> Input: L_{High}, L_{Low}, $Index_{Max}$, $Index_{Min}$, and $Index_{Cur}$
> Initial phase: $L_{High} = Index_{Max}$; $L_{Low} = Index_{Min}$;
> If to increase transmit power:
>   If $(L_{High} = L_{Low})$ { $L_{High} = Index_{Max}$ };
> $L_{Low} = Index_{Cur}$;
> $Index_{Cur} = \left\lceil \frac{L_{High} + L_{Low}}{2} \right\rceil$;
> If to decrease transmit power:
>   If $(L_{High} = L_{Low})$ { $L_{Low} = Index_{Min}$ };
> $L_{High} = Index_{Cur}$;
> $Index_{Cur} = \left\lceil \frac{L_{High} + L_{Low}}{2} \right\rceil$;

Fig. 3. Binary search algorithm of ATPA

As shown in Fig.3, the binary search algorithm is implemented with two index limits, i.e., L_{High} and L_{Low} (initialized with $Index_{Max}$ and $Index_{Min}$, respectively), which progressively narrow the search range. If the received ATPA command is to increase the transmit power, the current operating power level index, $Index_{Cur}$, is selected as L_{Low}. On the other hand, if the received ATPA command is to decrease the transmit power, the $Index_{Cur}$ is chosen as L_{High}. The intermediate power level index between the L_{High} and L_{Low} is obtained and the corresponding transmit power is selected at the ZigBee client. Compared to linear search that adjusts the power level by level, whose worst case requires N-1 iterations (N is the number of the power levels supported in the mote.), the binary search is substantially more efficient with a worst case of $\lceil log_2(N) \rceil$.

The ZigBee coordinator sends back ATPA commands to trigger the binary search operation and power adjustment until the PLR_{Total} is between the two PLR boundaries, i.e., PLR_{High} and PLR_{Low}. Once the external interference changes and the PLR requirement is not satisfied any more, a new ATPA power increase/decrease command will be generated and transmitted to trigger another binary search operation and transmit power adjustment.

4   Performance Evaluation Results and Discussion

In order to validate the performance improvement of the proposed ATPA mechanism, we performed an extensive set of experiments using the testbed shown in Fig. 1. For comparison, ZigBee's performance was also assessed when the transmit power of the ZigBee client mote was set at the maximum or minimum values. PLR and the energy consumption of the CC2420 transceiver in the packet transmission process were evaluated. For transmitting each ZigBee packet, the energy consumed by CC2420 can be expressed as:

$$E = A_i * V_{cc2420} * \frac{L_Z}{R_Z}, \tag{2}$$

with A_i denoting the current consumption of power level i (shown in Table 1), V_{CC2420} the supply voltage of 1.8V, L_Z the ZigBee packet length, and R_Z the transmit bit rate. Our custom-made ZigBee client firmware calculates the number of ZigBee packets transmitted at each power level so that the total energy consumption in the experiment can be calculated. In each experiment, the ZigBee client mote is programmed to send out 10000 data packets with 100 bytes/packet at 30ms intervals. The D-ITG generates UDP traffic with different segment payload, segment rate and IDT distribution, which are converted to varying IEEE 802.11g Wi-Fi interference by the WR. The corresponding results are illustrated and discussed in Figs. 4 to 9. All the data points are marked with a 95% confidence interval.

In Fig. 4 and Fig. 5, ZigBee's performance evaluation results are shown when the transmitted packets are not acknowledged, thus there is no packet retransmission. The required PLR (PLR_{High}) is set to be 10% and PLR_{Low} is assigned the value of 9%. D-ITG generated UDP traffic with constant segment IDT, payload size of 1400 bytes and different segment generation rates: 300 segments/second (Test 1), 500 segments/second (Test 2), and a combination of 300 segments/second in the first half of the experiment and 500 segments/second for the remaining half (Test 3).

As shown in Figs. 4 and 5, although using the minimum transmit power consumes the minimum energy for packet transmission, the ZigBee mote suffers from severe packet losses, resulting in PLRs far beyond the required value. While operating at the maximum power achieves the best PLR, the transmitting mote consumes the most energy. Obviously, if the PLR requirement has already been met, there is little or no use for ZigBee mote to sacrifice more energy in exchange of further PLR improvement. The proposed ATPA provides a simple but efficient trade-off algorithm to reduce the energy consumption while maintaining the required PLR. It can be observed from Fig. 5 that compared to maximum transmit power, ATPA reduces energy consumption from ~15% (Test 2) to ~ 33% (Test 1) depending on the external interference level; the less the interference, the more the energy savings are. In addition, ATPA handles the changing Wi-Fi interference very well as demonstrated in Test 3. The Wi-Fi traffic in Test 3 is an equal combination of traffic used in Test 1 and Test 2. Thus, in Fig. 4, the PLRs of minimum and maximum transmit power in Test 3 have values larger than those in Test 1 but smaller than those in Test 2. Since the transmit power adjustment of ATPA is for saving energy while maintaining the required PLR, the PLRs of ATPA in all three tests are about the same, but the energy consumption of ATPA in Test 3 is between the corresponding values in Test 1 and Test 2, which shows the ATPA adjusts the transmit power when interference changes. ATPA increases transmit power when interference increases so as to maintain the required PLR. ATPA could be particularly effective with bursty interference because it could temporarily boost transmit power when there is increased interference and decrease transmit power when interference goes down.

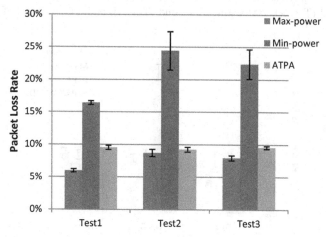

Fig. 4. Packet loss rate comparison of ZigBee without use of packet retransmission under interfering UDP traffic with different packet rates

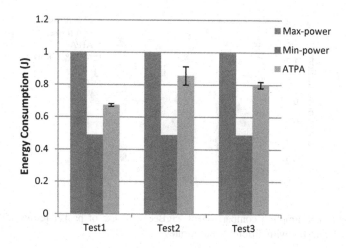

Fig. 5. Energy consumption comparison of ZigBee without use of packet retransmission under interfering UDP traffic with different packet rates

In Figs. 6 - 9, the ZigBee's performance is evaluated when allowing one ZigBee packet retransmission. The results of combining ATPA with our earlier proposed ACK with Interference Detection (ACK-ID) scheme [17] are also illustrated for comparison purposes. By performing interference detection before sending out ACK packets, ACK-ID can effectively reduce ACK losses and ZigBee packet retransmissions, thus consequently reduce the energy consumption in transmitting packets. The PLR_{High} and PLR_{Low} have assigned values of 3% and 2%, respectively. The assigned PLR threshold values are much lower compared to those used in the experiments of Figs. 4 and 5. This is because packet retransmission is adopted in this set of experiments, which significantly decreases PLR. In Fig. 6 and Fig. 7, D-ITG is set to generate traffic with constant UDP segment IDT, payload size of 1400 bytes and different segment rates: 500 segments/second (Test 4), 700 segments/second (Test 5), and a combined traffic with 500

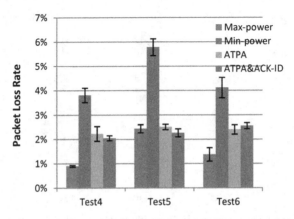

Fig. 6. Packet loss rate comparison of ZigBee with use of packet retransmission under interfering UDP traffic with different packet rates

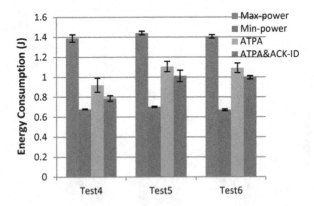

Fig. 7. Energy consumption comparison of ZigBee with use of packet retransmission under interfering UDP traffic with different packet rates

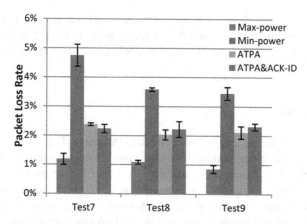

Fig. 8. Packet loss rate comparison of ZigBee with use of retransmission under interfering UDP traffic with payload sizes and arrival rates following three different random distributions

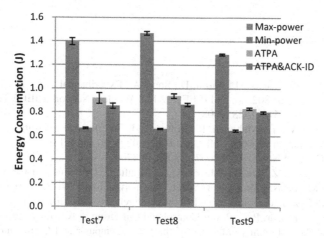

Fig. 9. Energy consumption comparison of ZigBee with use of packet retransmission under interfering UDP traffic with payload sizes and arrival rates following three different random distributions

segments/second in the first half of the experiment and 700 segments/second in the remaining half (Test 6). For the tests shown in Fig. 8 and Fig. 9, the UDP segment's payload size and IDT are both following three different random distributions, i.e., Poisson (Test 7), Uniform (Test 8), and Exponential (Test 9), with mean payload size of 1200 bytes and arrival rate of 600 segments/second. More specifically, uniform distributed traffic has a UDP payload size between 1000 to 1400 bytes, and a segment rate between 400 to 800 segments/second.

From Figs. 6 - 9, it can be seen that ATPA effectively reduces the energy consumption for ZigBee packet transmission while satisfying the predefined PLR requirement when there is varying interference from the collocated WLAN. As discussed in [17], ACK-ID can improve the performance of ZigBee packet transmission in terms of packet retransmission rate, which consequently saves energy. Based on the experimental results, the ACK-ID and ATPA techniques can be implemented together to achieve better usage of bandwidth and energy when there is varying Wi-Fi interference close by.

5   Conclusion

In this paper, we proposed a novel and effective Adaptive Transmit Power Adjustment (ATPA) technique that makes use of the configurable transmit power provided by the sensor nodes to dynamically and rapidly select the optimal transmit power according to the varying external Wi-Fi interference. The performance improvement has been validated and evaluated through extensive experiments carried out in our testbed. The experimental results confirmed that ATPA can improve the performance of ZigBee packet transmission in terms of energy consumption when there is varying interference from the collocated WLAN and in the meantime maintain the required PLR.

References

1. Angrisani, L., Bertocco, M., Fortin, D., Sona, A.: Experimental Study of Coexistence Issues between IEEE 802.11b and IEEE 802.15.4 Wireless Networks. IEEE Trans. Instrum. and Meas **57**(8), 1514–1523 (2008)
2. Petrova, M., Wu, L., Mahonen, P., Riihijarvi, J.: Interference Measurements on Performance Degradation between Collocated IEEE 802.11g/n and IEEE 802.15.4 Networks. In: 6th Intl. Conf. on Netw., (ICN 2007), pp. 93–98 (2007)
3. Tang, Y., Wang, Z., Du, T., Makrakis, D., Mouftah, H.T.: Study of Clear Channel Assessment Mechanism for ZigBee Packet Transmission under Wi-Fi Interference. In: 2013 IEEE 10th Consumer Commun. and Netw. Conference (CCNC 2013), pp. 765–768 (2013)
4. Kawadia, V., Kumar, P.R.: Power Control and Clustering in Ad Hoc Networks. In: Twenty-Second Annual Joint Conference of the IEEE Computer and Communications (IEEE INFOCOM 2003), vol. 1, pp. 459–469 (2003)
5. Kubisch, M., Karl, H., Wolisz, A., Zhong, L.C., Rabaey, J.: Distributed Algorithms for Transmission Power Control in Wireless Sensor Networks. Wireless Communications and Networking Conference (IEEE WCNC) **1**, 558–563 (2003)
6. Li, L., Halpern, J.Y., Bahl, P., Wang, Y., Wattenhofer, R.: A Cone-based Distributed Topology-control Algorithm for Wireless Multi-hop Networks. IEEE/ACM Trans. Netw. **13**, 147–159 (2005)
7. Wattenhofer, R., Li, L., Bahl, P., Wang, Y.: Distributed Topology Control for Power Efficient Operation in Multihop Wireless Ad Hoc Networks. In: Proc. INFOCOM 2001, vol. 3, pp. 1388–1397 (2001)
8. Ramanathan, R., Rosales-Hain, R.: Topology Control of Multihop Wireless Networks using Transmit Power Adjustment. In: Proc. INFOCOM 2000, vol. 2, pp. 404–413 (2000)
9. Xiao, S., Dhamdhere, A., Sivaraman, V., Burdett, A.: Transmission Power Control in Body Area Sensor Networks for Healthcare Monitoring. IEEE J. Sel. Areas Commun. **27**, 37–48 (2009)

10. Zhao, Z., Zhang, X., Sun, P., Liu, P.: A Transmission Power Control MAC Protocol for Wireless Sensor Networks. In: Sixth International Conference on Networking (ICN 2007), pp. 5–9 (2007)
11. Lin, S., Zhang, J., Zhou, G., Gu, L., He, T., Stankovic, J.A.: ATPC: Adaptive Transmission Power Control for Wireless Sensor Networks. In: Proceedings of the 4th International Conference on Embedded Networked Sensor Systems (SenSys 2006), pp. 223—236 (2006)
12. Kim, J., Chang, S., Kwon, Y.: ODTPC: On-demand Transmission Power Control for Wireless Sensor Networks. In: International Conference on Information Networking (ICOIN), pp. 1–5 (2008)
13. Masood, M.M.Y., Ahmed, G., Khan, N.M.: Modified on Demand Transmission Power Control for Wireless Sensor Networks. In: 2011 International Conference on Information and Communication Technologies (ICICT), pp. 1–6 (2011)
14. Zurita Ares, B., Park, P.G., Fischione, C., Speranzon, A., Johansson, K.H.: On Power Control for Wireless Sensor Networks: System Model, Middleware Component and Experimental Evaluation. In: IFAC European Control Conference (ECC 2007) (2007)
15. Botta, A., Dainotti, A., Pescapè, A.: A Tool for the Generation of Realistic Network Workload for Emerging Networking Scenarios. Computer Networks (Elsevier) **56**(15), 3531–3547 (2012)
16. Texas Instruments, 2.4 GHz IEEE 802.15.4 / ZigBee-ready RF Transceiver CC2420 data sheet, http://www.ti.com/lit/ds/symlink/cc2420.pdf
17. Wang, Z., Du, T., Tang, Y., Makrakis, D., Mouftah, H.T.: ACK with Interference Detection Technique for ZigBee Network under Wi-Fi Interference. In: 8th Intl Conf. Broadband and Wirel. Comput., Commun. and Appl., pp. 128–135 (2013)

Channel Switching Cost-Aware Resource Allocation for Multi-hop Cognitive Radio Networks with a Single Transceiver

Mustafa Çamurli and Didem Gözüpek[✉]

Department of Computer Engineering,
Gebze Institute of Technology, Kocaeli, Turkey
didem.gozupek@gyte.edu.tr

Abstract. Cognitive radio networks need to operate in a wide range of frequencies. This requirement brings up new challenges that do not exist in other wireless networks. Switching from a certain frequency to another frequency incurs a non-negligible cost in cognitive radio networks and depends on the distance between the previous and current frequencies. This cost is especially important in ad hoc cognitive radio networks when the cognitive devices have a single transceiver. Research studies related to green networks indicate the need for methods that address energy consumption in cognitive radio networks. In this paper, we analyze the impact of the channel switching cost in terms of energy consumption. We formulate an optimization problem that makes frequency and time slot allocation to the cognitive devices in an ad hoc cognitive radio network so that the energy cost related to frequency switching is minimized. We formulate our optimization problem as an integer linear program and comparatively evaluate the energy cost of varying switching energy consumption with constant switching energy consumption. Our simulation results indicate that taking into account the different energy consumption while switching to different frequency bands is vital for resource allocation in cognitive radio networks with a single transceiver.

Keywords: Cognitive radio · Ad-hoc networks · Energy efficiency · Channel switching · Frequency switching · Resource allocation

1 Introduction

Fixed spectrum assignment policy in current wireless networks leads to inefficiency in spectrum usage. To this end, researchers have proposed dynamic spectrum access concept, which refers to opportunistic usage of frequencies by intelligent devices called cognitive radios (CR) or secondary users (SU). Users who have exclusive rights to use the spectrum are called primary users (PU). SUs need to operate in such a way that the operation of PUs is not affected.

This work is supported by the Scientific and Technological Research Council of Turkey (TUBITAK) under grant no.113E567.

© Institute for Computer Sciences, Social Informatics and Telecommunications Engineering 2014
N. Mitton et al. (Eds.): ADHOCNETS 2014, LNICST 140, pp. 158–168, 2014.
DOI: 10.1007/978-3-319-13329-4_14

Availability of a particular frequency to a particular SU depends on the spectrum usage behaviors of the PUs in the vicinity of the SUs [1].

An SU consumes energy to change its operation frequency. This energy consumption in general depends on the distance between the previous and current frequency bands [2]. For instance, switching from central frequency of 700 MHz to 10 GHz leads to larger energy consumption than switching from 700 MHz to 750 MHz. This behavior is directly related to the different channel switching delay while switching to different frequency bands [3] since spending more time for switching naturally consumes more energy. This energy consumption might be negligible in wireless technologies that operate in a narrow band; however, cognitive radios are expected to operate in a wide range of spectrum and hence the energy consumption due to channel switching is crucial for cognitive radio networks [2]. The emerging green networking paradigm that focuses on energy efficiency of both wired and wireless technologies puts emphasis on techniques that enhance the energy efficiency of new technologies such as cognitive radio networks [4].

Studies in the literature analyzed the impact of channel switching in CRNs mostly in terms of delay [5–10]. Most of these works focus primarily on minimizing the number of channel switchings along the routing path; in other words, they assume constant switching delay whenever channel switching occurs irrespective of from which frequency and to which frequency the channel switching has taken place. Only [5] and [6] consider the dependence of channel switching delay on the distance between the previous and current frequencies. The work in [3], on the other hand, focuses on scheduling in centralized cognitive radio networks and analyzes the impact of channel switching delay on throughput. The authors propose a scheduling algorithm that considers the different hardware delay that occurs while switching to different frequency bands. The work in [11] focuses on minimizing the service interruption by taking into account the dependence of switching delay on the frequency distance. To the best of our knowledge, the work in [2] is the only work in the literature that considers the impact of frequency distance-aware channel switching on energy efficiency in cognitive radio networks. However, unlike our work, the work in [2] concentrates on scheduling in centralized cognitive radio networks.

Most works about routing in cognitive radio networks consider the case where the CR devices have multiple transceivers/interfaces [11–15]. However, having multiple transceivers is costly and therefore, scenarios where CRs have a single transceiver are more realistic. There are some works in the literature that focuses on the case with single transceivers [16–18]. In a multi-hop CRN, channel switching cost becomes especially important when each CR has a single transceiver. However, unlike our work, none of the works in [16–18] focus on the energy cost related to the channel switching of the single transceiver.

The rest of this paper is organized as follows: In Section 2, we provide our optimization problem formulation as an integer linear program. In Section 3, we present our numerical evaluation and then conclude the paper in Section 4.

2   Problem Formulation

We represent the ad hoc CRN as a graph $G = (V, E)$, where the vertices in V correspond to the SUs and the edges in E corresponds to the communication links between the SUs. We consider the situation where the routing is predetermined; in other words, if a link exists between a pair of SUs, it means that link is used to carry data along some route. The scheduling period consists of T time slots. There are a total number of F frequencies. A subset of these F frequencies is available for each SU in each time slot. Availability of the frequencies is determined by the PU spectrum occupancy behavior in the geographical region of the ad hoc CRN. The goal of our integer linear programming (ILP) formulation is to assign a time slot and frequency to each SU so that the total energy consumption of the SUs due to frequency switching is minimized.

Table 1 and 2 present the decision and input variables, respectively, of our ILP formulation. If $x_{vft} = 1$, it means the single transceiver of the SU corresponding to vertex v is tuned to use frequency f in one of its incident links (an incident link e with $x_{eft} = 1$) in time slot t. Besides, $y_{vff't}$ is the main decision variable used in the calculation of the objective function. If at the beginning of time slot t, vertex v switches to frequency f from frequency f', then $y_{vff't} = 1$. y_{vft} is another decision variable needed to model the behavior of $y_{vff't}$ by taking into account the silent (idle) time slots (will be explained in the sequel).

Table 1. Table for decision variables

Varible	Description	
x_{vt}	$=$ $\begin{cases} 1, & \text{if vertex } v \text{ is assigned some frequency in time slot } t \\ 0, & \text{otherwise.} \end{cases}$	
x_{eft}	$=$ $\begin{cases} 1, & \text{if edge } e \text{ is assigned frequency } f \text{ in time slot } t \\ 0, & \text{otherwise.} \end{cases}$	
x_{vft}	$=$ $\begin{cases} 1, & \text{if vertex } v \text{ is assigned frequency } f \text{ in timeslot } t \\ 0, & \text{otherwise.} \end{cases}$	
y_{vft}	$=$ $\begin{cases} 1, & \text{if } x_{vft} = 1 \text{ or } x_{vf(t-1)} = 1 \\ 0, & \text{otherwise.} \end{cases}$	
$y_{vff't}$	$=$ $\begin{cases} 1, & \text{if } y_{vft} = 1 \text{ and } y_{vf'(t-1)} = 1 \\ 0, & \text{otherwise.} \end{cases}$	

Table 2 shows input variables that are given to the ILP formulation. The value of switching cost $c_{ff'}$ denotes the energy consumption that occurs while switching from/to frequency f to/from f' and depends on the hardware of the cognitive nodes. Switching cost to/from the same frequency equals zero, whereas the switching cost between different frequencies has a nonzero and symmetric cost. Besides, the values of a_{vft} are determined by the spectrum usage behavior of the PUs.

Table 2. Table for input variables

Input Variable	Description
$c_{ff'}$	= Switching cost (in terms of energy consumption) to transition from/to frequency f to/from frequency f'
a_{vft}	$= \begin{cases} 1, & \text{if frequency } f \text{ is available for vertex } v \text{ in time slot } t \\ 0, & \text{otherwise.} \end{cases}$
G = (V,E)	= Network represented as a graph with vertex set V and edge set E
T	= Total number of time slots
F	= Total number of frequencies

Objective function of our ILP formulation is as follows:

$$\min \sum_{v=1}^{|V|} \sum_{f=0}^{F} \sum_{f'=0}^{F} \sum_{t=0}^{T} c_{ff'} \times y_{vff't} \tag{1}$$

The objective function in Equation (1) minimizes the switching cost of all vertices (nodes) in the graph (network). The decision variable $y_{vff't}$ indicates whether there has been a frequency switching at vertex v from f' to f at the beginning of time slot t; i.e., basically, $y_{vff't} = y_{vft} \times y_{vf'(t-1)}$. This relation will be modeled by the constraints and explained later.

Recall that routing is predetermined in our scenario. In other words, every edge $e \in E$ carries data and should therefore be assigned at least one time slot during the scheduling period. The following constraint achieves this behavior:

$$\sum_{f=1}^{F} \sum_{t=1}^{T} x_{eft} \geq 1; \forall e \in E \tag{2}$$

Since only available frequencies can be assigned to a particular vertex, we need the following constraint:

$$x_{vft} \leq a_{vft}; \forall v, f, t \tag{3}$$

Since each node (vertex) has a single transceiver, at most one incident edge can be given service in each time slot. Therefore, we need to ensure that $x_{vft} = \sum_{e \in E(v)}^{|E|} x_{eft}$. Furthermore, since the values of the decision variables $y_{vff't}$ depend on the frequency assignments in the previous time slot, in order to properly handle the situation in the first time slot, we define an auxiliary frequency $f = 0$ and an auxiliary time slot $t = 0$. The auxiliary frequency $f = 0$ is not assigned to any vertex for time slots $t \geq 1$. Besides, all vertices are assigned frequency $f = 0$ in time slot $t = 0$ (will be enforced in constraints (4) and (5)). The inputs $c_{ff'}$ are given such that the switching cost from frequency 0 to all other frequencies equals zero. This behavior is necessary in order to linearize our integer programming formulation and handle the border case in the first time slot. In other words, frequency $f = 0$ and time slot $t = 0$ are defined to handle the value of $y_{vff't}$ in the first time slot $t = 1$. All vertices are assigned frequency $f = 0$ in time slot $t = 0$. Switching cost between frequency $f = 0$ and any other frequency is zero. Frequency $f = 0$ cannot be used in other time slots $t \neq 0$. Hence, we need the following constraints:

$$x_{vft} = 1 ; \text{ for } f = t = 0 \text{ and } \forall v \tag{4}$$

$$y_{vft} = 1 ; \text{ for } f = t = 0 \text{ and } \forall v \tag{5}$$

$$x_{vft} = \sum_{e \in E(v)}^{|E|} x_{eft} = 0 ; \text{ for } f = 0 \tag{6}$$

$$x_{vft} = \sum_{e \in E(v)}^{|E|} x_{eft} \geq 1 ; \ \forall f \geq 1 \tag{7}$$

The following constraints ensure the multiplication of the decision variables such that $y_{vff't} = y_{vft} \times y_{vf'(t-1)}$. This way, if there is a switching between frequencies f' and f at vertex v, the variable $y_{vff't}$ is set to 1.

$$y_{vff't} \leq y_{vft}; \quad \forall v, f, t \geq 1 \tag{8}$$

$$y_{vff't} \leq y_{vf'(t-1)}; \forall v, f, f', t \geq 1 \tag{9}$$

$$y_{vft} + y_{vf'(t-1)} - 1 \leq y_{vff't}; \forall v, f, f', t \geq 1 \tag{10}$$

Notice that it is not a requirement that each vertex is assigned some frequency in every time slot; some vertices may not be assigned a frequency in some time slots. We refer to such a time slot as a *silent time slot* for that vertex. We assume that the transceiver of the node is tuned to the last used frequency in that time slot. When some other frequency is used in a tim eslot following the silent time slot(s), an energy consumption cost corresponding to frequency switching occurs. We need to make sure that the decision variable $y_{vff't}$ handles the silent time slots properly. To this end, we need to ensure the following set of nonlinear inequalities: a) If $x_{vft} = 0$, then $y_{vft} = y_{vf(t-1)}$ and b) If $x_{vft} = 1$, then $y_{vft} = 1$. These nonlinear constraints can be linearized as follows:

$$y_{vft} - y_{vf(t-1)} \leq x_{vft}; \ \forall v, f, t \geq 1 \tag{11}$$

$$y_{vf(t-1)} - y_{vft} \leq x_{vft}; \ \forall v, f, t \geq 1 \tag{12}$$

$$x_{vft} \leq y_{vft}; \ \forall v, f, t \geq 1 \tag{13}$$

Since each node has a single transceiver and a transceiver can tune to at most one frequency at a time, we need to ensure that at most one frequency is assigned to each vertex in each time slot:

$$\sum_{f=1}^{F} x_{vft} \leq 1; \ \forall v, t \tag{14}$$

We also need to model the relationship between the decision variables x_{vt} and x_{vft}. In particular, $x_{vt} = 1$ if and only if some frequency f is assigned to vertex v in timeslot t. We model this relation as follows:

$$\sum_{f=1}^{F} x_{vft} = x_{vt}; \ \forall v, t \tag{15}$$

In order to increase the utilization in the network and achieve more throughput, less queueing delay and more realistic network behavior, we need to avoid the situation that two adjacent vertices are idle. To this end, we ensure in the following that at least one of two neighboring nodes is assigned some frequency in each time slot:

$$x_{vt} + x_{v't} \geq 1; \ \forall v, t, \forall v' \in N(v) \tag{16}$$

where $N(v)$ denotes the neighborhood of vertex v, i.e., the set of vertices that are adjacent to vertex v.

3   Simulation Results

In this section, we present our simulation results and comparatively evaluate our ILP formulation solutions with different input parameter settings. We have implemented our ILP formulation introduced in Section 2 by using CPLEX [19]. We have made performance evaluation under different number of frequencies, primary users and secondary users. In our simulation environment, PUs and SUs are distributed randomly in a 400 m^2 two dimensional Euclidean space. As in [11], we set the operation range of each SU to a radius of 110 m. If two SUs are within the operation range of each other, then there is an edge connecting the two vertices corresponding to these SUs in the input graph G fed into our ILP formulation. Likewise, we set the operation range of each PU to 170 m radius. An SU within the operation range of a PU cannot use the frequency used by that PU in that time slot. Furthermore, each scheduling period consists of 20 time slots, i.e., $T = 20$. All PUs are assigned a random frequency at the beginning of the simulation. In every time slot, each PU changes its frequency with a probability of $P_c = 0.1$. If a PU changes its frequency, the probability of selecting each frequency is equally likely.

In 2009 full power analog TV ceased operation and hence, the frequency range between 54 MHz and 806 MHz were cleared due to the transition to digital TV [20]. In accordance with these frequency bands that became available for cognitive radio operation, we set the frequency range in our experiments between 460 MHz and 700 MHz with the bandwidth of each channel being 20 Mhz. In other words, the highest number of frequencies used in our experiments is 13. According to the work in [2], switching latency is 0.1 ms/MHz. In the same article, channel switching power is assumed to be 1 W. In accordance with this information, we set in our model the energy consumption incurred due to switching between two frequencies with a difference of 20 MHz as 0.002 Joule.

We have evaluated the impact of the following three parameters in our simulations: number of primary users, number of secondary users and number of frequencies. Values of the other parameters remain constant in all experiments. As a result, we calculate two separate solutions corresponding to two different cost schemes. Notice that the energy consumption due to frequency switching is proportional to the time it takes to complete the frequency switching, i.e., switching delay. We refer to the first scheme as *varying cost*. Varying cost scheme relies on the fact that switching delay and hence the energy consumption due to frequency switching depends on the distance between the previous and current frequencies. We refer to the second scheme as *fixed cost*. Fixed cost scheme relies on the assumption that switching delay and hence the energy consumption due to frequency switching is the same (constant value) as long as the previous and current frequencies are different. We have taken this constant value as 0.002 Joule in our simulations.

Table 3 displays the range of values for the evaluated parameters. When investigating the impact of a particular parameter, we set the value of the other parameters to their middle values, which are also shown in Table 3. We take the sample mean of 15 random experiments in each setup.

Table 3. Parameter names and range of values evaluated in the experiments

Parameter	Range Min	Range Max	Middle Value
Frequency	5	13	10
Secondary User	5	13	10
Primary User	3	7	5

Figure 1 shows that varying cost scheme is advantageous when the number of frequencies in the CRN is less than 7. Furthermore, when the number of frequencies is high, the cardinality of the frequency set that is available for the SUs also increases. This increasing availability makes it possible to switch to closer frequencies and hence decreases the energy consumption due to frequency switching.

In Figure 2, we observe that the number of secondary users does not have a consistent and stable impact on the performance of the fixed cost scheme, which fluctuates and is hence unpredictable. In contrast, the switching cost of varying cost scheme increases linearly with number of secondary users. In some parts, fixed cost scheme performs better than varying cost. However, its unpredictability can discourage cognitive radio systems to rely on fixed switching cost in order to schedule their networks. As a result, predictable and consistent performance of varying cost scheme (in addition to the fact that it is more realistic) can make it preferable.

Figure 3 shows the impact of increasing number of PUs. Since the frequencies that are available for the SUs decrease as the number of PUs increases, SUs become obliged to make frequency switching more often and between increasingly distant frequencies. Especially when we have more than 5 primary users,

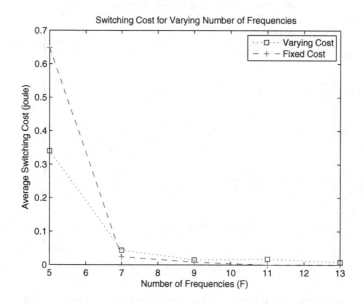

Fig. 1. Average switching cost for varying number of frequencies

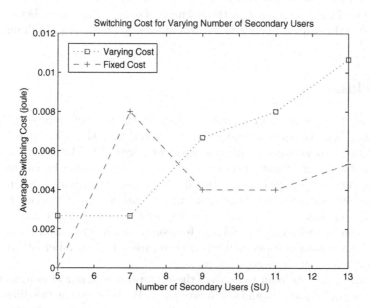

Fig. 2. Average switching cost for varying number of secondary users

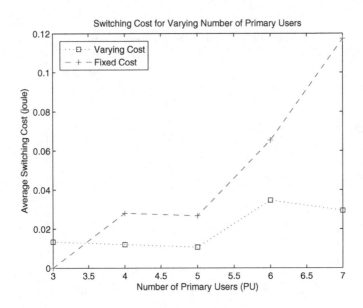

Fig. 3. Average switching cost for varying number of primary users

average switching cost of fixed cost solutions increases faster than varying cost solutions. This figure demonstrates the strength of our varying cost scheme since it outperforms the constant cost scheme especially when there are a high number of PUs.

4   Conclusion

In this paper, we present an optimization model in the form of an integer linear programming formulation that makes frequency and time slot allocation for ad hoc cognitive radio networks with a single transceiver. Our formulation aims to minimize the energy consumption due to frequency switching by taking into account the fact that energy consumption due to frequency switching depends on the distance between the previous and current frequencies. Our simulation results indicate that our idea of taking into account the different energy consumption that occurs during switching to different frequency bands is essential for ad hoc cognitive radio networks especially when there are a high number of primary users in the vicinity of the secondary users.

As a future work, we plan to analyze the performance of our algorithm with higher number of frequencies and secondary users. We believe that the difference between constant switching cost case and our suggestion of varying switching cost will be more evident in a network with a high number of secondary users and frequencies. Furthermore, we also plan to analyze the computational complexity of our integer linear programming formulation and propose a computationally efficient heuristic algorithm.

References

1. Akyildiz, I., Lee, W., Vuran, M., Mohanty, S.: Next generation/dynamic spectrum access/cognitive radio wireless networks: A survey. Computer Networks **50**(13), 2127–2159 (2006)
2. Bayhan, S., Alagoz, F.: Scheduling in centralized cognitive radio networks for energy efficiency. IEEE Transactions on Vehicular Technology **62**(2), 582–595 (2013)
3. Gozupek, D., Buhari, S., Alagoz, F.: A spectrum switching delay-aware scheduling algorithm for centralized cognitive radio networks. IEEE Transactions on Mobile Computing **12**(7), 1270–1280 (2013)
4. Gur, G., Alagoz, F.: Green wireless communications via cognitive dimension: An overview. IEEE Network Magazine **25**(2), 50–56 (2011)
5. Cheng, G., Liu, W., Li, Y., Cheng, W.: Spectrum aware on-demand routing in cognitive radio networks. In: IEEE DySPAN (2007)
6. Cheng, G., Liu, W., Li, Y., Cheng, W.: Joint on-demand routing and spectrum assignment in cognitive radio networks. In: IEEE ICC (2007)
7. Filippini, I., Ekici, E., Cesana, M.: Minimum maintenance cost routing in Cognitive Radio Networks. In: IEEE MASS (2009)
8. Chowdhury, K., Felice, M.: SEARCH: A routing protocol for mobile cognitive radio ad-hoc networks. Computer Communications **32**(18), 1983–1997 (2009)
9. Chen, J., Li, H., Wu, J., Zhang, R.: STARP: A novel routing protocol for multi-hop dynamic spectrum access networks. In: ACM Workshop on Mobile Internet Through Cellular Networks (2009)
10. Krishnamurthy, S., Thoppian, M., Venkatesan, S., Prakash, R.: Control channel based MAC-layer configuration, routing and situation awareness for cognitive radio networks. In: IEEE MILCOM (2005)
11. Arkoulis, S., Anifantis, E., Karyotis, V., Papavassiliou, S., Mitrou, N.: On the optimal, fair and channel-aware cognitive radio network reconfiguration. Computer Networks **57**(8), 1739–1757 (2013)
12. Chen, K.-C., Cetin, B.K., Peng, Y.-C., Prasad, N., Wang, J., Lee, S.: Routing for cognitive radio networks consisting of opportunistic links. Wireless Communications and Mobile Computing **10**(4), 451–466 (2010)
13. Pyo, C.W., Hasegawa, M.: Minimum weight routing based on a common link control radio for cognitive wireless ad hoc networks. In: ACM International Conference on Wireless Communications and Mobile Computing, pp. 399–404 (2007)
14. Zhu, G.-M., Akyildiz, I.F., Kuo, G.-S.: Stod-rp: A spectrum-tree based on-demand routing protocol for multi-hop cognitive radio networks. In: IEEE Global Telecommunications Conference (GLOBECOM), pp. 1–5 (2008)
15. Wang, X., Kwon, T.T., Choi, Y.: A multipath routing and spectrum access (mrsa) framework for cognitive radio systems in multi-radio mesh networks. In: ACM Workshop on Cognitive Radio Networks, pp. 55–60 (2009)
16. Ma, H., Zheng, L., Ma, X., et al.: Spectrum aware routing for multi-hop cognitive radio networks with a single transceiver. In: IEEE International Conference on Cognitive Radio Oriented Wireless Networks and Communications (CrownCom), pp. 1–6 (2008)

17. Zeeshan, M., Sattar, K., Shah, Z., Ullah, I.: Routing and spectrum decision in single transceiver cognitive radio networks. In: IEEE Vehicular Technology Conference (VTC), pp. 1–5 (2013)
18. Kamruzzaman, S., Kim, E., Jeong, D.G.: An energy efficient qos routing protocol for cognitive radio ad hoc networks. In: IEEE International Conference on Advanced Communication Technology (ICACT), pp. 344–349 (2011)
19. Cplex. In: CPLEX. http://www.ilog.com/products/cplex
20. FCC, E.: Fcc 10–174 (2010). https://apps.fcc.gov/edocs_public/attachmatch/FCC-10-174A1.pdf

Connectivity Provisioning Using Cognitive Channel Selection in Vehicular Networks

Elif Bozkaya, Müge Erel, and Berk Canberk[(⊠)]

Department of Computer Engineering, Istanbul Technical University,
Ayazaga Campus, 34469 Istanbul, Turkey
{bozkayae,erelmu,canberk}@itu.edu.tr

Abstract. High mobility of vehicles, limited transmission range of roadside units (RSUs), and channel status (busy or idle) cause dynamic topological changes in Vehicular Networks (VNs). Due to these dynamic topological changes, maintaining full connectivity arises as a main communication challenge in VNs. Moreover, the high number of channel switching also effects the quality of network connectivity causing an another significant problem in VNs. In order to overcome these challenges, we analyze the full connectivity provisioning in VNs by proposing four cognitive channel selection algorithms, parameterizing the vehicle satisfaction ratio and the number of channel switching. Specifically, the proposed channel selection algorithms provide minimal channel switching ratio while conserving full network connectivity. We also compare the results of multi-channel selection and single channel selection and simulation results show that network connectivity can be enhanced while optimizing the channel switching with our proposed cognitive channel selection algorithms.

Keywords: Vehicular networks · Network connectivity · Channel switching · Dynamic channel allocation

1 Introduction

With recent advances in online embedded mobile applications, traffic safety and efficiency have gained major importance in vehicular networks. Among them, online safety, monitoring, tracking and infotainment applications can be listed as leading examples. To support these applications and to enhance network performance, RSUs are deployed for vehicle to infrastructure (V2I) communication pattern. However, one of the main distinct characterization of vehicular networks is high mobility of vehicles. In addition to the high mobility of vehicles, limited transmission range of RSUs and channel status (busy or idle) cause dramatic changes behaviours of the network topology influencing network performance negatively. In such a dynamic network topology, maintaining continuous and robust connectivity will be significantly difficult in vehicular networks.

Specifically, after The U.S. Federal Communications Commission (FCC) has allocated bandwidth of 75 MHz in the 5.9 GHz frequency band for dedicated short range communication in 1999, many attractive applications have become

© Institute for Computer Sciences, Social Informatics and Telecommunications Engineering 2014
N. Mitton et al. (Eds.): ADHOCNETS 2014, LNICST 140, pp. 169–179, 2014.
DOI: 10.1007/978-3-319-13329-4_15

more popular in transportation system. However, although new applications and innovations emerged in transportation system, increasing bandwidth requirement in these online applications cause new problem; spectrum scarcity. To utilize unused spectrum bands, dynamic spectrum access (DSA) has been proposed in many researches to supply growing demand [1–3]. However, due to changing channel availability status, network connectivity is more challenging in vehicular networks.

Moreover, the number of channel switching effects the quality of network connectivity in vehicular networks. Each channel switching results with intermittent connectivity and communication duration continuously changes depending on network topology. Vehicles need to exploit the channel status to check availability of channels at all times. Therefore, when the number of channel switching increases, the quality of network connectivity will effect by causing communication disruptions. Therefore, the quality of communication is related to determine best available channels dynamically.

These aforementioned challenges, maintaining full network connectivity, channel switching and dynamic channel allocation, is investigated in many researches with different approaches in vehicular networks.

[4] presents a knowledge-based learning to service vehicular communications and proposes the use of Vehicular Dynamic Spectrum Access (VDSA). The authors investigate channel selection problem and calculate channel switching and channel access rate in a realistic simulation environment. [5] researches dynamic channel selection schemes and focus on channel switching in multi-hop vehicular ad hoc networking and evaluate the total time of transmission and the amount of transmitted data in DSA inter-vehicle networks. In [6], the authors study on the learning techniques to use in many applications in VDSA and determine channel availability status to analyze channel prediction and selection process. [7] presents channel allocation algorithm using game theory in Vehicular Ad hoc NETworks (VANETs).

Moreover, there exist many works related to connectivity in vehicular networks. [8] proposes an analytical model to improve connectivity in vehicular networks. The effect of road traffic parameters (traffic flow, speed), transmission range of vehicle on the connectivity is described with the proposed model. [9] investigates the relationship between mobility and network connectivity with different mobility models for realistic VANET by proposing an analytical framework. In [10], authors combine two concepts, cooperative communications and analog network coding (ANC), to improve network connectivity and capacity in vehicular networks.

Even though the connectivity challenge has been analyzed in these aforementioned studies, a full connectivity maintenance has not been investigated while optimizing continuous connectivity, channel switching and channel allocation simultaneously in vehicular networks.

Therefore, in this paper, we propose cognitive channel selection algorithms to evaluate the relationship between network connectivity and channel switching in vehicular networks. We analyze the connectivity problem with different traffic density in terms of satisfaction ratio and the number of channel switching. These two performance parameters are defined as follows.

- Satisfaction ratio: Total usage ratio of channels with respect to proposed dynamic channel selection algorithms in different traffic densities.
- The number of channel switching: The total number of channel switching throughout entire communication period in different traffic densities.

In our work, our main objective is to enhance network connectivity between vehicles and RSUs in vehicular networks. With this purpose, we maximize satisfaction ratio while minimizing the number of channel switching with the proposed cognitive channel selection algorithms. In the proposed algorithms, we define best available channels with two different approaches, multi-channel selection and single channel selection. Therefore, at first we propose a channel utilization map and then implement different cognitive channel selection algorithms, finally we compare the results with different approaches including single channel switching and multi-channel switching.

Specifically, this paper makes the following main contributions.

- We develop a channel utilization map using temporal usage characteristics of vehicles.
- Using this map, we derive analytics for channel utilization ratio, vehicle satisfaction ratio and channel switching.
- We propose four different cognitive channel selection algorithm by maximizing connectivity, maximizing channel utilization ratio, checking channel utilization table by selecting maximum channel utilization ratio and optimizing between satisfaction ratio and channel switching.

The results show the relationship between network connectivity and channel switching with the proposed algorithms to provide effective communication between vehicles and RSUs.

The rest of the paper is organized as follows. Section 2 gives the details of proposed system architecture. Section 3 describes the proposed cognitive channel algorithms for vehicular networks, Section 4 gives simulation results and evaluate the performance and finally Section 5 concludes the paper.

2   System Architecture

In this paper, we proposed a vehicular network architecture for the communication between vehicles and RSUs. In this architecture, RSUs units are deployed specific location with a limited transmission range, α, in order to communicate with vehicles.

We assume that there are c channels that are divided into fixed time slots, t, and m vehicles that can opportunistically access to channels depending on communication requests. Vehicles move at variable velocity, v', which are between v_1 and v_2 depending on traffic density. The movement of vehicles is considered normally distributed zero mean and unit variance.

Each vehicle registers to RSU when they come into the transmission range of a RSU. Moreover, vehicles sense multiple channels at a time in order to obtain the information of channel availability within the transmission range of a RSU and they can dynamically switch to another suitable channel when the channel is detected as unavailable. However, vehicles access only one channel in each time slot.

In the proposed architecture, network connectivity is required to establish communication and disseminate online information between vehicles and RSUs. RSU collects all network information by including channel availability status and communication requests of vehicles within the geographical area of itself. To maintain full connectivity, Fig. 1 is proposed which is implemented in RSU and each module is modelled as follows.

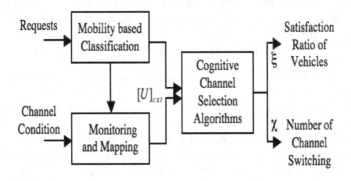

Fig. 1. Proposed System Model

2.1   Mobility Based Classification Module

This module characterizes communication requests of vehicles within the transmission range of RSU. Requests, R(t), are represented with binary variables and distributed according to Poisson process with the arrival rate λ_R in time interval $[1, t]$. Vehicles move at variable velocities, v', which are between v_1 and v_2 depending on traffic density and RSUs determine the time interval of vehicles, how long will remain in its transmission range, assuming that $\frac{\alpha}{v'}$. The movement of vehicles is considered normally distributed zero mean and unit variance.

2.2   Monitoring and Mapping Module

In this module, each channel is modelled as idle or busy in each time slot which is represented with binary variables, C(t), and distributed according to Poisson process with the arrival rate λ_C in time interval $[1, t]$.

In this module, after storing communication requests and monitoring channel condition in RSU, channel utilization map is derived and utilization ratio of channels are calculated for each vehicle. When a new vehicle moves into the transmission range of a RSU, it characterizes which time slots are idle and calculates channel utilization map as shown in Fig. 2.

Time

Communication Request, R(t)	no request	requested	no request	requested
Channel Availability, C(t)	idle	idle	busy	busy
Utilization Map, $[U]_{cxt}$	N/A	occupied	N/A	N/A

Fig. 2. Channel Utilization Map

When channel is idle and vehicle has a communication request in this specified time slot, then the channel can be occupied by a vehicle. It can be formulated by eq.1 as follows:

$$[U_{cxt}] = \begin{cases} 1, & R(t) = 1, \ C(t) = 0 \\ 0, & otherwise \end{cases} \qquad (1)$$

where $[U_{cxt}]$ is utilization matrix for each vehicle, R(t) and C(t) represent communication request and channel availability, respectively.

Then, utilization ratio of each channel is calculated for each vehicle in eq.2 as follows:

$$U_{c_i}^m = \frac{\sum_{j=1}^{t}[U]_{c_i}^m}{t} \qquad \forall i \in [1, 2, ..., c], \forall j \in [1, 2, ..., t] \qquad (2)$$

where $U_{c_i}^m$ is utilization ratio of channel i for vehicle m, $c_i \in c$ and $[U]_{c_i}^m$ is the utilization matrix of ith channel for vehicle m.

After obtaining the utilization map for each vehicle, vehicle determines available channels and decides a channel selection algorithm to maintain full connectivity with minimal channel switching.

3 Cognitive Channel Selection Algorithms

In this section, we defined four novel cognitive channel selection algorithms in order to maintain full network connectivity with two approaches, multi-channel selection and single channel selection. In single channel selection, vehicles can access only one channel throughout entire communication period and whenever channel is detected as unavailable, vehicles quit the channel and wait until channel is available. Due to the usage of only one channel, channel selection is the more significant when compared with multi channel operations. To evaluate the results with these approaches, we specified two main communication performance parameters described in the previous section and then elaborated them under different traffic density.

– Satisfaction ratio, ξ: Total usage ratio of channels with respect to proposed channel selection algorithms.
– The number of channel switching, χ: The total number of channel switching throughout entire communication period.

With the proposed algorithms, our aim is to maximize satisfaction ratio while minimizing the number of channel switching by defining best available channels. With these motivations, the following algorithms are derived.

3.1   Algorithm 1 (Connectivity Maximization)

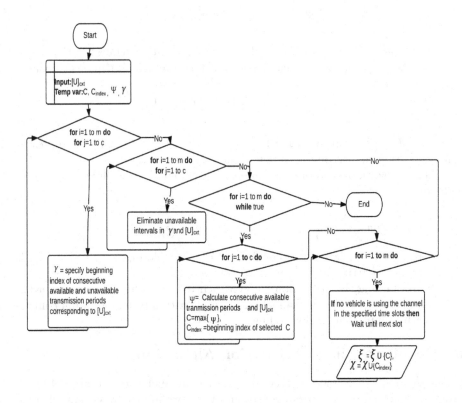

Fig. 3. Flowchart of algorithm 1

Algorithm 1 is based on multiple channel selection by maintaining maximum connectivity with maximum channel switching as flow diagram given in Fig. 3. In algorithm 1, each vehicle determines available and unavailable transmission periods in its utilization map and calculates consecutive available transmission intervals. At the end of the each transmission period, available channels are determined and then a large amount of transmission interval is selected for the next channel switching. Every selection is based on higher utilization in order to minimize channel switching. In this algorithm, vehicles dynamically switch to another suitable channel whenever channel is detected as unavailable and all idle time slots are used to obtain maximum satisfaction ratio resulting frequent channel switching.

3.2 Algorithm 2 (Maximum Channel Utilization Ratio)

Algorithm 2 is based on single channel selection approach. Channel utilization ratios, $U_{c_i}^m$, are calculated for each vehicle as given in eq.2 and each vehicle selects a channel that has maximum utilization ratio throughout entire transmission period in order to utilize the channel as long as possible. However, if the number of vehicle is higher than the number of channels, all vehicles cannot be access the channels. The flow diagram is given in Fig. 4(a).

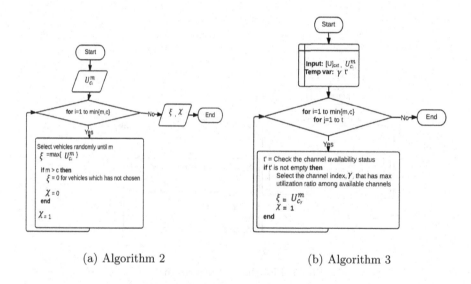

(a) Algorithm 2   (b) Algorithm 3

Fig. 4. Flowcharts of Algorithm 2 and 3

3.3 Algorithm 3 (Checking Channel Utilization Table by Selecting Maximum Channel Utilization Ratio)

Algorithm 3 uses only one channel selection approach. In this algorithm, channel utilization ratios, $U_{c_i}^m$, are calculated for each vehicle similar to algorithm 2 and each vehicle checks its utilization map by starting from initial time slot. When one or more channel is detected as available at a time, vehicle selects a channel that has maximum utilization ratio among available channels in this specific time as flow diagram given in Fig. 4(b).

3.4 Algorithm 4 (Optimization Between Satisfaction Ratio and Channel Switching)

This algorithm is proposed to avoid frequent channel switching in algorithm 1 with multiple channel selection approach.

To decrease the number of channel switching in algorithm 1, at first algorithm 1 is run in order to obtain performance parameters, satisfaction matrix and the number of channel switching, and then total amount of transmission periods in satisfaction matrix is calculated in each channel switching. With the help of obtaining these transmission intervals in each channel switching, the mean of all periods is calculated to compare with each transmission period. Then transmission periods that smaller than the mean value are eliminated to decrease the number of channel switching in algorithm 1. The flow diagram is given in Fig. 5.

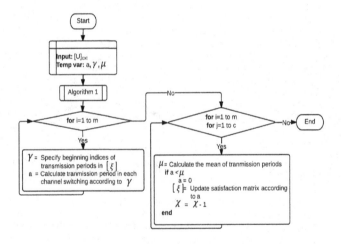

Fig. 5. Flowchart of algorithm 4

However, we can expect that while decreasing number of channel switching, satisfaction ratio is also decreased in algorithm 4. However, we observe that satisfaction ratio and number of channel switching are optimized by conserving full network connectivity.

4 Performance Evaluation

In this section, we evaluate the performance of the proposed system model and show the relationship between connectivity and channel switching with the proposed four cognitive channel selection algorithms. The results of proposed algorithms and all system modules are implemented in MATLAB environment. We look into the connectivity problem with two different approaches, multi channel selection and single channel selection. Moreover, we obtain the results with different traffic densities, low, medium and high. The number of vehicles varies between 1 to 10, 10 to 15 and 15 to 20 in low, medium and high traffic densities, respectively. The parameters used in the simulation are shown in Table.1.

Table 1. Simulation Parameters

Parameter	Value
Transmission Range of a RSU	5000 m
Velocity of Vehicles	10 to 20 m/s
Number of Channels	10
Number of Vehicles	1 to 20
Total Number of Time Slot	1000

We use a vehicular network architecture with one RSU and between 1 and 20 vehicles with variable velocity between 10 and 20 m/s. We assume that all vehicles are registered and connected to RSU when they come into its transmission range.

A total number of 10 channels are divided into 1000 time slots and vehicles opportunistically access to channels depending on channel status (busy or idle).

We compare the proposed algorithms in terms of satisfaction ratio and the number of channel switching according to different traffic densities with the following approaches.

- Multi-channel selection: Vehicles can sense multiple channels and access one channel at a time when the channel is detected as available and can switch to another suitable channel dynamically when channel is detected as unavailable.
- Single-channel selection: Vehicles can access only one channel throughout entire communication period depending on availability of channel.

In this respect, Fig. 6 shows the relationship between satisfaction ratio and number of channel switching depending on traffic density for each proposed algorithm. Algorithm 1 enables to maximum connectivity resulting frequent channel switching in each traffic density. However, the results of algorithm 4 is acceptable due to the decreasing the number of channel switching with a 47% rate by conserving network connectivity. Moreover, the satisfaction ratios of algorithm 2 and 3 is less than due to the usage of only one channel. We observe that maintaining connectivity is more challenging in high traffic density for all proposed algorithms.

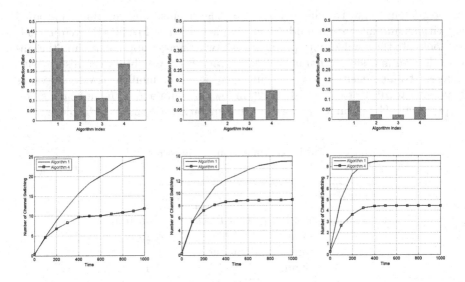

Fig. 6. Satisfaction ratio and the number of channel switching w.r.t. low, medium and high traffic density, respectively

5   Conclusion

In this paper, we propose four cognitive channel selection algorithms in order to maintain full connectivity between vehicles and RSUs in terms of satisfaction ratio and number of channel switching. The proposed multi-channel selection and single channel selection algorithms are evaluated in simulation environment separately. We observe in the proposed algorithms that multi-channel selection can significantly improve the network performance when compared with single-channel selection and simulation results show that there is a significant relationship between satisfaction ratio and the number of channel switching to maintain connectivity and connectivity can be enhanced the proposed cognitive multi channel selection algorithms.

References

1. Cheng, N., Zhang, N., Lu, N., Shen, X., Mark, W., Liu, F.: Opportunistic Spectrum Access for CR-VANETs: A Game-Theoretic Approach. IEEE Trans. Veh. Technol. **63**, 237–251 (2014)
2. Rzayev, T., Shi, Y., Vafeiadis, A., Pagadarai, S., Wyglinski, A.: Implementation of A Vehicular Networking Architecture Supporting Dynamic Spectrum Access. In: IEEE Vehicular Networking Conference (VNC), pp. 33–38. IEEE Press, Amsterdam (2011)
3. Niyato, D., Hossain, E., Wang, P.: Optimal Channel Access Management with QoS Support for Cognitive Vehicular Networks. IEEE Trans. Mobile Computing **10**, 573–591 (2011)

4. Rocke, S., Chen, S., Vuyyuru, R., Altintas, O., Wyglinski, A.: Knowledge?based Dynamic Channel Selection in Vehicular Networks. In: IEEE Vehicular Networking Conference (VNC), pp. 165–172. IEEE Press, Seoul (2012)
5. Tsukamoto, K., Omori, Y., Altintas, O., Tsuru, M., Oie, Y.: On Spatially-Aware Channel Selection in Dynamic Spectrum Access Multi-Hop Inter-Vehicle Communications. In: 70th IEEE Vehicular Technology Conference (VTC), pp. 1–7. IEEE Press, Alaska (2009)
6. Chen, S., Vuyyurut, R., Altintas, O., Wyglinski, A.: Learning in Vehicular Dynamic Spectrum Access Networks: Opportunities and Challenges. In: IEEE International Symposium on Intelligent Signal Processing and Communication Systems (ISPACS), pp. 1–6. IEEE Press, Chiang Mai (2011)
7. Kasdani, Y., Chew, Y.H., Yuen, C., Chin, W.H.: Channel Allocation in A Multiple Distributed Vehicular Users Using Game Theory. In: 71st IEEE Vehicular Technology Conference (VTC), pp. 1–5. IEEE Press, Taipei (2010)
8. Yousefi, S., Altman, E., El-Azouzi, R., Fathy, M.: Analytical Model for Connectivity in Vehicular Ad Hoc Networks. IEEE Trans. Veh. Technol. **57**, 3341–3356 (2008)
9. Ho, I.W.H., Leung, K.K., Polak, J.W., Mangharam, R.: Node Connectivity in Vehicular Ad Hoc Networks with Structured Mobility. In: 32nd IEEE Conference on Local Computer Networks, pp. 635–642. IEEE Press, Dublin (2007)
10. Khlass, A., Ghamri-Doudane, Y., Gacanin, H.: Combining Cooperative Relaying and Analog Network Coding to Improve Network Connectivity and Capacity in Vehicular Networks. In: Global Telecommunications Conference (GLOBECOM 2011), pp. 1–5. IEEE Press, Houston, TX (2011)

Using Location Services to Autonomously Drive Flying Mobile Sinks in Wireless Sensor Networks

Nicola Roberto Zema[2]([✉]), Nathalie Mitton[1], and Giuseppe Ruggeri[2]

[1] Inria, Paris, France
nathalie.mitton@inria.fr
[2] University "Mediterranea" of Reggio Calabria, Rome, Italy
{nicola.zema,giuseppe.ruggeri}@unirc.it

Abstract. The use of mobility in a Wireless Sensor Network has already been indicated as a feature whose exploitation would increase the performances and the ease of mantainance in these environments. Expecially in a event-based WSN, where is necessary a prompt response in terms of data processing and offloading, a set of mobile flying sinks could be a good option for the role of autonomous data collectors. For those reasons in this paper we propose a distributed algorithm to independently and autonomously drive a mobile sink through the nodes of a WSN and we show its preferability over more classical routing approaches expecially in the presence of a localized generation of large amount of information. Our result shows that, in the case of fairly complete coverage of the area where the nodes lie, it is possible to promptly notify a mobile sink about the presence of data to offload, drive it to the interested area and achieve interesting performances.

Keywords: Controlled mobility · Sensor networks · Network scalability and capacity · Network architectural and protocol design

1 Introduction

The delivery and diffusion of precious data in a multihop environment like the one of the Wireless Sensor Networks (WSNs) [29] pose a series of challenges to each of the designer, the maintainer and the user of these specific networks. Energy consumption linked with network lifetime and end-to-end delay are some of the most prominent and it is shown [11,18,27] that applying mobility as a degree of freedom in the network would enhance its performances while easing in the management of the aforementioned challenges. For example, with one or more fixed destinations scattered far apart in the network and with each node

The research of Nicola Roberto Zema is partially supported by European Union (EU), European Social Fund (ESF), Calabria Local Goverment and Inria Lille. This paper reflects the views only of the authors, and the EU, the ESF, Calabria Local Goverment and Inria Lille cannot be held responsible for any use which may be made of the information contained therein.

© Institute for Computer Sciences, Social Informatics and Telecommunications Engineering 2014
N. Mitton et al. (Eds.): ADHOCNETS 2014, LNICST 140, pp. 180–191, 2014.
DOI: 10.1007/978-3-319-13329-4_16

as a possible source of multihop traffic, there would be a strong imbalance in the paths taken by information. This difference would make the nodes around the fixed collectors deplete sooner their batteries and generate rings of unconnected free space around the data sinks [19]. In this situation, using a mobile solution for the collectors leads to balance the load distribution [3]. In reviewed studies, regardless using naive *direct* [13], *multihop*[22] or *hybrid* [27] routing schemes to deliver data to a mobile sink, it is usually supposed that the mobility is uncontrollable or at best predicted. In this paper we propose instead to allow the mobile node to manipulate its path guided by the network itself. We devise the use of a controlled mobility-enhanced sink in a Wireless Sensor Network for data offloading. This peculiar study would research the inferring of the trajectory by a mobile node from the information diffused by the other members of the network. We create an environment in which instead of relying on multihop data diffusion and routing, the nodes of the network will signal to a collector the presence of events associated with the consistent generation of data, like the necessity for a cluster head to unload all the collected values by its neighbor nodes, without requiring an *apriori* knowledge of its position. The collector will then schedule its movements to reach the interested areas. This is particularly useful in all the environments where a strict temporal response is needed and where large quantities of data are generated. We propose a practical, completely distributed, signaling and movement protocols for a mobile sink and, in support of our design, we present a simulation study where we analyze its performances and make comparisons against more used solutions. Results show that our approach outperform these latters regarding the overall energy expenditure and, up to a certain number of sources, the end-to-end delay. The paper is organized as follows. In Section 2 we overview the existing literature and solutions for the mobility of a sink in a WSN. In Sections 3 and 4 we present our proposal first in its environment and then in its details. Our results are shown in Section 5, while in Section 6 we describe our future proposal and possible research paths.

2   Related Literature

Studies regarding maximization of network lifetime in a WSN highlight several key features that need to be addressed apart from budget and coverage requirements. These include energy consumption distribution, energy hole problems and the discovery of efficient routes for data diffusion and dissemination [8,32]. It is also highlighted that the use of mobility could bring great benefits to the performances and lifetime of a WSN [15,16,20]. Bringing mobility in the network in form of a mobile sink shifts the priority of the routing problem. From the optimal and stable finding of efficient routes departing from any point in the network and arriving to a set of fixed sinks, the routing algorithms have to track their movements and try to deliver them the data [28]. The solutions to this problem are various and can be classified using various criteria. Some authors make distinction between the ones that employ the preliminary creation of hierarchical structures and the ones that do not use them [28]. Other authors instead propose the distinction between the routing protocols that use a pure multihop approach, the single-hop data collection and hybrid routing schemes [25]. The majority of those approaches however suppose that (i) the mobility of the sinks can at best be predicted and (ii), are tailored for value diffusion rather than multihop flow handling. Regarding the latter issue, there are different works that leverage the use of mobile entities for information gathering and delivering. Data MULES [17,26] and Message Ferries [23,31] propose the use of mobile elements to transport large quantities of offloaded data using mobile nodes with enhanced capabilities in respect to the rest of the network. Regarding the former issue, there is a set of works that employs actual controlled mobility for network enhancement. In [4] is proposed a framework comprising of a mathematical optimization, a centralized and distributed heuristic that define a predefined abstract set of movements for a group of mobile sinks improving the expected network lifetime. In [24] is proposed another scheme for the trajectory finding of a mobile sink that uses phased arrays antenna systems to orient itself in a network, given a set of predefined waypoints. Our work is different as we propose an on-demand scheme for sink movement rather than a collection trip, useful in event-driven situation where a prompt response is needed, and as we propose a practical direction finding scheme. We also take as a source the works on position discovery in WSN routing [6] and in particular the research on methods that use geographical properties of the network [7].

3   Overall Principle and Main Assumption

The use of the nodes' geographic properties in the design of network protocols is not new and a lot of solutions implement the exploitation of those properties for routing algorithms and data diffusion schemes [11]. However among the limitations highlighted are the scarce efficiency and the energy dispersion inherent in delivering amounts of data not limited to single values. In a sensor network covering an area where the nodes could sense an event, activate themselves and offload the collected data to a sink, that amount is not trivial and it is problematic to deliver it to its destination using the multihop schemes described in literature. Techniques including mobility in the sink help reduce the number of hops to travel for a packet to arrive at destination thus reducing the overall network resource consumption at the expenses of introducing an energy cost for the physical movement. It is pointed out that a good solution would be to use a controlled mobility environment where the sink entity is driven by information given by the network itself [28]. In an event-driven WSN, there would be geographically localized *events* that make the sensor covering the same area to start collecting environmental information and, possibly, deliver them to temporary storage. In such an environment whenever this localized data is generated and have to be quickly offloaded [9], it is possible for a mobile sink to move directly into the proximity of the temporary collector and reduce to the minimum the number of hops. Also, there would be cases where in addition to the offloading process, there is the need of bringing an external observer in the area of a sensed event even if there is no data to deliver. With these guidelines in mind we first devised a protocol for delivering the information about the presence of data to offload in a wireless sensor network and then included it in a controlled mobility framework where the sink can move to the advertised position and collect the data or perform some other local maintenance operations [21]. In our design the trajectory is directly inferred by the network and computed autonomously by the mobile sink. The assumptions we made about our network are that: (i) it is composed by static sensor nodes; (ii) it is dense enough, given the capabilities of a general sensor networking device, to uniformly cover the whole sensing area and (iii) that each node knows its position either because of the presence of a GPS device or because that value has been pre-set. In our proposal, we envision the use of mobile flying robots for the mobile sink role as the possibility to use them as an effective communication station is displayed [12,14,30]. In particular, for its capability to hover above a group of sensors waiting for the data offloading to finish, we envisioned the use of quadcopters [5] considering the movement capabilities accordingly.

4 Supporting Protocol Overview

Our protocol design takes its roots in the works on geographical data diffusion and in particular the research on the location services. If a node has data to transmit, each time interval Δt_{source} it broadcasts a *source advertisement* packet containing its ID and its absolute position. Upon reception, the packet is broadcast again only by nodes placed in the band parallel to the north-south absolute axis, whose median passes by the original broadcasting node and whose amplitude is defined by the parameter Δ_{width}. Also, the nodes that receive a packet, will check against its ID and broadcast it again only after the expiration of a timeout $\Delta t_{source\ expire}$. This is possible because the nodes keep track of the various sources of information they come in contact with, in terms of the tuple composed of the ID and the coordinates. In Figure 1 is displayed a working scenario with Δ_{width} equal as the node transmission range. The mobile sinks also are capable, upon the expiration of the time interval Δt_{sink}, to send *sink advertisement* packets along a stripe, this time parallel to the east-west absolute axis. Eventually those two stripes will intersect and in the geographical area of superposition there will be nodes that have been reached by both packet types, the shaded gray area of figure 1. In the case of a single collector, when a node has the information about both the position of the mobile sink and the source, it sends the information about the latter using *backtrace* packets, which contain the same information as the *source advertisement* with the addition of the sink ID. Those are broadcasted back to the sink only by the nodes that originally forwarded the *sink advertisement* packets. Whenever a mobile sink receives the information about a source of traffic it stores the value and, at the expiration of a timer $\Delta t_{movement\ control}$, it ranks the sources based on the distance and move to the nearest to initiate the offloading. After the offloading has expired, the mobile sink will check the position of the sources and move again to the new nearest destination if present. In this way it is possible to bypass completely the routing of large quantities of packets in an energy constrained multihop environment thus improving the whole performance of the network in terms of end-to-end delays and power consumption.

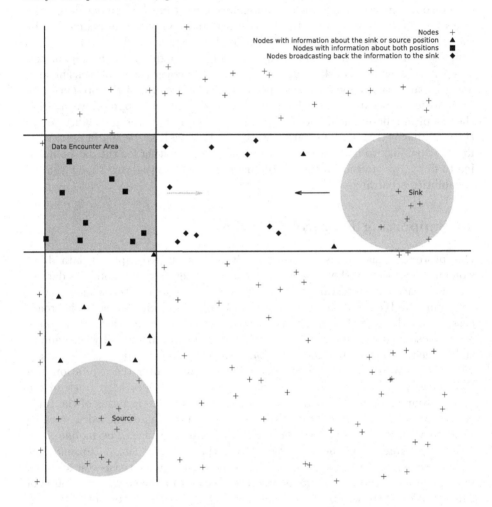

Fig. 1. Example working scenario

For testing the capability of our proposal to ease the network in cases of large quantities of data to offload, we tested our system against a WSN environment and an implementation of a common solution, the Greedy Geographical Routing.

5   Highlighted Results

For our purposes, we set up a network simulation with the wsnet environment [1,10]. We defined a topology of 600 uniformly distributed nodes on a

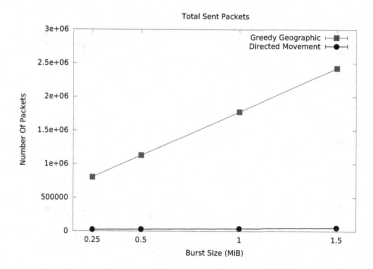

Fig. 2. Total number of sent packets

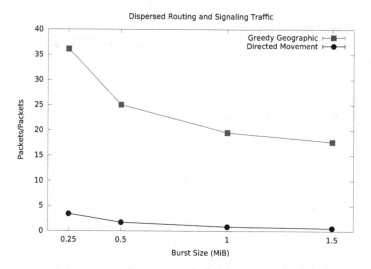

Fig. 3. Ratio between the application data sent by source and destination nodes and the total routing and movement signaling traffic

$500m \times 500m$ area. Each node is equipped with a 2400MHz bpsk 802.15.4 compliant radio and MAC interface working on a single channel. We set the values of Δt_{source}, Δt_{sink} and $\Delta t_{source\ expire}$ as the estimated time necessary for a packet to travel the network diameter with the current nodes' capabilities, while Δ_{width} was put as the averaged node's coverage umbrella diameter. The values of $\Delta t_{movement\ control}$ were set in order for the mobile sink to receive the information about the sources and move immediately after the completion of a

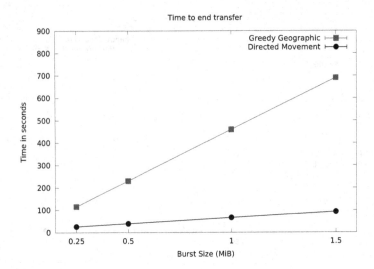

Fig. 4. Time to transfer completion

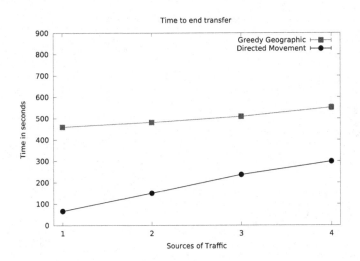

Fig. 5. Time to transfer completion, multiple sources

transfer. In a first set of simulations, for our tests we put a source and a sink at two opposite corners of the topology. We set up a bursty acked application where we made the source transmits a variable size data of 0.25, 0.5, 1 and 1.5 MB, representing the data that s to be offloaded, with the maximum rate and packets size possible for the 802.15.4 MAC [2]. Using our proposal, called *Directed Movement* in the graphs, the source and the destination will first signal each other and then the sink will move into position to offload the data. For making a comparison, we fed the same bursty traffic to the geographical rout-

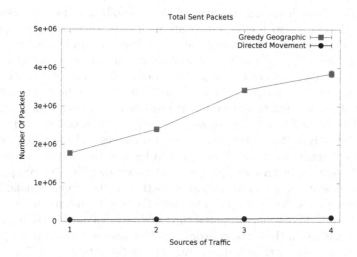

Fig. 6. Total number of sent packets, multiple sources

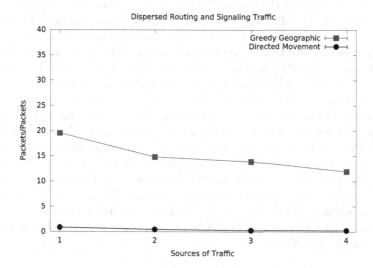

Fig. 7. Ratio between the application data sent by source and destination nodes and the total routing and movement signaling traffic, multiple sources

ing algorithm implemented in stock wsnet [1], that is indicated in the graphs as *Greedy Geographic*. Each value is the result of a 10 simulative runs whose outputs were processed using a student's t-distributions with 95% confidence intervals and shown where applicable. Figure 4 shows the time to complete the data offload for various burst sizes, defined as the difference in time between the first packet enqueue in the source and the last received ack. It can be seen that it is dependent of the burst size and it shows a great reduction using our system.

The reduction is high enough to suggest the possibility, using our system, to serve multiple sources with ease, especially with large burst size. It is possible to see from Figure 2 that the energy impact on the network is greatly reduced. The figure shows the total number of sent packets in the network, as a sum of application, routing and position signaling traffic where present, by all nodes. Again our proposal, reducing to just one hop the distance the information has to travel make consistent traffic reduction possible thus greatly augmenting the network lifetime. In figure 3 it is shown the ratio between the original application data sent only by the source and destination nodes and the routed, routing and movement traffic where applicable. It can be seen that our system achieves better performances in terms of packets sent and minor time to complete the transfer because it can perform a great reduction in the aforementioned ratio, relying only on our signaling protocol to make the mobile sink reach the sources. In a second set of simulations we tested the capabilities of our system in presence of multiple sources. In the same network topology and environment we put this time up to four sources that had, starting at the same time, to offload 1 MiB of application data to a sink placed in a corner of square area where the nodes were placed. We set up the sources in the other corners and in the center and activate them in the following order during different setups: first the adjacent corners, then the center and then the opposite corner increasing distance. Figure 5 is again a measure of the needed time to complete the transfer comparing our proposal and the greedy geographical routing. Even if in our proposal the time to serve all the sources increases faster than the greedy approach in respect to number of sources, it stills outperforms it up to four data generating nodes. It should be noted that, in the same conditions, the total number of sent packets and thus the network energy consumption is not only higher but also increasing faster as the number of sources increases. This aspect of our system can also be seen from figure 6, where the total traffic is shown. Increasing the sources create a dramatic increase in the packet generation for the greedy geographical approach due to congestion and retransmissions. In the last figure, 7, a replica of figure 3 for multiple sources, as the total transmitted data increase the ratio between original application data and the routed traffic decreases but our system still achieves better efficiency.

6   Conclusions and Possible Future Research Paths

In this paper we have proposed a practical, completely distributed, signaling and movement protocols for a mobile sink to collect data from advertizing nodes in a wireless sensor network. Our proposal is particularly useful when the quantity of data that needs to be offloaded is not negligible and our event pinpointing system can also be used to drive the mobile nodes towards designated areas where their physical presence is needed. Even if we have shown the feasibility of our driving framework and its advantages against a simple geographical routing system in the reliable delivery of application data, there are still some issues that we plan to address. We suppose that the network topology is dense enough to guarantee the coverage of the geometrical surface where the nodes are placed; else there would be points where the information about the sources and the sinks cannot travel. It should be devised so an obstacle avoidance system that is capable to make the packets carrying the positions route around coverage holes and continue in the same direction. It should also be analyzed the setup where are present multiple mobile sinks and how to apply to this situation an advanced algorithm that efficiently ranks the various source positions eventually detected by each sink. In this situation would also be necessary a careful tune of the parameters and an accurate evaluation of the mobility inherent cost. Another important research direction would be to abandon the dependence on absolute positioning systems and the introduction of a protocol that is capable to swiftly guide the mobile sink through waypoints in the network using only relative positions and inertial navigation, relaxing the assumptions on coordinate awareness.

References

1. WSNet / Worldsens Simulator - wsnet. available from http://wsnet.gforge.inria.fr
2. IEEE Standard for Information Technology- Telecommunications and Information Exchange Between Systems- Local and Metropolitan Area Networks- Specific Requirements Part 15.4: Wireless Medium Access Control (MAC) and Physical Layer (PHY) Specifications for Low-Rate Wireless Personal Area Networks (WPANs). Technical report (2006)
3. Basagni, S., Carosi, A., Melachrinoudis, E., Petrioli, C., Wang, Z.M.: Controlled sink mobility for prolonging wireless sensor networks lifetime. Wireless Networks 14(6), 831–858 (2008)
4. Basagni, S., Carosi, A., Petrioli, C., Phillips, C.A.: Coordinated and controlled mobility of multiple sinks for maximizing the lifetime of wireless sensor networks. Wireless Networks 17(3), 759–778 (2011)
5. Chen, Y., Chen, J., Zhou, L., Du, Y.: A data gathering approach for wireless sensor network with quadrotor-based mobile sink node. In: Wang, R., Xiao, F. (eds.) CWSN 2012. CCIS, vol. 334, pp. 44–56. Springer, Heidelberg (2013)
6. Cheng, W., Zhang, N., Cheng, X., Song, M., Chen, D.: Time-bounded essential localization for wireless sensor networks. IEEE/ACM Transactions on Networking (TON) 21(2), 400–412 (2013)
7. Das, S.M., Pucha, H., Hu, Y.C.: Performance comparison of scalable location services for geographic ad hoc routing. In: Proceedings of the IEEEINFOCOM 2005 24th Annual Joint Conference of the IEEE Computer and Communications Societies, vol. 2, pp. 1228–1239 (March 2005)
8. Keskin, M.E., Altınel, İ,K., Aras, N., Ersoy, C.: Wireless sensor network lifetime maximization by optimal sensor deployment, activity scheduling, data routing and sink mobility. Ad Hoc Networks (2014)
9. Filipponi, L., Vitaletti, A., Landi, G., Memeo, V., Laura, G., Pucci, P.: Smart city: an event driven architecture for monitoring public spaces with heterogeneous sensors. In: 2010 Fourth International Conference on Sensor Technologies and Applications (SENSORCOMM), pp. 281–286. IEEE (2010)
10. Fraboulet, A., Chelius, G., Fleury, E.: Worldsens: Development and prototyping tools for application specific wireless sensors networks. In: Proceedings of the 6th International Conference on Information Processing in Sensor Networks, IPSN 2007, pp. 176–185. ACM, New York (2007)

11. Gao, S., Zhang, H., Das, S.K.: Efficient data collection in wireless sensor networks with path-constrained mobile sinks. IEEE Transactions on Mobile Computing **10**(4), 592–608 (2011)

12. Giorgetti, A., Lucchi, M., Chiani, M., Win, M.Z.: Throughput per pass for data aggregation from a wireless sensor network via a uav. IEEE Transactions on Aerospace and Electronic Systems **47**(4), 2610–2626 (2011)

13. Gu, Y., Bozdag, D., Ekici, E., Özgüner, F., Lee, C.-G.: Partitioning based mobile element scheduling in wireless sensor networks. In: SECON, pp. 386–395. Citeseer (2005)

14. Guerriero, F., Surace, R., Loscri, V., Natalizio, E.: A multi-objective approach for unmanned aerial vehicle routing problem with soft time windows constraints. Applied Mathematical Modelling (2013)

15. Hamida, E.B., Chelius, G.: Strategies for data dissemination to mobile sinks in wireless sensor networks. IEEE Wireless Communications **15**(6), 31–37 (2008)

16. He, L., Pan, J.: A progressive approach to reducing data collection latency in wireless sensor networks with mobile elements. IEEE Transactions on Mobile Computing **12**(7), 1308–1320 (2013)

17. Jea, D., Somasundara, A., Srivastava, M.B.: Multiple controlled mobile elements (data mules) for data collection in sensor networks. In: Prasanna, V.K., Iyengar, S.S., Spirakis, P.G., Welsh, M. (eds.) DCOSS 2005. LNCS, vol. 3560, pp. 244–257. Springer, Heidelberg (2005)

18. Kansal, A., Somasundara, A.A., Jea, D.D., Srivastava, M.B., Estrin, D.: Intelligent fluid infrastructure for embedded networks. In: Proceedings of the 2nd International Conference on Mobile Systems, Applications, and Services, pp. 111–124. ACM (2004)

19. Li, J., Mohapatra, P.: Analytical modeling and mitigation techniques for the energy hole problem in sensor networks. Pervasive and Mobile Computing **3**(3), 233–254 (2007)

20. Liang, W., Luo, J., Xu, X.: Prolonging network lifetime via a controlled mobile sink in wireless sensor networks. In: 2010 IEEE Global Telecommunications Conference (GLOBECOM 2010), pp. 1–6. IEEE (2010)

21. Magklara, K., Zorbas, D., Razafindralambo, T.: Node discovery and replacement using mobile robot. In: Zheng, J., Mitton, N., Li, J., Lorenz, P. (eds.) ADHOC-NETS 2012. LNICST, vol. 111, pp. 59–71. Springer, Heidelberg (2013)

22. Papadimitriou, I., Georgiadis, L.: Energy-aware routing to maximize lifetime in wireless sensor networks with mobile sink. Journal of Communications Software and Systems **2**(2), 141–151 (2006)

23. Polat, B.K., Sachdeva, P., Ammar, M.H., Zegura, E.W.: Message ferries as generalized dominating sets in intermittently connected mobile networks. Pervasive and Mobile Computing **7**(2), 189–205 (2011)

24. Rao, J., Biswas, S.: Network-assisted sink navigation for distributed data gathering: Stability and delay-energy trade-offs. Computer Communications **33**(2), 160–175 (2010)

25. Rault, T., Bouabdallah, A., Challal, Y.: Wsn lifetime optimization through controlled sink mobility and packet buffering. In: Global Information Infrastructure Symposium, pp. 1–6. IEEE (2013)

26. Shah, R.C., Roy, S., Jain, S., Brunette, W.: Data mules: Modeling and analysis of a three-tier architecture for sparse sensor networks. Ad Hoc Networks **1**(2), 215–233 (2003)

27. Somasundara, A.A., Kansal, A., Jea, D.D., Estrin, D., Srivastava, M.B.: Controllably mobile infrastructure for low energy embedded networks. IEEE Transactions on Mobile Computing **5**(8), 958–973 (2006)
28. Tunca, C., Isik, S., Donmez, M.Y., Ersoy, C.: Distributed mobile sink routing for wireless sensor networks: A survey. IEEE Communications Surveys Tutorials **16**(2), 877–897 (2014)
29. Yick, J., Mukherjee, B., Ghosal, D.: Wireless sensor network survey. Computer Networks **52**(12), 2292–2330 (2008)
30. Younis, M., Senturk, I.F., Akkaya, K., Lee, S., Senel, F.: Topology management techniques for tolerating node failures in wireless sensor networks: A survey. Computer Networks (2013)
31. Zhao, W., Ammar, M.H.: Message ferrying: Proactive routing in highly-partitioned wireless ad hoc networks. In: Proceedings of the Ninth IEEE Workshop on Future Trends of the Distributed Computing Systems, FTDCS 2003, pp. 308–314. IEEE (2003)
32. Zorbas, D., Douligeris, C., Fodor, V.: Target location based sink positioning in wireless sensor networks. In: 2011 18th International Conference on Telecommunications (ICT), pp. 21–26 (May 2011)

Validation and Evaluation of the Chosen Path Planning Algorithm for Localization of Nodes Using an Unmanned Aerial Vehicle in Disaster Scenarios

Oleksandr Artemenko$^{(\boxtimes)}$, Alina Rubina, Oleg Golokolenko, Tobias Simon, Jan Römisch, and Andreas Mitschele-Thiel

Integrated Communication Systems Group, Technische Universität Ilmenau,
98693 Ilmenau, Germany
{Oleksandr.Artemenko,Alina.Rubina,Oleg.Golokolenko,
Tobias.Simon,Jan.Roemisch,Mitsch}@tu-ilmenau.de

Abstract. In this paper, a so-called LMAT (**L**ocalization algorithm with a **M**obile **A**nchor node based on **T**rilateration) path planning algorithm is being validated using simulations and evaluated in experiments using a real unmanned aerial vehicle (UAV). Our focus is to find out if the flying path used for our unique scenario, represented by a disastrous event, fulfills the required accuracy. In our scenario, we consider an UAV that moves around buildings and localizes "survived" devices inside a building. This can help to detect victims and to accelerate the rescue process. For this, fast and accurate localization is essential.

Keywords: Localization · Path planing algorithm · Mobile beacon · Disaster · Unmanned aerial vehicle · Simulation · Experiment

1 Introduction

With a rapid deployment of technology and usage of mobile devices, the role of object localization is increasing. Localization of wireless devices in wireless networks is an important and challenging task for many applications, such as healthcare monitoring, personnel and asset tracking, emergency rescue and recovery [2]. One very challenging scenario, that requires fast and accurate location estimation, is represented by the localization during or after a disastrous event. We assume a well-known Wi-Fi technology (IEEE 802.11 standard family) for the communication among nodes in this work. Furthermore, a scenario is considered in which unmanned aerial vehicle (UAV) is flying over an urban area that suffers from a disaster and measures received signal strength of 802.11 beacon frames, coming from nodes that need to be localized. The purpose of the UAV is to localize all survived devices that are Wi-Fi-enabled and can be represented by user mobile phones, notebooks, gadgets. Thus, this information might be very beneficial to accelerate the rescue process.

© Institute for Computer Sciences, Social Informatics and Telecommunications Engineering 2014
N. Mitton et al. (Eds.): ADHOCNETS 2014, LNICST 140, pp. 192–203, 2014.
DOI: 10.1007/978-3-319-13329-4_17

In our work, we concentrate on the anchor-based localization algorithms, i.e. there exists an external reference node which knows its position. The latter is represented by an UAV collecting the information for the position estimation process. Furthermore, this work focuses on a range-based localization approach that uses signal strength readings to calculate distances between nodes. Signal strength-based localization is very attractive despite its lower location accuracy in comparison to other methods. Its main benefits are low-complexity and no need in any additional hardware installations.

The related work in the field of anchor-based localization with moving beacons deals mainly with two problems: anchor placement (aka path planning) and anchor selection. Many anchor selection algorithms have been already investigated in our previous work [4]. This paper instead focuses on the validation and evaluation of a path planning algorithm which is represented by LMAT (**L**ocalization algorithm with a **M**obile **A**nchor node based on **T**rilateration) trajectory from [8]. The authors have shown that the LMAT trajectory outperforms many other trajectories in terms of localization accuracy. The goal of this paper is to confirm that the LMAT trajectory can be also applied to a new scenario represented by disasters. The main contribution of this paper is three-fold: (1) a validation of the trajectory is being provided with simulations using a signal propagation model that reflects disaster conditions, (2) an experimental evaluation using real hardware equipment that includes an UAV, smartphones and netbooks, (3) a detailed analysis and comparison of results obtained by simulations and experiments.

The rest of the paper is organized as follows. In Section 2, the overview on the anchor placement algorithms will be given. In Section 3, the simulation environment and results are presented. Then, the description of the experimental evaluation follows in Section 4. Section 5 presents a detailed analysis and comparison of the results obtained in simulations and experiments. In Section 6, conclusions are given.

2 Related Work

This work considers methods that fall into the category of localization algorithms using static nodes that need to be localized and mobile beacons (aka mobile landmarks). The latter are represented by UAVs in our scenario. Furthermore, we use geometrical relationships between a mobile beacon and static nodes in order to determine the coordinates of the latter. It has been shown in [8] that the trajectory of the mobile landmark can be crucial and has direct impact on the localization precision. For this, different path planning algorithms have been developed [5–10,13].

The idea of the path planning localization algorithms can be explained as follows. A landmark moves along some specific trajectory and broadcasts information about its position. The problem here is to find an optimal path in terms of localization accuracy and required time to complete the selected trajectory.

In [7], authors proposed three trajectories named SCAN, DOUBLE SCAN and HILBERT. It has been shown that the static trajectories help to improve localization accuracy in comparison to the random movements. Also, it was observed that SCAN performs better than HILBERT achieving a higher resolution defined as a relation between the average distance to anchors and the trajectory length. The smallest localization error was obtained using DOUBLE SCAN trajectory. However, the distance traveled must have been doubled as compared to SCAN.

In [5] and [6], authors suggest spiral-shaped and S-shaped (aka S-CURVE) trajectories. It has been shown with simulations that S-CURVE is shorter and the energy consumption is lower compared with other trajectories like CIRCLES, SCAN and HILBERT. However, due to difficult signal propagation, S-CURVE trajectory showed poor results in scenarios when unknown nodes are located close to the edges of the area of interest.

Another work in [8] compared the existing trajectories SPIRAL, SCAN, DOUBLE SCAN, and HILBERT to the so-called LMAT method (Localization algorithm with a Mobile Anchor node based on Trilateration) which was introduced by Jiang et al. The LMAT trajectory consists out of triangles that cover the whole area of interest. This guarantees that all nodes will receive beacons required for the localization process. The results show that LMAT outperforms the existing algorithms in terms of localization accuracy. Also, it has been proven that the localization error is the smallest when the triangles are equilateral.

Han et al. in [9] investigate the performance of already mentioned trajectories (LMAT, SCAN, DOUBLE SCAN, HILBERT, and SPIRAL) using a mobile anchor node. However, the authors do not use any signal propagation model. Instead, they add a noise variance to the distances between nodes being simulated during the localization process. This is not realistic since the relation between distance and estimated signal parameters is not directly proportional. It is not described explicitly how the range of the noise variance is chosen. The length of LMAT trajectory is assumed to be over 400 m. In our simulations, we consider a shorter trajectory length and much slower flying speed of an UAV to reduce negative effects of high speed movements that would destructively affect the localization results. Instead, we collect a bigger number of readings and apply a sophisticated algorithm to select the most beneficial constellation of these measurements. This results in saving energy of an UAV battery and increase of the localization accuracy. Also in our simulations, we apply an appropriate signal model that reflects a difficult signal propagation environment in case of a disaster scenario.

In [10], a pseudo formation control based trajectory algorithm is presented to determine an optimal trajectory of a moving beacon. Although authors are assuming a similar scenario as in our paper, simulations are performed using a free-space signal propagation model. For our scenario, this would result in higher localization uncertainty. A difficult signal propagation environment, that includes wall penetration, must be considered. In [10], the obtained trajectory has an adaptive character, while we are concentrating on a static path planning. Deterministic trajectories help to save energy as well as to keep the reconnaissance time predictable and as short as possible.

A so-called Z-curve path planning mechanism has been proposed in [13]. It has been proven that a Z-shaped trajectory ensures three consecutive non-collinear messages through the shortest possible path. Motivated by the need to build a path that avoids obstacles, authors developed a mechanism that uses known positions of obstacles and constructs a path with a high number of turns. However in our scenario, a lot of points, in which an UAV has to rotate changing the direction, would introduce a considerable overhead resulting in unnecessary time delays and energy waste. Furthermore, in disaster scenarios, it is not realistic to assume that there is a map of obstacles available before the reconnaissance.

Based on the above overview of the state-of-the-art path planning approaches as well as their strong and weak aspects, we have chosen LMAT trajectory for the validation and further experimental evaluations. According to the results in [13], the best efficiency with minor variations is presented by LMAT and Z-curve mechanisms. However for our scenario, Z-curve is considered to be unrealistic.

The effectiveness of the chosen path planning algorithm has to be validated. For this, simulations were performed in advance of experimental evaluation to confirm the correct choice. Next, we introduce the simulation setup.

3   Simulation Setup and Results

We assumed the following scenario: an UAV is flying over the 10x10 m area along the LMAT (see Fig.1). The trajectory consists of 500 points in which the UAV takes RSS (Received Signal Strength) measurements of signals coming from nodes to be localized. Location estimation is performed after every new measurement, building 500 intermediate results. In order to make simulations as close as possible to the reality, a state-of-the-art signal propagation model was included.

3.1   Signal Propagation Model

For our disaster scenario, it is important to consider a wireless communication between the outdoor and indoor devices. A similar scenario was investigated in [11] where RSS readings have been measured by an access point inside a building of signals emitted by a wireless device that was outside. The result of this campaign was a signal propagation model that additionally considers a wall attenuation factor:

$$P_r(d) = P_{r_o} - 10\alpha log(d) - W + X_\sigma \ [dBm], \tag{1}$$

where P_{r_o} is the path loss on a distance 1 m from a transmitter, α is the path loss exponent, W is a wall attenuation factor. X_σ represents shadowing, which is modeled as Gaussian random variable with zero mean and standard deviation σ dB [11]. This model has been applied to the experimental results obtained in our previous work [4], where a similar scenario has been investigated. It was found that the best fit is represented by the following parameters:

$P_{r_o} = -40$ dBm, $\alpha = 3.32$, $W = 4.8$ dBm, $\sigma = 3.1$ dB.

These parameters together with eq. (1) have been used in the simulation to generate RSS readings and to calculate distances according to these readings.

3.2 Anchor Selection Technique

The main idea of anchor selection is to choose the most effective constellation of the reference data sets from redundant data available for the location estimation. In our simulations, a Joint Clustering (JC) method has been used. It has been proven in our previous work in [4] that JC shows better results in terms of localization accuracy and complexity compared to other anchor selection algorithms.

The Joint Clustering method was first introduced by Youssed et al. [12]. The main idea of this method is to choose k anchors from the m strongest signal strength levels among a set of available anchors to perform a location estimation. Authors proposed to choose three measurements each from the three strongest RSS levels. In our simulation however, we extended the number k to ten in order to increase the localization precision.

Furthermore, a multilateration technique from [4] was used for the calculation of nodes' coordinates using location information of up to ten anchors and the estimated distances to these anchors. In our studies, multilateration is referred to as an algorithm that incorporates multiple reference points by minimizing the mean square distance error of these points to the unknown target position.

3.3 Simulation Results

Massive simulations were performed. For the LMAT trajectory, simulations have been repeated 1000 times, each time changing the position of the target node randomly using uniform distribution inside the area of interest. In this way, we excluded any co-dependencies. Furthermore, the simulation process was repeated twice, each time resulting in the same statistical interpretation. The simulation results in form of the Cumulative Distribution Functions (CDFs) are given in Fig. 4(a) and (b) where simulation results are presented with dashed lines. While the plot in Fig. 4(a) represents all intermediate results (500 localizations for every from 1000 repetitions), the plot in Fig. 4(b) is only based on the 500th iteration.

We observed that the average localization error less than 1 m obtained in our simulations corresponds to the order of magnitude of the localization error obtained in other works [9,10,13]. With this, we confirm that the LMAT trajectory can also be used for our scenario. For that reason, we applied LMAT trajectory to our real time experiment which is described in the next section.

4 Experimental Evaluation

There is a lot of theoretical work about path planning algorithms, but to the best of our knowledge, there are very few of them that present evaluation using experiments. For our experiments, we used a four-rotor quadrocopter (QC) that will be described below.

4.1   Experimental Setup

The experiment was conducted at the Ilmenau University of Technology, Germany. The chosen trajectory was mapped to the area of 10x10 m, according to Fig. 1.

Weather conditions at the time of the experiments are summarized in Table 1.

Table 1. Environmental conditions at the time of the experiments

Atmospheric conditions	Index
Air temperature	17.9 °C
Humidity	38,7 %
Speed of wind	5 m/s
Strength of sunlight	362,4 W/ m^2
Air pressure	985,5 hPa

During the real-time experiments a QC was flying around the area of interest according to the LMAT trajectory. Both experimental (a snapshot of one trajectory that the QC flew) and theoretical trajectories are shown in Fig. 1. Five netbooks of model ASUS Eee PC Seashell series and five Samsung Galaxy S smartphones, running Android 4.2 were chosen for our experiment. Netbooks were equipped with Wi-Fi IEEE 802.11 b/g antennas, configured to run in an ad-hoc mode. Smartphones were launched in Wi-Fi IEEE 802.11 access point mode. We have chosen the location of the nodes, in a way that four of the nodes were positioned in the corners of the area of interest and the rest were spread randomly. In this way, obtained results will show how the position of nodes influences the localization precision. The detailed coordinates of all devices is presented in Table 2. The setup of our experiment is seen in Fig. 3.

Table 2. Positions of unlocalized nodes

Equipment	Coordinates (x,y)
Smartphones	(2.5,2.5); (2,8); (10,0); (5,5); (9.5,4)
Netbooks	(0,0); (10,10); (5,1); (2.5,5); (0,10)

The description of the main QC parameters can be found in Table 3. QC was operated remotely. The experiment was repeated six times.

Next, we present a detailed analysis and comparison of the results obtained with both simulations and experiments.

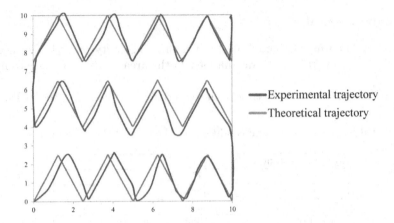

Fig. 1. Comparison of theoretical and experimental trajectories (red-colored: experimental, blue-colored: theoretical)

Table 3. Technical parameters of the quadrocopter

Technical Characteristic	Model or Parameter
Processor	600MHz Cortex A8
RAM	256MB
Gyroscope/Acceleration Sensor	MPU6050
Magnetic Field Sensor	HMC5883L
GPS Receiver	UBLOX6
Barometric Pressure Sensor	MS5611
Ultrasonic Sensor	MaxSonar I2CXL
Operating System	Gentoo Linux
Flight and Measurement Software	PengPilot (www.github.com/PenguPilot)

5   Detailed Analysis and Comparison of the Results

To evaluate the performance of the chosen trajectory and the signal propagation model used in both simulations and experiments, we have used several metrics. First, we compare the heat diagrams of the signal strength derived with simulations and experimental data. Next, we calculate an average localization error in meters, to obtain the accuracy of the localization. For the selection of anchors, we have applied three different anchor selection algorithms, which will also be reflected in the plots. Since both netbooks and smartphones were used in our experiments, we compare the location estimation accuracy between these two device types. Moreover, we observe a relationship between nodes' positions and localization error.

1. **Accuracy of the applied signal propagation model:** According to the data collected by QC, the heat diagram of the received signal strength was

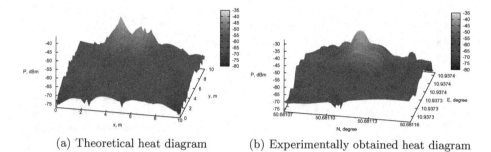

(a) Theoretical heat diagram   (b) Experimentally obtained heat diagram

Fig. 2. Heat diagrams of the signal strength for the target node located at the coordinate (4.9 m, 6 m) in simulations and (5 m, 5 m) in experiments

Fig. 3. The working area of the performed experiment. Size of the marked area is 10x10 m.

created. It can be observed in Fig. 2(b). In comparison to the heat diagram derived from our simulation results (Fig. 2(a)), the experimental one shows higher and more frequent fluctuations. The simulated signal strength is decaying more or less equally in all directions, which is different in Fig. 2(b). This happens due to the fact that in the simulation, shadowing is assumed to be normally distributed. In the reality this is not the case.

However, we can see that both have approximately the same received strength range, varying from -35 dBm to -70 dBm. This shows that implemented signal propagation model gives results which are close to the reality due to two factors. First of all, the wall attenuation factor was taken into account and secondly shadowing was modeled as a random Gaussian variable, the importance of which was discussed earlier. This shows that implemented signal propagation model can be applied to disaster scenarios.

2. **The type of anchor selection algorithm**: Fig. 4(a) and Fig. 4(b) show the cumulative distribution function of the localization error obtained from simulation and experimental data. While the plots in Fig. 4(a) represent all

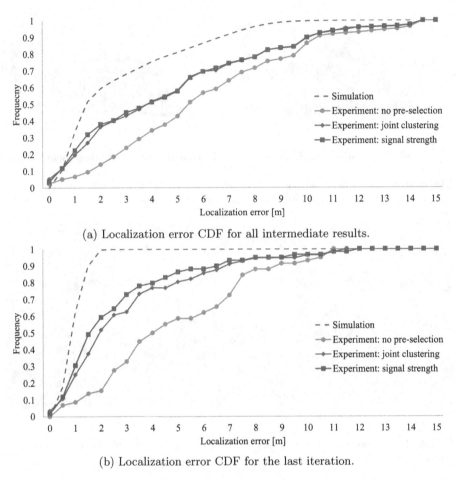

(a) Localization error CDF for all intermediate results.

(b) Localization error CDF for the last iteration.

Fig. 4. Simulated and experimentally obtained localization error CDFs. Three different anchor selection algorithms were applied to the experimental data.

intermediate results, plots in Figure 4(b) are only based on the last iteration. Here, we also compare the performance of different anchor selection algorithms. In our simulation we used Joint Clustering (JC) method only which was explained in the previous chapter. For experimentally obtained data, besides JC, we applied further two methods from our previous work in [4]: (1) signal strength-based method (SS) and (2) algorithm which does not have any pre-selection criteria and incorporates all available data sets using multilateration method to calculate a corresponding coordinate. The key observations here are the following. The smallest localization error less than 2 m was obtained by the SS method. SS method chooses data sets with the strongest signal strength for calculating the distances, ensuring the accuracy of the localization. Those data sets can all contain the signals of the same level. The selection based on JC method cannot choose the strongest readings and just selects data sets with different signal strength levels. In the real world, this can lead to a collinear constellation of data sets selected because, as we have seen in the heat diagram (Fig. 2), the signal strength drops not uniformly in all directions.

The worst results in terms of the accuracy are presented by the method with no pre-selection criteria. Due to the obvious bias in the distribution of signal strength over the area of interest, the precision of this method will always depend on the overall picture of the signal strength distribution and not only on the data sets with strongest signals. The higher the bias of the overall signal distribution is, the higher the resulting localization error will be.

3. **Location of the nodes**: Here, we investigated how the position of nodes affects the localization precision. We placed four nodes in the corners of the area of interest and other six were located randomly inside the area. Figure 5 plots the difference between the CDFs for the nodes located inside the area and in the corners ($CDF_{difference} = CDF_{inside} - CDF_{incorners}$). It was observed that, basically, the devices which are inside the area are localized better than the nodes in the corners. For small localization errors (less than 2 m) difference is around 20 %. For JC and SS methods, difference varies in the range of 10-20 % also for medium errors (3-10 m). As a conclusion, both JC and SS approaches tolerate, to some extend (10-20 %), even such obviously difficult positions like the corners.

For the multilateration with no pre-selection, we get the biggest difference in the localization precision depending on the location of nodes. As can be seen in Fig. 5, the difference reaches even 65 %. Obviously, this is due to the fact that the position estimation deals in such a case with a big number of data sets that all are located on one side of the node presenting a trend: the bigger the number of readings is, the bigger the localization error will be.

Concluding, the trajectory has to be constructed considering an UAV going beyond the borders of the area where unlocalized nodes are expected to be found. This will ensure non-collinear data sets, even though it will increase the path length and flying time.

4. **The type of the device**: Analysis of the obtained data from experiments for smartphones and netbooks has shown that there is almost no obvious relationship in localization precision between these two types of devices. This can be seen in the Fig. 6. The difference varies in the range of 0-30 %. The overall difference is not significant. However, smartphones tend to be localized better than netbooks. This can be due to following reasons. The signals emitted by smartphones are generally weaker and show significantly bigger standard deviation in signal strength than the netbooks. As a result, obvious picks are constructed within the area of interest leading to a smaller uncertainty. It is expected that this effect will neglect if the area of interest will increase.

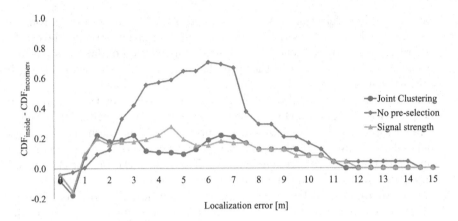

Fig. 5. Difference between localization error CDFs of nodes located inside the area of interest and in the corners as $CDF_{difference} = CDF_{inside} - CDF_{incorners}$

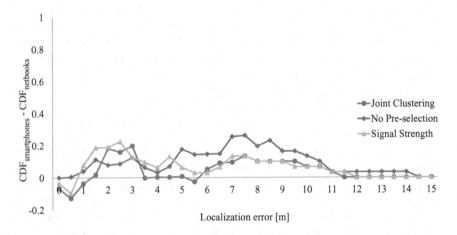

Fig. 6. Difference for localization error CDFs of smartphones and netbooks as $CDF_{difference} = CDF_{smartphones} - CDF_{netbooks}$

6   Conclusions

In this paper, the LMAT trajectory has been validated using simulations and evaluated using experiments with a flying UAV. It is to conclude that this path planning algorithm can be applied for disaster scenarios. Furthermore, our experimental evaluation has shown that implemented signal propagation model allows performing simulations which are very similar to the real world. In the experiments, the most accurate results have been obtained using a simple signal strength-based selection algorithm. This algorithm performs the best in tolerating signal strength readings highly biased by the environment.

Furthermore, we observed a clear relationship in localization error between nodes positioned inside the area of interest and in its corners. The nodes inside the area are localized significantly better than the nodes in the corners. Constructing a path, one has to consider an UAV going beyond the borders of the area where unlocalized nodes are expected to be found to ensure equal localization precision of all nodes.

References

1. Huang, L., Wang, F., Ma, C., Duan, W.: The Analysis of Anchor Placement for Self-localization Algorithm in Wireless Sensor Networks. In: Wang, R., Xiao, F. (eds.) CWSN 2012. CCIS, vol. 334, pp. 117–126. Springer, Heidelberg (2013)
2. Zekavat, S.A., Buehrer, R.M.: Handbook of position location: Theory, Practice, and Advances. Wiley-IEEE Press (2011)
3. Yick, J., Mukherjee, B., Ghosal, D.: Wireless sensor network survey. Comput. Netw. **52**(12), 2292–2330 (2008)
4. Artemenko, O., Simon, T., Mitschele-Thiel, A. Schulz, D., Ta, R.S.: Comparison of anchor selection algorithms for improvement of position estimation during the wi-fi localization process in disaster scenario. In: IEEE LCN, pp. 44–49 (2012)
5. Zhen Hu, Z.S., Gu, D., Li, H.: Localization in wireless sensor networks using a mobile anchor node. In: IEEE ASME (2008)
6. Huang, R., Zruba, G.V.: Static path planning for mobile beacons to localize sensor networks. In: PerCom Workshops. IEEE Computer Society, pp. 323–330 (2007)
7. Koutsonikolas, D., Das, S.M., Hu, Y.C.: Path planning of mobile landmarks for localization in wireless sensor networks. Computer Communications **30**(13), 2577–2592 (2007)
8. Jiang, J., Han, G., Xu, H., Shu, L., Guizani, M.: Lmat: Localization with a mobile anchor node based on trilateration in wireless sensor networks. In: IEEE GLOBE-COM. IEEE, pp. 1–6 (2011)
9. Han, G., Xu, H., Jiang, J., Shu, L., Hara, T., Nishio, S.: Path planning using a mobile anchor node based on trilateration in wireless sensor networks. Wireless Communications and Mobile Computing **13**(14), 1324–1336 (2013)
10. Miles, J., Kamath, G., Muknahallipatna, S., Stefanovic, M., Kubichek, R.F.: Optimal trajectory determination of a single moving beacon for efficient localization in a mobile ad-hoc network. Ad Hoc Networks **11**(1), 238–256 (2013)
11. Faria, D.B.: Modeling Signal Attenuation in IEEE 802.11 Wireless LANs - vol. 1, Kiwi Project, Stanford University, Tech. Rep. TR-KP06-0118 (2006)
12. Youssed, M., Agrawala, A.: Location-clustering techniques for energy-efficient wlan location determination systems. The International Journal of Computers and Applications 28(3) (2006)
13. Rezazadeh, J., Moradi, M., Ismail, A., Dutkiewicz, E.: Superior Path Planning Mechanism for Mobile Beacon-Assisted Localization in Wireless Sensor Networks. IEEE Sensors Journal **PP**(99), 1–13 (2014)

Efficient Algorithms for Characteristic Wireless Power Transfer Problems in Sensor Networks

Sotiris Nikoletseas[1,2] and Theofanis P. Raptis[1,2(✉)]

[1] Department of Computer Engineering and Informatics,
University of Patras, Patras, Greece
nikole@cti.gr
[2] Computer Technology Institute and Press "Diophantus", Patras, Greece
traptis@ceid.upatras.gr

Abstract. In Wireless Rechargeable Sensor Networks, one or more special mobile entities (called the Mobile Chargers) traverse the network and wirelessly replenish the energy of sensor nodes, using wireless power transfer technology. In this paper, we present some state of the art algorithms that apply to characteristic problems in such networks, namely efficient use of wireless power transfer using i) one Mobile Charger, ii) multiple Mobile Chargers, iii) collaborative mobile charging.

Keywords: Wireless Power Transfer · Wireless Sensor Networks · Energy Management · Distributed Algorithms · Mobility

1 Introduction and Model

Wireless Rechargeable Sensor Networks have recently attracted much research interest (e.g. [2], [3], [4], [6]). In this paper, we review some state of the art algorithms that apply to characteristic problems in Wireless Rechargeable Sensor Networks: (a) how can we use a single Mobile Charger efficiently ([1]), (b) how can we use multiple Mobile Chargers efficiently ([5]) and (c) how can we use multiple Mobile Chargers, capable of charging each other, efficiently.

Our model features three types of devices: stationary sensors, Mobile Chargers and one stationary Sink. We assume that there are N sensors of wireless communication range r distributed at random in a circular area of radius R. We virtually divide the network into Slices, the number of which is equal to the number of the Mobile Chargers. K Mobile Chargers initially deployed at coordinates $(x, y) = (\frac{R}{2} \cos(\frac{\pi}{K}(2j-1)), \frac{R}{2} \sin(\frac{\pi}{K}(2j-1)))$ of the circular area, where

S. Nikoletseas: Research supported by the European Social Fund (ESF) and Greek national funds through the Operational Program "Education and Lifelong Learning" of the National Strategic Reference Framework (NSRF) - Research Funding Program: Thalis-DISFER, Investing in knowledge society through the European Social Fund.

T.P. Raptis: Research supported by the EU/FIRE IoT Lab project - STREP ICT-610477.

© Institute for Computer Sciences, Social Informatics and Telecommunications Engineering 2014
N. Mitton et al. (Eds.): ADHOCNETS 2014, LNICST 140, pp. 204–215, 2014.
DOI: 10.1007/978-3-319-13329-4_18

$j = 1, 2, ..., K - 1$ (one Mobile Charger per Slice). In the case where $K = 1$, the Mobile Charger is initially deployed at the centre of the circular area. The Sink lies at the centre of the circular area. In our model we assume that the Mobile Chargers do not perform any data gathering process.

We denote by E_{total} the total available energy in the network. Initially, $E_{total} = E_{sensors} + E_{MC}(t_{init})$ where $E_{sensors}$ is the amount of energy shared among the sensor nodes and $E_{MC}(t_{init})$ is the total amount of energy that the Mobile Chargers have and may deliver to the network by charging sensor nodes. The maximum amount of energy that a single node and a single charger may store is E_{sensor}^{max} and E_{MC}^{max} respectively. Energy is split among the sensor nodes and the chargers as follows: $E_{sensor}^{max} = \frac{E_{sensors}}{N}$ and $E_{MC}^{max} = \frac{E_{MC}(t_{init})}{K}$. We denote as E_i and E_j the residual energy of sensor node i and Mobile Charger j respectively.

In our model the charging is performed point-to-point, i.e. only one sensor may be charged at a time from a Mobile Charger by approaching it at a very close distance so that the charging process has maximum efficiency. The time that elapses while the Mobile Charger moves from one sensor to another is considered to be very small when compared to the charging time; still the trajectory followed (and particularly its length) is of interest to us, since it may capture diverse cost aspects, like gas or electric power needed for charger movement. We assume that the charging time is equal for every sensor and independent of its battery status.

We assume a quite heterogeneous data generation model. Each sensor node chooses independently a relative data generation rate $\lambda_i \in [a, b]$ (where a, b constant values) according to the uniform distribution $\mathcal{U}[a, b]$. Values of λ_i close to a imply low data generation rate and values close to b imply high data generation rate. The routing protocol operates at the network layer, so we are assuming appropriate underlying data-link, MAC and physical layers.

1.1 Energy/Flow Criticality

In order to develop efficient algorithms for the Mobile Charger and address the corresponding trade-offs, we introduce *an attribute that captures a node's "importance"* in the network, under any given routing protocol. This attribute relies on two factors, (a) the *traffic served* by the node and (b) the *energy consumed* by the node.

The need for combining these two factors emerges from the fact that the traffic served by a node captures different aspects than its energy consumption rate. A node may consume a large amount of energy either because it serves a high network flow, or because its transmissions have high cost (e.g. long ranged transmissions) (or both). The purpose of the attribute is to indirectly prioritize the nodes according to their flow rate and energy consumption; a node serving high traffic and/or having low residual energy should be charged at higher energy level.

We denote as $c_i(t)$ the *energy/flow criticality* (also referred as criticality for simplicity) of node v_i at time t, with $c_i(t) = f_i(t) \cdot \rho_i(t)$. Given the time t_{MC}

when the last charging of the node occurred,

$$f_i(t) = 1 - \frac{generation\ rate\ of\ node\ v_i}{traffic\ rate\ of\ v_i\ since\ t_{MC}} = 1 - \frac{\lambda_i}{\lambda_i + \frac{m_i(t)}{t - t_{MC}}}$$

is the *normalized traffic flow* served by node v_i, where $m_i(t)$ *is amount of traffic (number of messages) that v_i has processed (received and forwarded) towards the Sink by time t since time t_{MC}*, and

$$\rho_i(t) = \frac{energy\ consumed\ since\ last\ charging}{max\ node\ energy\ since\ t_{MC}} = \frac{E_i(t_{MC}) - E_i(t)}{E_i(t_{MC})} = 1 - \frac{E_i(t)}{E_i(t_{MC})}$$

is the *normalized energy consumption* by time t, since the last charging. The criticality is thus a number in $[0, 1]$ which captures the importance of a given node by taking into account its flow rate, its energy consumption, its possible special role in the network and its influence to the routing protocol; nodes serving high traffic (large $m_i(t)$) and/or having consumed a lot of energy (low $E_i(t)$) have high criticality $c_i(t)$ at time t and *are "prioritized"* by the Mobile Charger.

2   Algorithms Using a Single Mobile Charger

2.1   Global Knowledge Algorithm GK

The global-knowledge charger we suggest is an on-line method that uses criticality as a ranking function. In each round, the charger moves to the sensor that minimizes the product of the negation of each node's criticality times its distance from the current position of the Mobile Charger. More specifically, in each moving step the GK minimizes the product

$$\min_i \left\{ (2 - c_i(t)) \cdot \left(1 + \frac{dist_i}{2R} \right) \right\}$$

where $dist_i$ is the distance of each sensor from the Mobile Charger and D is the network radius, with the minimum taken over all sensors in the network (or at least a large part of it). In other words, *this algorithm prioritizes nodes with high criticality and small distance to the Mobile Charger.* Since this algorithm requires *a global knowledge of the state of the network,* it is expected to outperform all other strategies that use only local or limited network information, thus somehow representing an on-line centralized performance upper bound. However, it would not be suitable for large scale networks as it introduces great communication overhead (i.e. every node has to propagate its criticality to the Mobile Charger) and does not scale well with network size.

2.2   Limited Reporting Algorithm LR

The Sink is informed about the status of some representative nodes scattered throughout the network and is able to provide the Mobile Charger with some guidance. In other words, this algorithm distributively and efficiently "simulates" the global knowledge algorithm. We assume that the Sink can transmit to the Mobile Charger wherever in the network the latter might be. The algorithm follows a limited reporting strategy, since it exploits information from the whole network area but from a limited number of nodes. The nodes of each Slice periodically run a small computation overhead algorithm in order to elect some special nodes, the *reporters* of the Slice; in particular, each node becomes a reporter independently with some appropriate probability (thus, the number of reporters is binomially distributed). The reporters act as the representatives of their Slice and their task is the briefing of the Sink about their criticality.

The *percentage of the nodes that will act as reporters* brings off a trade-off between the representation granularity of the network and the communication overhead on each message propagated in the network. If we set a large percentage of reporters, the Sink will have a more detailed knowledge of each Slice's overall criticality but the message overhead will highly increase, since each message should carry the Slice reporter's current criticality. On the contrary, if we set a small percentage of reporters, the overhead will be tolerable, but the representation of a Slice will be less detailed.

In order to maintain *a small set of reporters* for each Slice (for communication overhead purposes) we propose that Slice i which contains n_i nodes elects $\kappa_i = \frac{n_i}{N} \cdot \kappa_{total}$ reporters, with the global number of reporters being

$$\kappa_{total} = h \frac{R}{r} \log N, \text{ where } h = 1 - \frac{a}{b}$$

is a network density heterogeneity parameter. Clearly, a highly heterogeneous deployment (large b compared to a) will necessitate a higher number κ_{total} of reporters. Also, κ_{total} must be large in large networks with many sensors. Each node periodically with probability p_i becomes a reporter. In order to have an expected number of κ_i reporters in Slice i we need:

$$\kappa_i = n_i \cdot p_i \Rightarrow p_i = \frac{\frac{n_i}{N} \cdot \kappa_{total}}{n_i} \Rightarrow p_i = \frac{\kappa_{total}}{N}$$

The reporter selection is meant to happen in a local and distributed manner, i.e. each node becomes a reporter with the above suitably, independently chosen probability. This random independent generation of reporters is captured by Bernoulli trials (one per node) i.e. a binomial distribution. In order to figure out possible good values for κ_{total} that maximize the LR performance we carry out a comparison operating the protocol between several reporter numbers (Fig. 1).

2.3   Reactive Trajectory Algorithm RT

In this algorithm, a node v_i is propagating an *alert message* to its neighbours each time its energy drops below a set of some crucial limits. The messages are propagated for some hops and are stored at every node passed, in order for a *tree structure* rooted at v_i to be formed that can be *detected by the Mobile Charger*

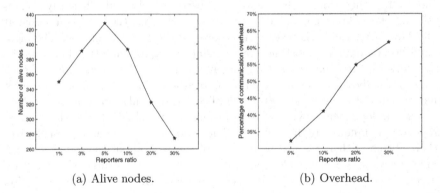

(a) Alive nodes.   (b) Overhead.

Fig. 1. Alive nodes and communication overhead for various κ_{total} values in LR, after 6000 generated events

when passing through some tree node. Every node can root a tree and the strategy followed (towards a small tree management overhead) is the maintenance of a small tree degree with a larger tree depth.

The tree that is formed for each node is gradually growing, in an analogous way to the criticality of the root node, as the gradual increase of a node's criticality is an indication of either high traffic or high energy consumption. *We use criticality as a measure of the gradual expansion of the tree,* since its value depicts both the importance of the node in the network and its energy consumption rate. We propose a strategy of message propagations that aims at covering a relatively large area of the network, while keeping energy consumption due to communication overhead low.

More specifically, each node v_i can alter among $\left\lceil \log\left(N\frac{R}{r}\right)\right\rceil$ alert levels which determine the characteristics of the v_i's rooted tree. We denote as al_i the current *alert level* of node v_i. The tree rooted at v_i is formed in a way that the *degree* = $al_i - 1$ and the *depth* = $2^{al_i-1} - 1$. The duration of each successive alert level is increased by a constant ratio from the previous level:

$$al_i = \begin{cases} 1 & \text{if } 0 \le c_i(t) < 0.5 \\ 2 & \text{if } 0.5 \le c_i(t) < 0.75 \\ \vdots & \quad\vdots \\ \left\lceil \log\left(N\frac{R}{r}\right)\right\rceil & \text{if } 1 - \frac{1}{2^{\left\lceil \log\left(N\frac{R}{r}\right)\right\rceil - 1}} \le c_i(t) < 1 \end{cases}$$

$$= \left\{ \mu \mid \mu \in \left[1, 2, ..., \left\lceil \log\left(N\frac{R}{r}\right)\right\rceil\right]\right\}$$

with $1 - \frac{1}{2^{\mu-1}} \le c_i(t) < 1 - \frac{1}{2^{\mu}}$ where $1 - \frac{1}{2^{\mu-1}} = \sum_{j=1}^{\mu-1}\frac{1}{2^j}, 1 - \frac{1}{2^{\mu}} = \sum_{j=1}^{\mu}\frac{1}{2^j}$.

The tree management procedure aims at providing a high level information about the local trees' state and at the same time at maintaining the node memory reservation at relatively low levels. For this reason, nodes store information solely about their parent nodes in emerging tree structures (i.e. one record per parent). Node v_i which is already a tree member, may receive alert messages coming from nodes that belong to other trees. In this case, v_i stores the received alert messages from surrounding parents, the number of which is at most equal to the number of v_i's neighbors (since a parent node of v_i can only be in its transmission range). Nodes that participate in multiple trees, propagate messages concerning solely the highest alert level and redirect the Mobile charger (when the latter is near the current node) to follow the highest alert level tree links. In short, each node can participate in multiple trees, reserves memory at most equal to the number of its neighbors, propagates messages about the highest priority tree and redirects the Mobile Charger to it.

The Mobile Charger alters its state between a *patrol mode* and a *charging mode*. When in patrol mode, it follows a spiral patrol trajectory centred at the Sink and does not charge any nodes until notified that the area traversed is low on energy. When so notified by a node in such an area, it pauses the patrol mode and enters the charging mode, in which it follows a different trajectory in order to accomplish the charging process in this area. If the Mobile Charger detects simultaneously different trees, then by a check on the *depth* of each structure it can decide which is the most critical. After the completion of the charging process the Mobile Charger resumes the patrol mode.

3 Algorithms Using Multiple Mobile Chargers

3.1 Centralized Coordination Algorithm CC

The CC protocol performs centralized coordination among the chargers and assumes no knowledge on the network. In particular, the coordination process is able to use information from all Mobile Chargers (energy status, position etc), but is agnostic of the underlying network and sensor nodes attributes (energy status, position etc.). This approach virtually partitions the network elements in two completely separate levels, the Mobile Chargers level and the sensor nodes level.

Coordination phase. Each Mobile Charger is assigned to a network region. Since the initial charger deployment coordinates are $(x, y) = (\frac{R}{2} \cos(\frac{\pi}{K}(2j - 1)), \frac{R}{2} \sin(\frac{\pi}{K}(2j - 1)))$, where $j = 1, 2, ..., K$, we can split the network area in Slices, with one charger assigned to each Slice. When the coordination process is initialized, the region of each charger is computed. Each charger should be assigned to a region of size analogous to its current energy level, so that the energy dissipation among the chargers is balanced. In order to compute the size of the region of charger j, it suffices to compute the central angle ϕ_j corresponding to the charger's Slice. In particular

$$\phi_j = 2\pi \cdot \frac{E_j}{\sum_{j=1}^{K} E_j}, \text{ where } \sum_{j=1}^{K} \phi_j = 2\pi.$$

Charging phase. During this phase, charger j traverses the network region it is assigned to (Slice defined by angle ϕ_j) and charges the corresponding sensor nodes. The CC algorithm assumes no knowledge on the network. For this reason the path followed by the Mobile Charger is restricted to several naive alternatives. In our approach we use a "blind" scanning of the region where the Mobile Charger starts form the Sink and traverses an exhaustive path until it reaches the boundaries of the network area. The advantage of this movement is that due to its space filling attributes, the Mobile Charger covers the whole Slice and almost every node is charged, until the energy of the Mobile Charger is totally depleted. On the other hand, due to lack of knowledge, this movement is not adaptive, i.e. it does not take into account differences of the energy depletion rates of the network area caused by the underlying message propagation.

3.2   Distributed Coordination Algorithm DC

Coordination phase. The DC algorithm performs distributed coordination among chargers and assumes no network knowledge. We split the network area in Slices and assign one Slice per charger. Angle ϕ_j corresponds to the central angle of jth charger's Slice. The chargers distributively define their Slice limits (i.e. the two radii that define the Slice), according to the size of the region each one can handle, w.r.t. their energy status. Each charger can shift their right and left Slice limits resulting in either a widening or a shrinkage of the region of interest. This task is performed distributively and each region limit movement is determined through a cooperation of the two adjacent Mobile Chargers. A limit movement of j's region is expressed as a change of ϕ_j. The coordination process uses two critical charger parameters for definition the region of interest, the charger's current energy level E_j and the charger's energy consumption rate since the last coordination ρ_j. The change $\Delta\phi_j^l$ of ϕ_j for the left Slice limit and the change $\Delta\phi_j^r$ of ϕ_j for the right are defined by the following computations:

if $\min\{E_j, E_{j-1}\} = E_j$ then
$$\Delta\phi_j^l = -\phi_j \cdot \frac{|\rho_{j-1}-\rho_j|}{\max\{\rho_{j-1},\rho_j\}}$$
else
$$\Delta\phi_j^l = \phi_{j-1} \cdot \frac{|\rho_{j-1}-\rho_j|}{\max\{\rho_{j-1},\rho_j\}}$$
end if

if $\min\{E_j, E_{j+1}\} = E_j$ then
$$\Delta\phi_j^r = -\phi_j \cdot \frac{|\rho_j-\rho_{j+1}|}{\max\{\rho_j,\rho_{j+1}\}}$$
else
$$\Delta\phi_j^r = \phi_{j+1} \cdot \frac{|\rho_j-\rho_{j+1}|}{\max\{\rho_j,\rho_{j+1}\}}$$
end if

The new angle (denoted by ϕ_j') is computed as $\phi_j' = \phi_j + \Delta\phi_j^l + \Delta\phi_j^r$. Note that, between two adjacent chargers j_1 and j_2, the change of their common slice limit is $\Delta\phi_{j_1}^r = -\Delta\phi_{j_2}^l$ so that the charger with the lower energy level provides its neighbor with a portion of its region of interest. Also, it is their energy level that determines which charger should reduce its region of interest and the energy consumption rate that determines the size of the reduced area. The size of the angle change is not computed by considering the energy levels of the two chargers because energy consumption rate shows how quickly will this energy level be reduced. For example, if ρ_j is high then j's Slice is critical, causing a rapid reduction of E_j, independently of its current level.

Charging phase. Since this algorithm operates under the no knowledge assumption, the charging phase follows the same pattern with the CC algorithm (Slice scanning).

3.3   Centralized Coordination Global Knowledge Algorithm CCGK

The CCGK algorithm, similarly to the CC algorithm, performs centralized coordination. However, the assumption of global knowledge on the network further extends the Mobile Chargers' abilities. For this reason, it is expected to outperform all other strategies that use only local information, thus somehow representing a performance bound. The global knowledge assumption would be unrealistic for real large-scale networks, as it introduces large communication overhead (i.e. nodes and chargers have to propagate their status over large distances).

Coordination phase. Instead of using the same coordination process with the CC algorithm, we integrate the global knowledge assumption in the coordination phase. As a result, the network is not partitioned in two separate levels (Mobile Chargers, sensor nodes) and the Mobile Chargers are allowed to use network information during this phase. Each Mobile Charger is assigned to a network region. The region of interest of charger j is a cluster of nodes. Node i belongs to the cluster of charger

$$j' = \arg\min_{j} \left\{ \left(1 + \frac{dist_{ij}}{2R}\right) \cdot \left(2 - \frac{E_j}{E_{MC}^{max}}\right) \right\}$$

where $dist_{ij}$ is the distance between node i and charger j. In other words, a node selects a charger which is close and with high amount of energy. Note that the centralized computation of the charger region in the CCGK algorithm is more powerful compared to other methods, since it uses information about the distance among every charger with every node.

Charging phase. The global knowledge charging phase we suggest uses energy and distance in a ranking function. In each round the charger moves to the sensor in the corresponding cluster, that minimizes the product of each node's energy times its distance from the current position of the Mobile Charger. More specifically, in each moving step the charger j charges node

$$i' = \arg\min_{i \in C_j} \left\{ \left(1 + \frac{dist_{ij}}{2R}\right) \cdot \left(1 + \frac{E_i}{E_{sensor}^{max}}\right) \right\}.$$

In other words, this algorithm prioritizes nodes with low energy and small distance to the Mobile Charger.

3.4   Distributed Coordination Local Knowledge Algorithm DCLK

Coordination phase. The coordination phase follows the same pattern with the coordination phase of DC algorithm (distributed ϕ_j angle computation).

Charging phase. The DCLK algorithm operates with local knowledge assumption. The Slice corresponding to charger j is divided into k Sectors S_{jk} of the same width. Charger j prioritizes its Sectors w.r.t. high number of sensor nodes with low level of residual energy.

Definition 1. $E_{jk}^{\min}$ *is the lowest nodal residual energy level in the Sector S_{jk}.*

Definition 2. $E_{jk}^{\min+\Delta}$ *is an energy level close to $E_{jk}^{\min}$:*

$$E_{jk}^{\min+\Delta} = E_{jk}^{\min} + \delta \cdot \frac{E_{sensor}^{\max}}{E_{jk}^{\min}}, \delta \in (0,1).$$

Definition 3. $N(S_{jk})$ *is the number of nodes in Sector S_{jk} with residual energy between $E_{jk}^{\min}$ and $E_{\min+\Delta}^{jk}$:*

$$N(S_{jk}) = \sum_{e=E_{jk}^{\min}}^{E_{jk}^{\min+\Delta}} N(e)$$

where $N(e)$ is the number of nodes with energy level e.

Charger j charges Sector S_{jk} which maximizes the product $\max_{S_{jk}}\{N(S_{jk}) \cdot (E_{sensor}^{\max} - E_{jk}^{\min})\}$. The intuition behind this charging process is the grouping of nodes in each Slice and the selection of a critical group. A critical group is a Sector containing a large number of sensor nodes that require more energy than other nodes throughout the network.

4   Algorithms Using Hierarchical Collaborative Mobile Charging

4.1   Model Variation

In this case, Mobile Chargers can either charge nodes or charge other Mobile Chargers. Initially, $E_{total} = E_{sensors} + E_{MC}(t_{init}) + E_{SC}(t_{init})$, where $E_{sensors}$ is the total amount of energy shared among the sensor nodes, $E_{MC}(t_{init})$ is the total amount of energy shared among the Mobile Chargers and $E_{SC}(t_{init})$ is the total amount of energy shared among the Special Chargers. The maximum amount of energy that a single node, a single Mobile Charger and a single Special Charger may store is $E_{sensor}^{\max}$, $E_{MC}^{\max}$ and $E_{SC}^{\max}$ respectively. Energy is uniformly split among the sensor nodes and the chargers as follows: $E_{sensor}^{\max} = \frac{E_{sensors}}{N}$, $E_{MC}^{\max} = \frac{E_{MC}(t_{init})}{M}$ and $E_{SC}^{\max} = \frac{E_{SC}(t_{init})}{S}$.

At first, we deploy the sensor nodes uniformly in the circular network. Then, we divide our network into M equal sized Slices, one for each Mobile Charger. Thus, every Mobile Charger is responsible for charging nodes that belong to its Slice. We denote by D_j the set of sensor nodes that belong to Slice j, i.e. to the jth Mobile Charger's group. Finally, we divide the Mobile Chargers into S groups, one for each Special Charger. Thus, each Special Charger is responsible for charging the Mobile Chargers that belong to its group, denoted as C_k (for SC_k). Initially, these S groups are equally sized, i.e. $|C_k| = \frac{M}{S}$ $(1 \leq k \leq S)$ and the Mobile Chargers that belong to each group are given by the following formula: $C_k = \left\{ j : j \in \left[(k-1)\frac{M}{S} + 1 , \ k\frac{M}{S} \right] \right\}$, $(1 \leq k \leq S)$

These groups may change during the algorithm's coordination phase. More specifically, the Special Chargers communicate with each other and decide, according to their energy status, if they are still able to be in charge of the Mobile Chargers that belong to their group or they should delegate some of them to other Special Chargers.

4.2 1-Level Knowledge Distributed Coordination 1KDC

The 1KDC algorithm performs a distributed coordination among Special Chargers, i.e. every Special Charger can communicate with adjacent neighbors. Also, it assumes 1-level network knowledge, i.e. it can use information only about Mobile Chargers' energy status (and not about the sensors' which lie one level lower). **Coordination phase**: In distributed coordination, we assume that a Special Charger knows which are the adjacent Mobile Chargers on the boundaries of its region. We call next the first Mobile Charger that belongs to the SC_{k+1} and previous the last Mobile Charger that belongs to SC_{k-1}. More specifically,
$$n_k = \min_{j \in C_{k+1}} \{j\}: \text{next Mobile Charger (belongs to } SC_{k+1}) \quad p_k = \max_{j \in C_{k-1}} \{j\}: \text{pre-}$$
vious Mobile Charger (belongs to SC_{k-1})

The Special Charger SC_k, in order to coordinate with each of its neighbors (SC_{k-1} and SC_{k+1}), calculates which of them has the highest energy supplies so as to charge the Mobile Chargers in its group and the additional Mobile Charger of its left or right neighbor. Thus, every Special Charger k estimates the residual energy in both cases (including a Mobile Charger of its left and right neighbor) by the following equations:

$$e_k^p = E_{SC_k} - \sum_{j \in C_k} E_{MC_j}^{lack} - E_{MC_{p_k}}^{lack}, \ \ e_k^n = E_{SC_k} - \sum_{j \in C_k} E_{MC_j}^{lack} - E_{MC_{n_k}}^{lack}$$

where $E_{MC_j}^{lack} = E_{MC}^{\max} - E_{MC_j}$ is the amount of energy that MC_j can receive until it is fully charged.

Between two adjacent Special Chargers the one with the higher energy supplies takes the other's boundary Mobile Charger in its group. Thus, the Special Charger with lower energy supplies is responsible for a smaller area. In the case that their energy supplies are the same they do not exchange any Mobile Chargers. More precisely, the coordination algorithm is the following:

(SC_k, SC_{k-1})

    if $(e_k^p > e_{k-1}^n)$ **then**
        $C_k = C_k \bigcup \{MC_{p_k}\}$
        $C_{k-1} = C_{k-1} \setminus \{MC_{p_k}\}$
    else if $(e_k^p < e_{k-1}^n)$ **then**
        $C_{k-1} = C_{k-1} \bigcup \{MC_{n_{k-1}}\}$
        $C_k = C_k \setminus \{MC_{n_{k-1}}\}$
    else
        No Mobile Chargers exchange
    end if

(SC_k, SC_{k+1})

    if $(e_k^n > e_{k+1}^p)$ **then**
        $C_k = C_k \bigcup \{MC_{n_k}\}$
        $C_{k+1} = C_{k+1} \setminus \{MC_{n_k}\}$
    else if $(e_k^n < e_{k+1}^p)$ **then**
        $C_{k+1} = C_{k+1} \bigcup \{MC_{p_{k+1}}\}$
        $C_k = C_k \setminus \{MC_{p_{k+1}}\}$
    else
        No Mobile Chargers exchange
    end if

Trajectory: Special Charger k should determine which Mobile Charger will be the next that will be charged prioritizing a Mobile Charger based on minimum energy and minimum distance. Considering this, SC_k chooses to charge MC_m where

$$m = \arg\min_{j \in C_k} \left\{ \left(1 + \frac{E_{MC_j}}{E_{MC}^{\max}} \right) \cdot \left(1 + \frac{d_{k_j}}{2R} \right) \right\}.$$

Charging phase: A Special Charger charges a Mobile Charger j according to its energy consumption rate r_{MC_j}. More specifically, a Mobile Charger with higher consumption rate (compared to the rest Mobile Chargers that belong to the Special Charger's group) should be charged with a higher amount of energy. Motivated by that, if by MC_m we denote the Mobile Charger that Special Charger k chose to charge, then the amount of energy that the Special Charger will give to it is $e = c_m \cdot (\min\{E_{MC_m}^{lack}, E_{SC_k}\})$ where $c_m = \frac{r_{MC_m}}{\sum_{j \in C_k} r_{MC_j}}$.

4.3   2-Level Knowledge Centralized Coordination 2KCC

The 2KCC algorithm performs centralized coordination and assumes 2-level network knowledge, i.e. it can use information both about Mobile Chargers' and about the sensors' energy status. It assigns to each Special Charger an amount of Mobile Chargers according to their residual energy. More precisely:
Coordination: $|C_k| = \mathcal{E}_k \cdot M$ where $\mathcal{E}_k = \frac{E_{SC_k}}{\sum_{i=1}^{S} E_{SC_i}}$, $(1 \leq k \leq S)$.
Trajectory: Since each Special Charger assumes 2-level network knowledge, it takes into account information from both Mobile Chargers and sensor nodes in order to find good trajectories. Thus, SC_k prioritizes MC_m where

$$m = \arg\min_{j \in C_k} \left\{ \alpha \cdot \frac{E_{MC_j}}{E_{MC}^{\max}} + (1 - \alpha) \cdot \frac{\sum_{i \in D_j} E_i}{|D_j| \cdot E_{sensors}^{\max}} \right\}$$

with $\alpha \in (0,1)$ a constant allowing to select the weight of each term in the sum. We use network lifetime (one of the most indicative performance metrics) to decide which is the appropriate value of parameter α in 2KCC protocol that achieves the best performance. As shown in Fig. 2 the most suitable value is $\alpha = 1$, which is explained by the fact that when a Special Charger charges a Mobile Charger, it should take into account its energy status only.

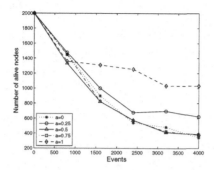

Fig. 2. Alive nodes over time (Varying α)

Charging phase: Each Special Charger computes the percentage of energy to transfer, according to the lack of energy in the Slice of the selected Mobile Charger compared to the total energy lack in all Slices that this Special Charger is responsible for. More precisely, Special Charger k transfers to MC_m an amount of energy $e = c_m \cdot \left(\min\{E_{MC_m}^{lack}, E_{SC_k}\} \right)$ where

$$c_m = \frac{\sum_{i \in \mathcal{D}_m} E_i^{lack}}{\sum_{j \in \mathcal{C}_k} \sum_{i \in \mathcal{D}_j} E_i^{lack}} \in (0, 1)$$

where $E_i^{lack} = E_{sensor}^{max} - E_i$ is the amount of energy that sensor i can receive until it is fully charged.

References

1. Angelopoulos, C.M., Nikoletseas, S., Raptis, T.P.: Wireless energy transfer in sensor networks with adaptive, limited knowledge protocols. Computer Networks **70**, 113–141 (2014)
2. Angelopoulos, C.M., Nikoletseas, S., Raptis, T.P., Raptopoulos, C., Vasilakis, F.: Improving sensor network performance with wireless energy transfer. International Journal of Ad Hoc and Ubiquitous Computing (in press, 2014)
3. Dai, H., Liu, Y., Chen, G., Wu, X., He, T.: Safe charging for wireless power transfer. In: Proceedings of the 33rd Annual IEEE International Conference on Computer Communications, INFOCOM (2014)
4. Dai, H., Wu, X., Chen, G., Xu, L., Lin, S.: Minimizing the number of mobile chargers for large-scale wireless rechargeable sensor networks. Computer Communications **46**, 54–65 (2014)
5. Madhja, A., Nikoletseas, S., Raptis, T. P.: Efficient, distributed coordination of multiple mobile chargers in sensor networks. In: Proceedings of the 16th ACM International Conference on Modeling, Analysis and Simulation of Wireless and Mobile Systems, MSWiM (2013)
6. Wang, C., Li, J., Ye, F., Yang, Y.: Netwrap: An NDN based real-time wireless recharging framework for wireless sensor networks. IEEE Transactions on Mobile Computing **13**(6), 1283–1297 (2014)

WAMN

A Proposal of the Gage-Free Safety Assessment Technique for the Steel Beam Structure Under Uncertain Loads and Support Conditions Using Motion Capture System

Jun Su Park[1,2], Byung Kwan Oh[1,2], Se Woon Choi[3], Tongjun Cho[2], Yousok Kim[2], and Hyo Seon Park[1,2(✉)]

[1] Department of Architectural Engineering, Yonsei University, Seoul, Korea
[2] Center for Structural Health Care Technology in Buildings, Yonsei University, Seoul, South Korea
{junsu,aeioobk,tjcho,yskim1220,hspark}@yonsei.ac.kr
[3] Department of Architecture, Catholic University of Daegu, Gyeongsan-si 712, South Korea
watercloud@cu.ac.kr

Abstract. Estimating the maximum stress through stress distribution of a structure is an important indicator for structural safety evaluation. Structural health monitoring can be used to do this with a variety of measuring equipment such as strain gage, LVDT, LDS. All the measuring equipment, however, has some weakness in the configuration of complex wire network and some inconvenience of replacing faulty sensors. Therefore, this paper suggests a technique that can estimate stress distribution of steel beam structure under uncertain load and support conditions by using motion capture system (MCS). MCS is a Vision-based Monitoring System, which measures 3D coordinates of multiple markers attached to the surface of steel beam without installing the complex wire network. In this study, the stress distribution is estimated from an analytic model by using displacement values measured by MCS. For the evaluation of the estimated stress distribution, comparing with the measured stress from ESG is performed.

Keywords: Structural health monitoring · Strain estimation · Structural safety · Steel beam · Maximum stress · Vision based monitoring · Motion capture

1 Introduction

In this study, a gage-free safety assessment technique for the steel beam structure is proposed. This proposed technique estimates stress distribution of the steel beam structure because the maximum stress is an important indicator for structural health monitoring. Stress distribution can be estimated from an analytic model using displacement values measured by motion capture system (MCS). MCS is a vision based monitoring system without complex wire network unlike conventional sensors such as strain gages, LVDTs, and laser displacement sensors (LDS).

© Institute for Computer Sciences, Social Informatics and Telecommunications Engineering 2014
N. Mitton et al. (Eds.): ADHOCNETS 2014, LNICST 140, pp. 219–227, 2014.
DOI: 10.1007/978-3-319-13329-4_19

As shown in figure 1, there is no complex wire network between steel beam structure and MCS. Because MCS is a vision based monitoring system that can measure
3D coordinates of markers by using reflected light from each marker.

So, this system can measure 3D coordinates of markers under the gage-free condition. But, partially, MCS Camera, Server and computer is connected by wires. In this
study, this issue is left for future research topic.

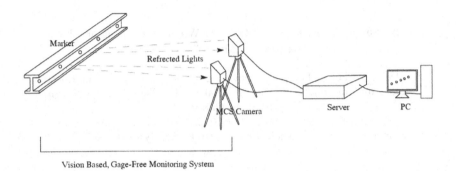

Fig. 1. Motion Capture System

From measured 3D coordinates measurement of each marker, stress distribution of
the steel beam can be estimated by interpolation as well as deformed shape of the
steel beam structure.

In order to estimate stress distribution, the radiuses of curvature of every point
should be calculated first. In this study, a cubic smoothing spline is used for interpo-
lating deformed shape of the steel beam structure, and numerical differentiation is
used for calculating the radiuses of curvature at every point of the steel beam.

Consequently, only 3D coordinates measured by MCS are needed to estimate stress
distribution, so this suggested technique in this paper is applicable to the steel beam
under uncertain load and support conditions.

2   Proposed Stress Distribution Estimating Model Using MCS

2.1   Estimate Structural Deformed Shape Using MCS

With the use of MCS, a structural deformed shape can be estimated, when 3D coordinates of markers are measured which are attached to the surface of the steel beam
structure. The markers should be attached to the measurement points on the steel
beam structure, and more than two motion capture cameras should be installed in full
view of the markers.

When the installation is complete, 3D coordinate system can be generated by wand
calibration. Then, the installed cameras measure 3D absolute coordinates of the markers on the basis of generated 3D coordinate system. Once 3D coordinates of the
markers are measured, a structural deformed shape can be estimated by finding the
difference between 3D coordinates of initial state and deformed state, and by interpo-
lating these data. In this research, cubic smoothing spline interpolation was used.

However, the generated 3D coordinate system through wand calibration may differ from the total coordinate system. Thus, it needs to be calibrated by coordinate transformation.

2.2 Estimate the Radius of Curvature from Structural Deformed Shape

When structural deformed shape is obtained, strain values at every point of structural deformed shape can be calculated from the radiuses of curvature at the same points. The relationship between strain and radius of curvature is as below.

$$\varepsilon(x) = -\frac{y}{\rho(x)} \tag{1}$$

Where y is the distance from the neutral axis and ρ is the radius of curvature.

Also, the radiuses of curvature at every point of structural deformed shape can be calculated by equation (2)

$$\rho(x) = \frac{(f'(x)^2 + 1)^{3/2}}{f''(x)} \tag{2}$$

In order to use the equation (2), it is necessary to calculate both the first derivatives and the second derivatives at every point of structural deformed shape.

For conducting numerical differentiation, structural deformed shape should be interpolated with very small intervals. In this research, cubic smoothing spline interpolation with 0.0001mm interval was used, and the first derivatives and the second derivatives at each point are calculated by numerical differentiation using Four-point central difference method (3) and Five point central difference method (4) respectively. These numerical method's equations are as below.

$$f'(x_i) = \frac{f(x_{i-2}) - 8f(x_{i-1}) + 8f(x_{i+1}) - f(x_{i+2})}{12h} \tag{3}$$

$$f''(x_i) = \frac{-f(x_{i-2}) + 16f(x_{i-1}) - 30f(x_i) + 16f(x_{i+1}) - f(x_{i+2})}{12h^2} \tag{4}$$

2.3 Estimate Strain and Stress from Radius of Curvature

Once the radiuses of curvature at each point are estimated, strain values at each point could be calculated by using equation (2).

And then, finally stress can be estimated by multiplying strain by elastic modulus. This relationship between strain and stress is as below.

$$\sigma(x) = E\varepsilon(x) = -E\frac{y}{\rho(x)} \tag{5}$$

3   Application to Stress Estimation Model of Steel Beam

3.1   Simply Supported Steel Beam Experiment

To evaluate this proposed technique of estimating stress distribution, simply support-ed steel beam experiment was conducted. In this experiment, H-shape Steel beam(100 x 100 x 6/8) was used and it was tested under two central concentrated load cases, one was 0.285tonf, and the other was 0.600tonf. Central concentrated load cases were generated by actuator.

4 motion capture cameras were installed to measure 3D coordinates at each meas-urement point of the steel beam and 17 motion capture markers (250mm space apart) were attached on the center of the web plate of the steel beam.

In order to verify applicability of estimated strain values, 14 strain gages were used as reference sensors. And these were attached on the top flange of the steel beam, 250mm space apart except for both ends and center of the steel beam.

Also, for verifying applicability of MCS as displacement measuring equipment, 5 La-ser displacement sensors were used, at 500mm, 1250mm, 2000mm, 2750mm. 3500mm, respectively. The installation view of the steel beam experiment is shown below.

Fig. 2. The Installation View of The Steel Beam Experiment

3.2   The Results of Experiment

Although 17 motion capture markers (250mm space apart) were attached to the center of steel beam web plate, only 9 markers (500mm space apart) were used for analysis. It is because cubic smoothing spline interpolation with too large number of markers resulted in distortion of curvature.

So, in this research, the structural deformed shape of the steel beam under central concentrated load was interpolated from 9 markers' 3D coordinate data (500mm space apart) by using cubic smoothing spline interpolation. From this interpolated structural deformed shape, 17 displacement data (250mm space apart) was re-estimated.

Then, as mentioned earlier, radiuses of curvature and strain values at each point (250mm space apart) were estimated. Since stress at each point can be calculated by multiplying strain of elastic modulus, the evaluation of strain values was performed only. The results of this experiment are shown below.

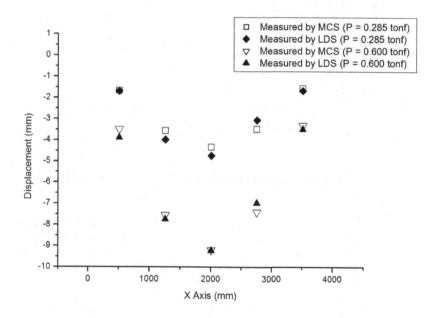

Fig. 3. Comparing with the Z-axis Displacements measured by MCS from measured by LDS

Table 1. The Error between Displacements measured by MCS from measured by LDS

X-axis (mm)	P = 0.285 tonf		P = 0.600 tonf	
	Absolute Error (mm)	Relative Error (%)	Absolute Error (mm)	Relative Error (%)
508.7	0.014	-0.839	0.397	-10.208
1256.0	0.418	-10.491	0.196	-2.533
2007.4	0.401	-8.472	0.025	-0.269
2756.5	-0.427	13.979	-0.422	6.046
3506.4	0.110	-6.603	0.191	-5.484
Average	0.274mm	8.077%	0.246mm	4.908%

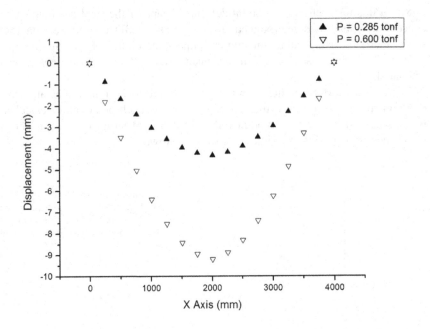

Fig. 4. Estimated Structural Deformed Shape for Each Load Case

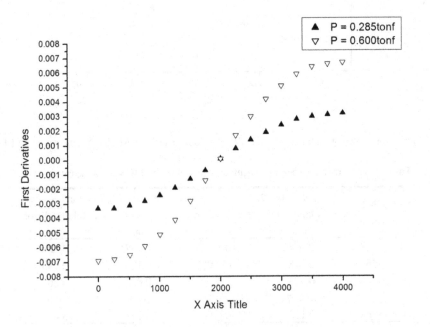

Fig. 5. Calculated First Derivatives using Four-Point Central Difference Method

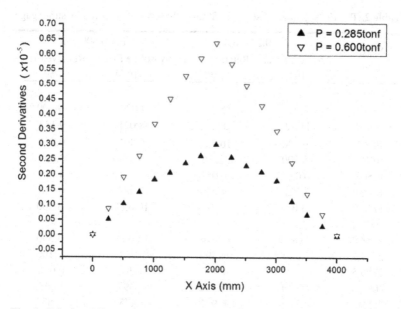

Fig. 6. Calculated Second Derivatives using Five-Point Central Difference Method

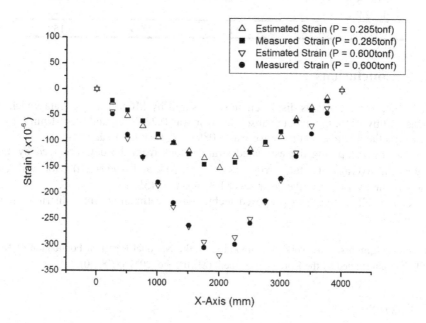

Fig. 7. Comparing with The Estimated Strain values from Measured by Strain Gages

Table 2. The Error between Estimated Strain values from measured by strain gages

X-axis (mm)	P = 0.285 tonf		P = 0.600 tonf	
	Absolute Error ($\times 10^{-6}$)	Relative Error (%)	Absolute Error ($\times 10^{-6}$)	Relative Error (%)
0.1	-	-	-	-
256.4	-3.511	15.811	4.627	-9.600
508.7	-11.422	28.280	-8.021	9.133
758.1	-9.930	16.246	-0.407	0.311
1007.0	-5.300	6.116	-5.551	3.099
1256.0	0.054	-0.052	-8.121	3.719
1506.9	5.327	-4.279	-2.482	0.948
1756.0	13.016	-9.015	10.657	-3.500
2007.4	-	-	-	-
2258.8	10.845	-7.746	13.672	-4.590
2504.7	5.910	-4.899	7.972	-3.106
2756.5	-4.404	4.382	-1.380	0.646
3007.7	-9.794	12.222	-2.497	1.463
3256.0	4.117	-6.926	7.475	-5.852
3506.4	5.046	-13.158	15.868	-18.900
3757.4	6.124	-29.994	9.268	-21.262
4002.9	-	-	-	-
Average	6.771×10^{-6}	11.366%	7.000×10^{-6}	6.152%

4   Conclusions

By comparing the Z-axis displacements measured by MCS from the data which was measured by LDS, the average absolute error was 0.2739mm and 0.2461mm for each case, and the average relative error was 8.08% and 4.91% for each case.

Also, by comparing the estimated strain values from the data obtained by strain gages, the average absolute error was 6.7715×10^{-6} and 6.9999×10^{-6} for each case, and and the average relative error was 11.37% and 6.15% for each case.

As a result of this, this proposed technique of estimating stress distribution was evaluated.

Acknowledgments. This work was supported by the National Research Foundation of Korea (NRF) Grant funded by the Korea government (MSIP) (no. 2011-0018360).

References

1. Lee, H.M., Choi, S.W.: Jung, Dong-jo., Park, H.S.: Analytical Model for Estimation of Maximum Normal Stress in Steel Beam-Columns Based on Wireless Measurement of Average Strains from Vibrating Wire Strain Gages. Computer-Aided Civil and Infrastructure Engineering **28**, 707–717 (2013)

2. Park, H.S., Kim, J.Y., Kim, J.G., Choi, S.W., Kim, Y.: A New Position Measurement System Using a Motion-Capture Camera for Wind Tunnel Tests. Sensors **13**, 12329–12344 (2013)
3. Fraser, C.S., Rieedel, B.: Monitoring the thermal deformation of steel beams via vision metrology. J. Photogramm. Remote Sens. **55**, 268–276 (2000)
4. Choi, S.W., Lee, Jihoon., Oh, B.H., Park, H.S.: Measurement Model for the Maximum Strain in Beam Structures Using Multiplexed Fiber Bragg Grating Sensors. International Journal of Distributed Sensor Networks (2013)
5. Lee, H.M., Park, H.S.: Measurement of Maximum Strain of Steel Beam Structures Based on Average Strains From Vibrating Wire Strain Gages. Experimental Techniques. **37**, 23–29 (2013)
6. Lee, J.J., Shinozuka, M.: A vision-based system for remote sensing of bridge displacement. NDT. E. Int. **39**, 425–431 (2006)
7. Corradini, M.L., Fioretti, S., Leo, T.: Numerical differentiation in movement analysis: How to standardize the evaluation of techniques. Med. Biol. Eng. Comput. **31**, 187–197 (1993)
8. Choi, S.W., Kim, B.R., Lee, H.M., Kim, Y.: A deformed Shape Monitoring Model for Building Structures Based on 2D Laser Scanner. Sensors **13**, 6746–6758 (2013)
9. Lee, H.M., Park, H.S.: Estimation of Deformed Shapes of Beam Structures using 3D Coordinate Information from Terrestrial Laser Scanning. CMES. **29**, 29–44 (2008)
10. Kang, D.S., Lee, H.M.: Computing Method for Estimating Strain and Stress of Steel Beams using Terrestrial Laser Scanning and FEM. Key Engineering Materials. **347**, 517–522 (2007)
11. Park, H.S., Jung, H.S., Kwon, Y.H., Seo, J.H.: Mathematical models for assessment of the safety of steel beams based on average strains from long gage optic sensors. Sensors and Actuators A. **125**, 109–113 (2006)
12. Hampshire, T.A., Adeli, H.: Monitoring the behavior of steel structures using distributed optical fiber sensors. Journal of Constructional Steel Research. **53**, 267–281 (2000)
13. Gere, James M.: Mechanics of Materials. Thomson-Engineering (2003)
14. GILAT, A., SUBRAMANIAM, V.: Numerical Methods for Engineering and Scientists: An Introduction with Applications using matlab. Wiley (2007)

Structural Health Monitoring of Infrastructure Using Wireless Sensor System

Dae Woong Ha[1], Jun Su Park[1], Jong Moon Kim[2], Hyo Seon Park[1(✉)]

[1] Department of Architectural Engineering, Yonsei University,
50 Yonsei-ro, Seodaemun-gu, Seoul, Korea
{dwha,junsu,hspark}@yonsei.ac.kr
[2] D S Tek, Inc., 1112, 30, Digital-ro 32-gil, Guro-gu, Seoul, Korea
dstek@dstek.biz

Abstract. In recent years, developments in construction technology have resulted in structures increasing in both size and height, with related safety concerns also increasing. These structures may pose significant risks in scenarios where they suffer significant damage, for example, from external shock or the influence of aging. This paper proposes a wireless sensor structural health monitoring (SHM) system construction and operation method for the verification of structural safety and risk determination in real time. The method first selects the sensor location and type via a simulation of the response of the structure for the construction of the SHM system. The system wirelessly receives the data from the data acquisition system used to collect the data from the sensors attached to the structure. Empirical results obtained by applying the proposed system to the monitoring of the concrete wall of a liquefied natural gas (LNG) tank and measuring the response of the structure confirm the feasibility of our proposed method.

Keywords: Structural health monitoring · Wireless sensor system · Safety of infrastructures · LNG tank

1   Introduction

Concomitant with technological developments in the construction arena, construction of huge high-rise structures is on the increase around the world. Among the high-rise buildings built recently is the Burj Khalifa in Dubai, the tallest building at 828 m. Further, several other buildings around the world have heights in excess of 400 m.

Bridges spanning seas or rivers are also increasing in length and size. One such bridge is the Su-Tong Bridge in China, which has a length of 1088 m. In addition, there are several bridges that are over 800 m in length. Dams, power plants, and gas storage facilities are also constructed as large and complex structures.

When damage occurs in these kinds of infrastructure, the ripple effect is substantial. For example, the damage to the Fukushima nuclear power plant in Japan caused by the earthquake and tsunami in 2011 has led to an ongoing global threat of exposure to radiation.

© Institute for Computer Sciences, Social Informatics and Telecommunications Engineering 2014
N. Mitton et al. (Eds.): ADHOCNETS 2014, LNICST 140, pp. 228–234, 2014.
DOI: 10.1007/978-3-319-13329-4_20

Thus, monitoring is essential to ensure that structures and infrastructure are safe. In recent times, structural health monitoring (SHM) systems are being employed to manage structures and ensure that they are safe through real-time measurements.

In the construction of an SHM system, producing the greatest effect at the lowest cost is essential. Consequently, choosing appropriate sensors and the optimal placement position through response analysis of the structure are very important. In addition, a suitable system to obtain accurate data from the sensor is also necessary.

In this paper, we propose a wireless sensor SHM system and discuss empirical measurements of the response of the concrete wall of a liquefied natural gas (LNG) tank. We also discuss the structure of the data acquisition system and the wireless sensor system utilized. In addition, we examine the economy and reality of wireless sensor systems and the SHM system, and outline how they can be usefully applied to other infrastructure.

2   Sensor Specification

In the construction of an SHM system for structure monitoring, the type of sensor employed is important. It is necessary to select a sensor that is able to measure the response of the structure to changes in the ambient environment. Thus, in this section, we discuss several types of sensors that are capable of measuring such responses.

The first type of sensor is the strain gauge sensor, which can measure the strain on the structure. Strain refers to the deformation of a material. Thus, it is possible to measure the deformation of the section on which the sensor is installed using the strain gauge. Further, because strain can be converted to mechanical stress, it is also possible to simultaneously measure the stress on those sections. The strain gauge sensor can be used electrical resistance type, voltage type, and vibrations type according to the method used to obtain the data.

An accelerometer is a sensor that can measure the dynamic response of the structure. This type of sensor can be used to measure the response of a structure to earthquake and wind. Acceleration data are important for understanding the mode shape of the structure due to environmental changes. Piezoelectric, moving coil, and micro-electro-mechanical system (MEMS) sensor types are based on this measurement principle.

A displacement sensor can measure the horizontal and vertical movements of a structure. It is used to measure the displacement of the structure by an external force both during and after construction of the structure. In the case of high-rise structures, in particular, the horizontal displacement can affect usability. Therefore, the data obtained from this type of sensor are very important. There are both contact and non-contact displacement sensors; non-contact displacement sensors are used in the case of structures.

A load cell sensor measures the load on an installation position. It is used primarily to measure the axial force applied to the vertical members of a structure. If the structure is concrete, the deformation generated in response to the axial force acting on the material are used in measuring the amount of deformation.

An inclinometer is a sensor that measures the vertical structure and the horizontal tilt. In order to measure the perpendicularity during the construction of high-rise structures, it is installed on the vertical member. It is also installed on the horizontal member in order to measure the horizontal tilt of the structure. It can also be used to measure the horizontal displacement of the ground below, especially uneven settlement of the ground, in order to guarantee safety. This sensor can be electric type, MEMS type, or optic type, according to the measuring element.

An anemometer is a sensor that is placed on the top of the structure. This sensor measures the wind speed and wind direction. The influence of the wind varies according to the shape and position of the structure; therefore, wind speed data are required. It is possible through analysis of the data to also know if the wind results in vertical and horizontal displacement of the structure

3   Proposed Wireless Sensor System

Because the structures we want to monitor are large, the amount of data obtained from the many sensors installed is also significant. In order to transfer such large amounts of data, more cable is required than the number of sensors installed.

However, cable installation is expensive and it is also difficult to work with cabling. Further, if the amount of cable used for data transfer is large, the accuracy of the data may decrease.

Consequently, we propose using a wireless sensor system in order to avoid these problems. A wireless sensor system is economical because there is no need for cables, and it is also suitable for structures that are difficult to access

The wireless sensor system proposed in this paper comprises sensors, sensor nodes and a monitoring server. The sensor nodes comprise slave nodes and master nodes.

The wireless sensor system can be divided into three stages.

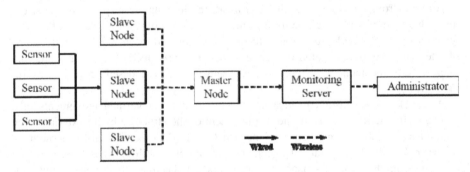

Fig. 1. Wireless sensor system

The first stage consists of slave nodes connected by wires to sensors. These slave nodes have multiple channels; consequently, they can receive data from multiple sensors concurrently.

The second stage comprises short-range wireless communication between the master and slave nodes. The slave nodes transmit sensor data to the master node via radio-frequency (RF) waves.

The third stage comprises wireless communication with the monitoring server and the master nodes. In long distance communication scenarios, code division multiple access (CDMA) is used.

The sensors are connected in parallel by wire to the slave nodes; the length of wire used is minimized. The slave nodes convert the analog data measured by the sensors into digital data. The sensor data collected in this way are sent to the master node over a relatively short distance. Short-range communication, 424 MHz ultra-high frequency (UHF) RF, is used. Texas Instruments CC1020 microprocessors are used in the wireless data conversion devices.

Each master node is installed in a position where it is possible to communicate with multiple slave nodes. Further, each master node is responsible for transmitting the data received from the slave nodes directly to the monitoring server in a remote location via CDMA, the long-range communication method used. CDMA effectively minimizes the effect of several disorders around the structure.

The monitoring server analyzes the data coming from each location and reports to the administrator in real time. The administrator subsequently uses the analyzed data to determine the safety of the structure.

4   Application to the Concrete Wall of an LNG Tank

We applied the wireless SHM sensor system to the monitoring of the concrete wall of an LNG tank. We simulated the responses of the structure through structural analysis of the LNG Tank to construct the SHM system, and thereby determined the best sensing position for the sensor. Figs. 2(a) and (b) show the position of the sensor installed on the structure.

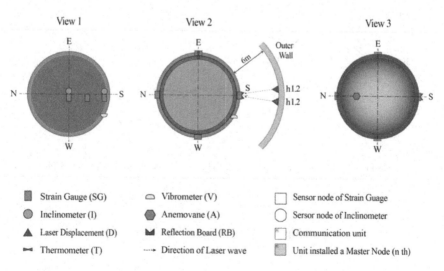

Strain Gauge (SG)	Vibrometer (V)	Sensor node of Strain Guage
Inclinometer (I)	Anemovane (A)	Sersor node of Inclinometer
Laser Displacement (D)	Reflection Board (RB)	Communication unit
Thermometer (T)	Direction of Laser wave	Unit installed a Master Node (n th)

Fig. 2. (a) The installed sensor position (plane)

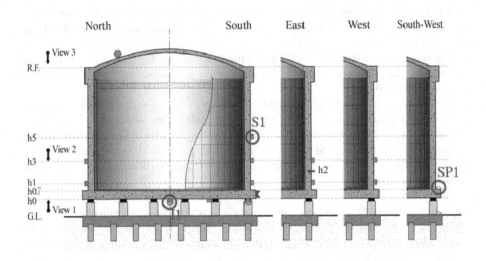

Fig. 2. (b) The installed sensor position (elevation)

Examples of the resulting data from each sensor measured over a period of time are displayed in Fig. 3.

The strain and temperature data were measured once every 5 h, about five times per day. The speed data were measured approximately six times per hour via a dynamic sensor. Further, the inclination was measured once every 5 h, about five times per day.

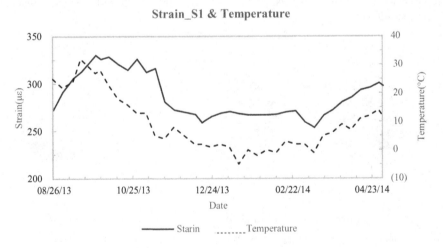

Fig. 3. Strain and Temperature data

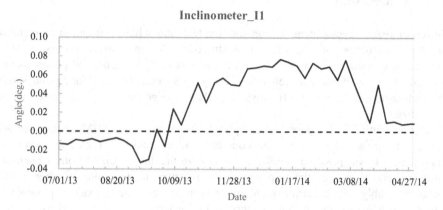

Fig. 4. Inclination data

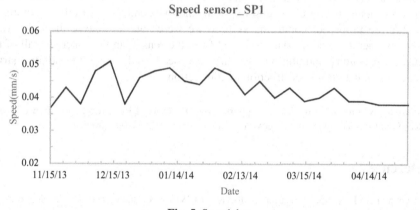

Fig. 5. Speed data

Fig. 3 shows that the strain is directly proportional to the temperature changes. Considering that it is a concrete structure, the strain value between 250 με and 350 με is a relatively small value. Thus, the strain occurring at the installation can be accorded to temperature changes.

We used a speed sensor instead of an accelerometer. A speed sensor can also be a part of an accelerometer. The results of the data analysis indicate that the speed range, 0.03 mm/s to 0.05 mm/s, is safe. The value obtained by the inclinometer placed on the floor of the structure does not exceed 0.077°, the maximum value, which indicates safety.

There were no major problems affecting the measurement because no significant meteorological activity occurred during the measurement period.

5   Conclusion

In recent years, developments in construction techniques have resulted in an increase in the construction of large high-rise structures. When damage occurs in such structures, especially social infrastructures such as bridges, dams, and power plants, the effect of the damage is felt over a very wide area. By monitoring the safety of such structures using an SHM system, when emergencies occur, damage can be minimized.

Consequently, in this paper, we proposed a wireless sensor SHM system and applied it to an actual structure (the concrete wall of an LNG Tank), an examined its efficacy. It was possible to collect and analyze the data obtained from the sensors installed, and to predict the response of the structure to determine whether it was behaving stably within certain standards. Our proposed system made it possible to observe at a glance the changes occurring in the structure overall, and to perform efficient monitoring. Further, our proposed system makes it possible to ensure safety by immediately responding to any risk factor observed consequent to viewing the data in real time using the wireless sensor system, and to extend the life of the structure.

Using the proposed monitoring system, we were able to analyze the LNG Tank during its operation via the data collected from the sensors in the concrete wall of the LNG Tank. Future monitoring systems will need to be able to monitor structures continuously from construction to completion.

Acknowledgments. This work was supported by the National Research Foundation of Korea (NRF) Grant funded by the Korea government (MSIP) (no. 2011-0018360).

References

1. Lynch, J.P., Loh, K.J.: A Summary Review of Wireless Sensors and Sensor Networks for Structural Health Monitoring
2. Chang, P.C., Flatau, A., Liu, S.C.: Review Paper : Health Monitoring of Civil Infrastructure, SAGE journals (2003)
3. Joseph, P., Robert, S., Alan, M., David, C., John, A.: Analysis of Wireless Sensor Networks for Habitat Monitoring, Wireless Sensor Networks, pp 399–423 (2004)
4. Farrar, C.R., Worden, K.: An introduction to structural health monitoring. Phil. Trans. R. Soc. A **365**, 303–315 (2007)
5. Jerome Peter Lynch: An overview of wireless structural health monitoring for civil structures, Phil. Trns. R. Soc. A **365**(345), 372 (2007)

Video Surveillance Applications Based on Ultra-Low Power Sensors

Valeria Loscrí[1]([✉]), Michele Magno[2,3], and Rosario Surace[4]

[1] Inria Lille, Lille, France
valeria.loscri@inria.fr
[2] ETH Zurich, Zurich, Switzerland
[3] University of Bologna, Bologna, Italy
[4] University of Calabria, Arcavacada di Rende CS, Italy

Abstract. Power consumption is an important goal for many applications, expecially when the power can be wasted doing nothing. Video surveillance is one of this application where the camera can be on for long period without "see" nothing. For this reason several power management techniques were carried out in order to reduce the activities of the camera when it is not needed. In this work we focus on surveillance applications performed through Video Surveillance Camera (VSC) that are not permanently active, but need to be properly "woken-up", by specific ultra Low Power wireless Sensor Nodes (LPSN) able to monitor continuously the area. named. The LPSN are equipped by Piezoelectric "Passive" Infrared (PIR) sensors to detect the movement, thus they have a specific transmission range (to wirelessly send the "wake-up" messages to the camera sensor device) and a sensing range to detect events of interest (i.e. a man that crosses a specific area). Different deployments may highly impact not only in terms of events detectable, but also in terms of the number of VDS that can be woken-up. In this work, we propose a neural/genetic algorithm, that tries to compute the best deployment of the LPSN, based on two weight factors that "prioritize" the first objective, that is the number of VSC that can be woken-up or the second objective, namely the events detectable. The two objectives can be opposite and based on the different values assigned to the weight factors, different deployments can be obtained. The performance evaluation is realized through a simulation tool and we will show the effectiveness of our approach to reach very effective deployments in different scenarios.

Keywords: Surveillance · PIR sensors · Neural/genetic algorithm · Coverage · Connectivity

1 Introduction

In the last few years, a significant effort has been made in the context of wireless networks, by effectively exploiting their ability to monitor real-world phenomena

This work has been partially supported by a grant from CPER Nord-Pas-de-Calais/FEDER Campus Intelligence Ambiante and by the FP7 VITAL project.

© Institute for Computer Sciences, Social Informatics and Telecommunications Engineering 2014
N. Mitton et al. (Eds.): ADHOCNETS 2014, LNICST 140, pp. 235–244, 2014.
DOI: 10.1007/978-3-319-13329-4_21

[2], [4]. The applications involving wireless sensor networks are several and with different features, but one common factor of many applications, is the energy-constrained aspect of battery-powered devices. Normally, the wireless networks based on battery-powered devices, are mostly influenced by an effective and valid deployment of the nodes in the space. Deployment is concerned with setting up an operational heterogeneous wireless network in a real-world environment. Usually, the realization of an effective deployment is a labor-intensive and cumbersome task. Since energy is a limited and very precious resource, the extension of the lifetime of a battery-powered nodes network has to be addressed from different levels: 1) at the device level, by considering circuits with specific features; 2) at the network level, by implementing effective medium access solutions [12], routing protocols, deployments etc. IIn this work we try to devise a solution that combines an effective deployment of specific ultra low power wireless sensors nodes with LPSN sensors for monitoring objects' movements of specific areas. Specifically, LPSN nodes [6] are able to sense motion. Since VSC are energy-expensive nodes, it would be useful, for surveillance purpose [9], to wake-up video-camera [10] if and only if there is an interesting event that occurs (i.e. human being presence detected). In order to increase the "detectable" area, namely the zone where the events of interest can occur, and realize the maximum connected VSC nodes with the sensors (each VSC has to be connected to at least a LPSN sensor in order to be woken-up), we propose a neural/genetic approach. Neural/genetic approaches can be very effective for the solution of multi-objective problem as shown in [11]. This algorithm has the capability to consider in a synergistic way two "opposite" objectives. Usually, the greater is the area to be covered, the smaller is the number of VSC that are connected with at least a LPSN node. In order to take into account the two goals in a simultaneous way, two weight factors are introduced that give a kind of priority to the objectives. The rest of the paper is organized as follows. Section 2 describes the problem we claim to resolve and the specific scenario considered. Section 3 presents the neural network exploited by each node to self-compute its best position. Section 4 describes the genetic algorithm used as training phase for the neural network. Section 5 presents the simulation results in different scenarios. Finally, we conclude this work in Section 6.

2   Reference Model and Problem Formulation

In this section, we will describe the specific characteristics of the LPSN sensors and the deployment problem. As described in [1] and [8], the Pyroelectric passive InfraRed (PIR) nodes, can be used as a trigger to wake-up a node from "sleep" mode to a power-hungry video capture mode. LPSN sensors are exploited in this specific context for event detection purpose [13], [14]. Specifically, they allow to sense motion and are able to detect if a human being is moving in or out of the sensor range. In the Figure 1, we show the architecture of LPSN nodes considered in this work. The hardware architecture is divided into three modules, powered by a single source:

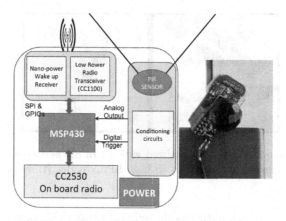

Fig. 1. Architecture and image of the implemented LPSN sensor node

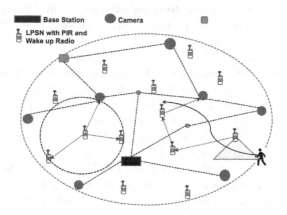

Fig. 2. Ultra-low power sensor network overlayed on an existing WSN

- The sensor module which hosts a LPSN sensor, and the conditioning circuitry to give an analog and a digital output
- Microcontroller board, the controller module built around a TI MSP430, which includes the power harvester module and batteries
- The communication module consisting of a nanoWatt WUR circuit and an ADF7020 transceiver to send information and/or to wake-up the neighbo

More details about each module can be found in [1].

In this work the low-power LPSN sensor, that can sense the motion, is used to detect the presence through continuous low-power sampling. Once motion is detected, a signal is sent to turn on the video camera for higher resolution sensing of the event. The main motivation beyond the combined use of LPSN nodes and video camera, is that LPSN sensors exhibit significantly lower energy consumption. An example of how LPSN network can be inserted in an existing energy expensive sensor network is shown in Figure 2.

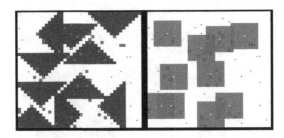

Fig. 3. (left) Example of coverage realized with 10 LPSN nodes (sensing radius = 8 meters); (right) connectivity exampke with 10 LPSN nodes (transmission range = 4 meters)

From Figure 2, we can notice as the existing network is not modified with the additional LPSN nodes and the LPSN sensor network is overlayed to the primary network. When a LPSN sensor detects an intruder, it broadcasts a message to its neighbourhood (the set of nodes that are in the cover range). The message is to wake-up the reachable nodes.

Associated with the LPSN nodes are two different ranges: 1) transmission range to send broadcast messages (to the video camera) to wake-up them. We will refer to it as *wake-up radius*; 2) directional sensing range to detect events of interest. Whether a VSC is in the *wake-up radius* of a LPSN, this means that this node can be woken-up, since there is at least one LPSN able to wake-up it if some event occurs. We will refer to the number of video camera that can be woken-up with the term "connectivity" and our goal is to maximize it by the mean of a good deployment of the overlayed LPSN network. If the percentage of VSC that can be woken up is not equal to the maximum (100%), this means that some VSC can not react to some events and are isolated. On the other hand, we are also interested tor each the maximum coverage, namely to maximize the areas covered through the sensing range of the LPSN nodes. This means, that we ensure that all the events will be detected by at least a LPSN.

In the Figure 3, we show a deployement example realized with 10 LPSN nodes (yellow nodes in the picture) and 54 VSC (pink nodes). By setting a directional sensing radius (blue area) equal to 8 meters and an omnidirectional *wake-up radius* equal to 4 meters(green area), the LPSN sensors will be capable to wake-up a certain number of VSC (pink nodes with red squares) by covering an area (the covered area is the total blue area). The VSC that are out form the coverage of at least a LPSN (pink nodes), will be isolated and then cannot be woken-up. Follow this reasoning, we can argue that the objectives to maximize the number of video camera that can be woken up and the maximization of the detection areas are opposite. Based on these considerations, we formulate a neural/genetic approach, where we formulate the problem by considering two weight factors, that can be adapted to the specific requirements of the user (that would give priority to the connectivity, that is the number of VSC that can be woken up, or to the coverage).

In the next Section we will give the details for this approach.

3   Discrete Model for an Evolving Neural Network Based Controller for Self-Deployment

The model proposed in this work is discrete in both time and space, so will refer as a step a discrete time unit and cell as a square discrete unit of area represented by a grid. In this scenario is suitable depict the range of coverage of a node by a square rather than a circumference. Given the sensing radius r of a node, expressed in number of cells, the area covered by one node is a square of $(2r + 1)^2$ cells centered in the current position of the same node. We focus on achieve single coverage consequently when the number of nodes in not enough to assure complete coverage, k-coverage is not desirable. We make the following assumptions:

- in each step each nodes is able to move only from one cell to a neighbor cell;
- each node knows the coordinates of the grid;
- each node knows its own initial position and heading (otherwise a low cost GPS is needed);
- even if there is no association between communication and sensing range from the hardware point of view to assure connectivity the communication range is at least twice the sensing range, in this case as shown in [5] we only need to guarantee coverage and also connectivity will be satisfied.

The behavior of each node of the network is controlled by a fully connected, recurrent and time-discrete artificial neural network. Each neuron unit in the network has a directed connection to every other unit. Each unit has a time-varying real-valued activation. Each connection has a modifiable real-valued weight. The network is composed by a layer of input neurons and a layer of output neurons and in the middle there are several layer of hidden neurons. Usually the number of these layer is related to the problem's complexity, for our problem two hidden layer seem enough. The architecture of the proposed neural network is depicts in Figure 4. The neural network is responsible of the mapping between the n-dimensional input and the m-dimensional output where the input of the networks is detected from the environment and is related to the goal of interest. Each drones can start from a position (grid's cell) and in each step is able to move in one of four admitted direction (north, south, est, west). The movement could be easily extended to all eight possible directions.

The input layer of the neural network is build starting from local information collected by each node from the environment and through messages exchange with neighbors. Such information needed for the learning process are the following:

- distance from obstacle if it is present in the coverage range in each of four direction expressed in terms of number of grid cells (4 inputs);
- number of cells in the coverage range covered also from others nodes in each of four direction (4 inputs);
- number of nodes in the same cell (1 input).

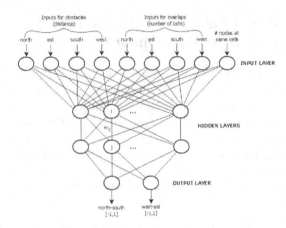

Fig. 4. Neural network architecture for drone's mobility controller

First set of inputs is needed to learn how to avoid the obstacles that constitute an impediment to movements, sensing and communication operations. The second and third sets of inputs regarding the k-covered cells and are useful to spread out the nodes when they are to close each other to extend the covered area. In particular the third one is very useful in the case when all nodes start from the same position.

Self-deployment usually need accurate location information acquired by each node by GPS or others location techniques. The proposed neural network approach is able to learn how to place using only poor location information provided to neural network for learning about the final position. This is an advantage because no accurate GPS equipment or complex location algorithms is required and at the same time the grid, if necessary, could be used as a landmarks where nodes are placed to get some location information.

All these information are used for the learning process in particular, through the weighted neural network connections these input are mapped into the output that is simply the new position for the node chosen among the four admitted neighbor cells. In particular at each step, each neuron i computes the sum over the current output of the neurons j feeding the connection weighted by the factor w_{ji} of the incoming connection and its bias b_i (see eq. 1). Weights can have either an excitatory or inhibitory effect.

$$o_i(k+1) = F(\sum_{j=0}^{n} w_{ji}o_j(k) + b_i) \tag{1}$$

The output of the neuron for next step $k+1$ is calculated through an activation function F over the weighted sum. In our case F is a simple linear threshold function as expressed in equation 2:

$$F(x) = \begin{cases} -1.0 \ if & x \leq -1.0 \\ x \quad if & -1.0 < x < 1.0 \\ 1.0 \ if & x \geq 1.0 \end{cases} \tag{2}$$

Obviously the input of the input neurons is caught from environment while the output of the output neurons will be adapted to the range of the actuators to realize the desired behavior so equation 1 is responsible for the matching neuron by neuron among inputs and outputs.

4 Evolutionary Algorithm for the Neural Network Training Phase

In order to train the network, in a self-organizing perspective, unsupervised reinforcement learning is used. Instead of a supervisor a fitness function is provided to evaluate the neural network's performance.

The global optimization method used for training the neural network is a genetic algorithms. The genetic algorithm is encoded with the neural network weights in a predefined manner where one gene in the chromosome represents one weight link. There are many chromosomes that make up the population, therefore, many different neural networks are evolved until a stopping criterion is satisfied as in our case the maximum number of training generations has been reached. The goal of the genetic algorithm is to maximize the fitness function that is evaluated during the training phase and influences the genetic selection process.

Since the goal of genetic algorithm is to find a population that permit to achieve the maximum value of a given fitness function, we need to relate the fitness function to a measure of coverage and time needed for coverage. To this scope the fitness function proposed for our scheme to make possible the evolution of the neural network is the following:

$$fitness\_function = achieved\_coverage - time \qquad (3)$$

At each generation the fitness function (3) is evaluated and the new population encoding the weights's value of the neural network is generated by selection, mutation and crossover of the previous member of population that guarantee an high fitness function's value. In this sense the fitness function is used as feedback for next generation. Notice that since time and space are discretized in this equation we're not summing seconds and meters but just counting how many cells are covered with current generation taking into account how many time steps are needed. Increasing the fitness function value by one unit in respect to previous generation means that evolution has led to cover one more cell or to cover the same number of cells but with one time step less. Table 1 shows the parameters used for the genetic algorithm.

5 Performance Evaluation

In order to compute effectively and adaptively a deployment of LPSN nodes that overlays the VSC network, we considered the neural/genetic technique described above. This algorithm is effective to compute the best deployment of the LPSN

Table 1. Parameters of genetic algorithms

Population size	100
Number of generation	100
Percentage of elite selection	15
Percentage of mutation	45
Percentage of crossover	30
Percentage of randomly created offsprings	5
Percentage of randomly selecting an offsprings from previous generation	5

nodes, by responding to the specific requirements of the user, by taking into account the environment and the number of devices available. The simulation tool considered is FREVO [7]. The synergistic combination of the neural network and the genetic algorithm is able to take into consideration different objective in a simultaneous way, by introducing two weights with value ranging from 0 to 1 (the sum of these two weight factors has to be equal to 1). As for instance, if we assign to the coverage weight 1, the weight connectivity will be 0, and this means that the coverage will be "prioritized", and the connectivity will be not considered at all and viceversa. We tested the algorithm, by varying the weights between 0 and 1., the number of the LPSN nodes (10,20,30) and the wake-up radius (4,8,12 meters).

In the Figure 5[left] we show the results we obtain when the weight assigned to the coverage is 0 and the *connectivity* weight is 1.

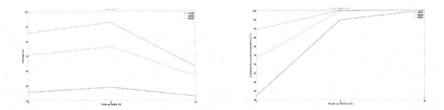

Fig. 5. [left]Coverage and [right]Connectivity when the coverage is 0 and the connectivity is 1

In Figure 5[right], we show the results concerning the "connectivity", when the weight factor associated with the coverage is equal to 0 and the connectivity factor is 1.

In Figure 6[left] we show the results we obtain when the weight assigned to the coverage is 1 and the *connectivity* weight is 0.

In Figure 6[right], we show the results concerning the "connectivity", when the weight factor associated with the coverage is equal to 1 and the connectivity factor is 0.

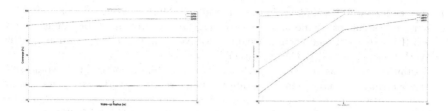

Fig. 6. [left]Coverage and [right]Connectivity when the coverage is 1 and the connectivity is 0

As we can remark from the Figures 5, when the user requires to the algorithm to prioritize the connectivity, the algorithm will deploy the nodes in a way to achieve the 100% of the VSC that can be woken up. In practice, the technique will try to cover a VSC with at least a LPSN node. This means that the coverage is not required to achieve the 100%. On the other hand, in the Figures 6, we can observe that the area can not be totally covered, by considering the specific number of LPSN nodes and the correspondent sensing radius to detect the events, but in any case, the coverage achieved is greater than in the previous case. On the other hand, the connectivity will achieve the maximum value by increasing the wake-up radius.

6   Conclusion

In this work we have investigated on effective deployment of an overlayed network inserted over a network of Video Surveillance Camera. The overlayed network is constituted by specific types of sensor, namely Low Power wireless Sensor Nodes (LPSN). The deployment is dynamically computed through a neural/genetic approach, that allow to consider a synergistic combination of two parameters, named here "connectivity" and "coverage", that normally are opposite. Through the neural/genetic approach we can ask the LPSN nodes to redeploy in order to improve the number of VSC that can be woken-up and also the covered zone (where events of interest occur). Finally, we demonstrated the effectiveness of this approach via simulation. In future works we are planning to realize a proof-of-concept, by implementing a test-bed with real devices.

References

1. Magno, M., Zappi, P., Brunelli, D., Benini, L.: A Solar-powered Video Sensor Node for Energy Efficient Multimodal Surveillance. In: 11th EUROMICRO Conference on Digital System Design (2008)
2. Yan, T., He, T., Stankovic, J.A.: Differentiated surveillance for sensor networks. In: SenSys, pp. 51–62 (2003)
3. Oh, S., Chen, P., Manzo, M., Sastry, S.: Design of a Completely Wireless Security Camera System. Instrumenting wireless sensor networks for real-time surveillance. In: Proc. of the International Conference on Robotics and Automation (May 2006)

4. D. Mendez, A. J. Prez, M. A. Labrador, and J. J. Marron, P-Sense: a participatory sensing system for air pollution monitoring and control. In: Proceedings of the 9th IEEE International Conference on Pervasive Computing and Communications Workshops, pp. 344–347 (March 2011)

5. Costanzo, C., Loscrí, V., Natalizio, E., Razafindralambo, T.: Nodes-self-deployment for coverage maximization in mobile robot networks using an evolving neural nettwork. Special issue: Wireless Sensor and Robot Networks: Algortihms and Experiments, in Computer Communications 35(9), 1047–1055 (2012)

6. http://www.ladyada.net/learn/sensors/pir.html (accessed online on June 15, 2014)

7. http://sourceforge.net/p/frevo/wiki/Tutorials/ (accessed online on June 15, 2014)

8. Magno, M., Boyle, D., Brunelli, D., Popovici, E., Benini, L.: Ensuring Survivability of Resource-Intensive Sensor Networks Through Ultra-Low Power Overlays. IEEE Transactions on Industrial Informatics 10(2), 946–956 (2014)

9. Magno, M., Tombari, F., Brunelli, D., Di Stefano, L., Benini, L.: Multimodal Video Analysis on Self-Powered Resource-Limited Wireless Smart Camera. IEEE Journal on Emerging and Selected Topics in Circuits and Systems 3(2), 223–235 (2013)

10. Jelicic, V., Magno, M., Brunelli, D., Bilas, V., Benini, L.: Benefits of Wake-up Radio in Energy-Efficient Multimodal Surveillance Wireless Sensor Network. IEEE Sensors Journal (99), 1 (2014)

11. Loscri, V., Pace, P., Surace, R.: Multi-Objective Evolving Neural Network supporting SDR Modulations Management. In: 24th IEEE International Symposium on Personal, Indoor, Mobile and Radio Communications (PIMRC 2013) (September 2013)

12. Iera, A., Ruggeri, G., Tripodi, D.: Providing Throughput Guarantees in 802.11e WLAN Through a Dynamic Priority Assignment Mechanism. In: Kluwer Wireless Pers. Commun. J. Special Issue on Advances in Wireless LANs and PANs (2005)

13. Magno, M., Tombari, F., Brunelli, D., Di Stefano, L., Benini, L.: Multimodal Abandoned/Removed Object Detection for Low Power Video Surveillance Systems. In: Sixth IEEE International Conference on Advanced Video and Signal Based Surveillance, AVSS 2009, September 2-4, pp. 188–193 (2009)

14. Kerhet, A., Leonardi, F., Boni, A., Lombardo, P., Magno, M., Benini, L.: Distributed video surveillance using hardware-friendly sparse large margin classifiers. In: IEEE Conference on Advanced Video and Signal Based Surveillance, AVSS 2007, September 5–7, pp. 87–92 (2007)

A Low-Overhead Localized Target Coverage Algorithm in Wireless Sensor Networks

Dimitrios Zorbas[1]([✉]) and Christos Douligeris[2]

[1] Inria Lille, Nord Europe, France
`dimitrios.zormpas@inria.fr`
[2] Department of Informatics, University of Piraeus, Piraeus, Greece
`cdoulig@unipi.gr`

Abstract. The scope of this paper is to present a low-overhead localized algorithm for the target coverage problem in wireless sensor networks. The algorithm divides the sensors into active and sleep mode nodes in order to conserve energy and extend the network lifetime. The set of active mode nodes provide full coverage to a set of targets (points) in the field. The decision of which sensors will remain active at any time is locally taken by the nodes by exchanging messages with each other. This kind of messages add overhead in the network, while high overhead can dramatically decrease the network lifetime especially in case of high node density environments. To tackle this problem we propose two variations of a localized algorithm with low communication complexity. Finally, the operational effectiveness of the proposed approaches is evaluated through simulation, while their superiority against other relevant proposed solutions in the literature is illustrated. The results show a great improvement in terms of communication cost while achieving an adequate network lifetime.

1 Introduction

Wireless Sensor Networks (WSNs) consist of energy constrained devices which are used in different kind of surveillance applications. One of them is the monitoring of a set of targets in the field. The targets are specific points of high interest since their coverage provides important information to the remote users. For example, in an agricultural application, a point can be a plant whose growth, soil humidity and temperature must be identified every some hours. In a military application, a point can be a piece of road where the opponent passes by and must be detected.

The presence of the targets may be known to the sensor nodes before their deployment or may be communicated and updated throughout the monitoring process. In all cases, a localization method is essential for the application, especially when the nodes are deployed randomly and their location is not predefined. GPS devices are ideal for outdoor applications, since most of the time they provide an accurate enough location (1-2 meters divergence to the actual position). Considering indoor applications other GPS-free methods are required [1].

© Institute for Computer Sciences, Social Informatics and Telecommunications Engineering 2014
N. Mitton et al. (Eds.): ADHOCNETS 2014, LNICST 140, pp. 245–254, 2014.
DOI: 10.1007/978-3-319-13329-4_22

The energy efficiency is important in WSNs and usually localization techniques, like GPS, consume a lot of energy. However, if the nodes are considered static, the computation of the position takes places only once, thus, the energy cost is minimal. In case of mobile nodes, the position must be updated regularly, thus, energy efficient localization solution must be used [2].

Depending on the type of the application, the surveillance of a part or of all the targets is required. This work focuses on the full target coverage problem with static nodes, where the main goal is to extend the lifetime of the involved sensor nodes, while at the same time guaranteeing 100% coverage of the targets. Since the sensor nodes are battery equipped, energy-efficient protocols should be developed. Aiming at achieving energy conservation, a certain quantity of unused nodes can remain in sleep mode (very low energy consumption mode), while the rest of the available devices used to provide coverage. Smart alternation of the nodes status between the active and the sleep mode – assuring coverage at the same time – leads to energy conservation.

In order to achieve the above described goal, the nodes must be divided into a number of sets, called cover sets. Each cover set is capable of covering all monitored targets, but only one set is active at any time. There is no restriction regarding the participation of a node in multiple sets. However, the monitoring process is divided in one or more rounds and in each round the nodes elect the current active set of sensors. The duration of the rounds is known to the sensors and they use an appropriate timer to wake up.

The majority of the existing solutions in the literature are centralized or in case of a distributed algorithm the election process exhibits a high communication overhead. Centralized solutions suffer from scalability issues, while high overhead can fast waste the nodes energy. In this paper, we overtake these problems by proposing a fully localized and low overhead algorithm for the election of the active sensor nodes. Each node is capable of deciding its status by acquiring information of its 1-hop neighbors and by keeping this information in its memory.

The remainder of the paper is structured as follows. Section 2 summarizes the related work, emphasizing at target coverage algorithms. In Section 3 the proposed problem is formulated and its solution is provided in Section 4. Section 5 evaluates the proposed algorithm and compares its performance to other works in the literature. Finally, Section 6 concludes the paper.

2   Related Work

In this section, we cite the most recent works in the area of target coverage and we classify them according to the nature of the proposed algorithms.

The target coverage problem has been extensively studied in the literature as a problem of generating the maximum number of cover sets. The problem has been proven to be NP-Complete [3,4], thus, finding the optimal number of sets is a hard process with high complexity. For that reason, many suboptimal solutions with or without performance guarantees have been proposed.

A set of mathematical optimization problems related to target coverage has been presented in the following works. In [3] linear programming is used to determine the optimal number of sets, while in [5] an algorithm based on the column generation theory is introduced. An automata based solution is described in [6], while a polynomial time approximation solution is presented in [7]. Both linear and approximation solution are used in [8] to find near optimal network lifetime. Bio-inspired and genetic approaches are presented in [9] and [10], respectively.

On the other hand, a high number of heuristic algorithms which provide a very fast solution without guaranteeing that the determined solution is the optimal one, can be found in the literature. In [11], a general methodology of how to construct a centralized coverage algorithm is described, along with some fast heuristics. Energy-efficient algorithms for different variations of the target coverage problem are also presented in [12–16].

Solving the target coverage problem using a localized or a distributed approach is an important task which has not been yet thoroughly examined in the recent literature. In [17] the authors show that when the communication range is at least two time the sensing range, the target coverage problem can be solved locally. Based on this observation they propose a localized solution. Other distributed coverage techniques are presented in [18–20], however, they are out of the scope of this paper.

3   The Target Coverage Problem

Let $T_0 = \{t_1, t_2, \ldots, t_k\}$ be the set of targets and $S_0 = \{s_1, s_2, \ldots, s_n\}$ the set of sensor nodes. Each target in T_0 is covered by at least one sensor node in S_0.

Each sensor has a sensing range equal to R_s and any target lying within the circle defined by the location of a sensor and the range R_s can be monitored with high probability by this particular sensor. On the other hand, targets outside this range cannot be accurately detected (or they cannot be detected at all) and they are considered uncovered. The covered targets are kept in P_i for each i in S_0.

Moreover, each node can communicate with other neighboring nodes which lie within a range R_c and exchange messages.

Each node's initial energy is equal to l_0 and this energy can be spent by participating in one or more generated cover sets. We assume that the energy cost during the sleep mode is negligible compared to the coverage cost in active mode. The maximum number of times each node can participate in the rounds is w ($w \in \mathbb{N}^*$) and in every round each active node consumes l_0/w amount of energy.

The coverage algorithm produces a collection $C = \{C_1, \ldots, C_m\}$ of m cover sets. Each cover set C_p is a subset of the available sensors ($C_p \subseteq S_0$) and covers all targets found in T_0.

The main objective of a coverage algorithm is to extend the lifetime of the network by maximizing $|C|$, where $|C|$ is the cardinality of the generated collection C of cover sets. The theoretical maximum number of sets is computed by the product $|min\_t| \frac{l_0}{w}$, where $|min\_t|$ is the cardinality of the target which is covered by the minimum number of sensors in the network.

4   The LOLOCA Solution

In this section, we introduce "LOLOCA" (Low Overhead LOcalized Coverage Algorithm), an algorithm which bases its functionality on three characteristics: (a) the control of the messages and how often the nodes communicate with their neighbors, (b) the coverage status of each node's neighbors, and (c) the node's own coverage status. We present the general characteristics of LOLOCA and we distinguish two ways to handle the the poorly covered targets in the network (targets that are not covered by many nodes).

In LOLOCA, the monitoring process is divided in rounds and each round consists of the initialization and the coverage phase. The initialization phase takes place at the beginning of each round and the nodes elect a set of nodes who will be active and provide coverage until the next election. The initialization phase is short and its duration is considered negligible compared to the coverage period.

In the following lines we describe how the nodes control the communication with their neighbors, how they elect the active nodes, and they handle the poorly covered targets.

4.1   Neighbor Discovery and Coverage Status

LOLOCA considers four types of nodes regarding their election status. Nodes that have been elected as active and have sent their status to their neighbors, have status equal to 2. Nodes that have been elected as active but they have not sent yet their decision to the other nodes, have status equal to 1. Nodes that are still during their decision have status equal to 0, while nodes that will remain in sleep mode during the round have status equal to -1.

It is obvious that at the beginning of the process, all the nodes have status equal to 0. This status can change to 1 if the node is elected as active or to -1 if a node decides to go sleeping. The status can change from 1 to 2 once an active node has communicated with its neighbors and declared his status.

The nodes are allowed to communicate with other nodes and exchange their status and their P sets in two cases:

- at the beginning of the first round while their election status is 0,
- their status is 1.

It practically means that, each node can communicate at most two times during the construction of the first cover set and only once for each of the next rounds.

Each node i in S_0 keeps the received messages in set N_i. This set is kept in node's memory. Each received message contains the list of the targets the neighboring node j covers (i.e., P_j), its current lifetime and its current status. Since the node's memory may be limited, N_i is updated every time the node receives new neighboring messages and only the double entries are deleted keeping only the most recent ones (the ones with the higher election status).

Based on the sets in N, each node keeps control of its own coverage status and the coverage status of its neighbors. Each time a node receives a message from a neighbor who has been elected as active, it updates each coverage status and the coverage status of its neighbors in N. The coverage status is used later in the computation of the contribution of each node and the status decision.

The communication complexity of LOLOCA is $O(n + nm)$, where n is the number of sensors and m the number of rounds (generated sets).

4.2 Election Process

The election process is a local decision process where each node decides if it will be active or in sleep mode during the current round. Each node compares its own contribution against the other nodes in the neighborhood, thus, the information kept in N is crucial during this process.

The node with the highest contribution in the neighborhood will be active in this round, will set its election status to 1, and will declare its decision to its neighbors. On the contrary, the rest of the neighboring nodes (nodes with lower contribution) will wait until they receive a message, will update their N set and will recompute their contribution. If all the targets in P have been covered by other elected nodes, then the node will remain in sleep mode. The initialization phase terminates when all the nodes have decided to remain active or in sleep mode.

The decision of staying active or not can be taken in two different ways. Considering the first way, each node computes its own contribution as well as the contribution of its neighbors with which it has common covered targets. Based on this approach, each node knows who will be active in this round and it just waits to receive a message from the active node and recompute its contribution. An alternative way to decide a node's status is to compute a waiting time before it declares itself active or inactive node and sends a message to its neighbors. This waiting time is higher for low contribution values and vice versa. If the node does not receive any message from neighboring nodes during this waiting period, it declares itself as active, otherwise it remains inactive and recomputes the contribution formula. The first method requires some more computations from the nodes as well as predefined communication slots during the initialization phase. The second way may cause synchronization issues due to network delays (buffer delays etc.).

4.3 Contribution and Poorly Covered Targets

The contribution of a node is measured using a cost function. The cost function handles the coverage status of the nodes and their association with the poorly covered targets. Since this type of targets sets an upper limit on the maximum possible generated number of cover sets, the cost function should be aware of avoiding double-covering such targets during a single round.

LOLOCA distinguishes two ways to deal with poorly covered targets. We name the two instances "Critical" and "Badness" which are based on the works presented in [21] and [11] respectively.

In LOLOCA-Critical, the poorly covered targets are handled by computing the most critical ones (the ones covered by the minimum number of nodes [15]). This process is repeated every time a target in P_i is covered by another node with higher status in N_i. Note that the critical targets may be more than one and all of them are taken into account. Each node i computes the cost function described by Formula (1).

$$CF_i = |P_i| - |PN_i| + \frac{l_i}{l_0} + \frac{i}{\texttt{max\_int}} \qquad (1)$$

where $|PN_i|$ denotes the number of targets in P_i that are already covered (by other nodes in N). The term $\frac{i}{\texttt{max\_int}}$ is used to avoid having two nodes with the same contribution. Node i uses the same formula to compute the contribution of its neighbors. Only neighbors with at least one common target with i are used. The corresponding P_j, PN_j, and l_j for each neighbor j are taken from N_i.

Additionally, LOLOCA-Critical penalizes the nodes which cover critical targets by reducing their contribution by x points for each critical target they cover ($x \gg CF$). Node i's contribution is penalized only for the already covered targets in P_i (by nodes in N_i). This action promotes nodes with no association with critical targets.

On the other hand, LOLOCA-Badness evaluates the nodes' association with poorly covered targets by assigning a weight to each node called "badness" and is represented by b_i [11]:

$$b_i = \sum_{p=1}^{|P_i|} (\mu_i - |t_p| + 1)^3, \qquad (2)$$

where μ_i is the maximum target cardinality found in the neighborhood of i and $|t_p|$ denotes the cardinality of target t_p.

Badness is higher for nodes which cover poorly covered targets and vice versa. Involving its value into the cost function the node's contribution can be affected:

$$CF_i = \alpha \frac{|P_i| - |PN_i|}{|PN_i| + 1} + \beta(1 - \frac{b_i}{max\_b_i}) + \gamma \frac{l_i}{l_0} + \frac{i}{\texttt{max\_int}}, \qquad (3)$$

where α, β are coefficients whose value is predefined [11] and max_b_i is the maximum badness in the neighborhood of i.

The weakness of LOLOCA-Badness is that each node must broadcast its badness value to its 1-hop neighbors once it has computed it. To tackle this weakness, each node can compute the badness for each other node in the neighborhood by using its N set. However, this can cause network instability and deadlocks since the exact cardinality of targets outside the neighborhood is not known to the nodes.

Both LOLOCA-Critical and LOLOCA-Badness elect the node with the highest contribution in the neighborhood. The elected node broadcasts its election status to its neighbors and they consequently update their N set. Nodes whose all the targets in P are already covered, change to sleep mode, while the rest of the nodes continue with a new evaluation. Apparently, nodes with no remaining energy do not take part anymore in the next elections. We assume that the last election (round) takes place when at least one target is not covered anymore by any sensor.

5   Evaluation and Discussion of the Results

In this section, we evaluate the proposed solutions and we compare their performance to a centralized approach called "Dynamic-CCF" [11] and to a localized one called "DOCA" [17]. Specifically, we measure the number of generated sets (network lifetime), the number of sent messages (overhead), and the average execution time per node and per generated set (computation cost).

We evaluate the algorithms in two scenarios. In the first scenario, we keep constant the number of nodes and we vary the number of targets, while in the second scenario, we keep constant the number of targets and we vary the number of sensors. In these two cases, we assess the target or sensor density on the algorithms' output. Each instance of the simulation has been executed 50 times and the average results are presented as well as the 95% confidence intervals.

The terrain area is fixed and equal to 100x100m, the sensing range is 10m, and the communication range is 30m. All the targets and sensors are randomly deployed in the area using the uniform distribution. α, β and γ coefficients of LOLOCA-Badness are set equal to 0.4, 0.1, and 0.5, respectively. The maximum number of node participations is set to 2. All simulations were carried out on a Intel Xeon 2.67Ghz host, running the Debian GNU/Linux operating system, and no parallel processing of the same instance was allowed.

5.1   Numerical Results

In the first scenario, the network consists of 200 static nodes and variable number of targets. The results are illustrated in Figure 1. The first figure shows that the number of generated sets decreases as the number of targets increases, since more sensors remain active to cover all the targets. The produced network lifetime is almost equivalent for all the approaches. DOCA performs slightly better when many targets are deployed, however, it sends more than three and two times more messages than LOLOCA-Critical and LOLOCA-Badness, respectively (see Figure 1(b)). For the rest of the cases our localized solutions exhibit the same network lifetime with the centralized approach which achieved the theoretical maximum lifetime for the 99% of the instances. The overhead is also kept in very low levels. Our proposed approaches have higher computation cost, however this cost can be easily carried out by a modern node CPU unit [22].

In the second scenario, we assess the algorithms' behavior on node density by varying the number of sensors between 100 and 300 with an increment of 50 considering a fixed number of targets. The results of this simulation are presented in Figure 2. As discussed in the previous scenario, the algorithms achieve an

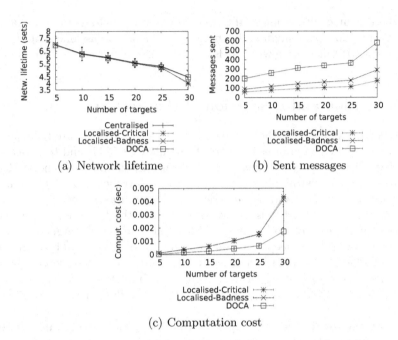

(a) Network lifetime

(b) Sent messages

(c) Computation cost

Fig. 1. Different measurements for a scenario with 200 sensors and variable number of targets

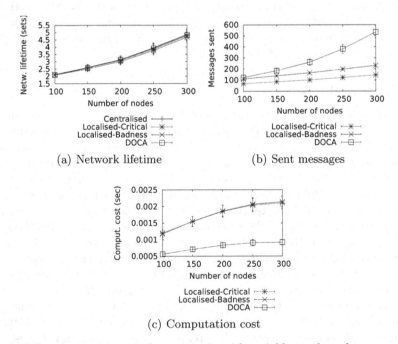

(a) Network lifetime

(b) Sent messages

(c) Computation cost

Fig. 2. Different measurements for a scenario with variable number of sensors and 20 targets

almost adequate performance in terms of network lifetime which is very close to the optimal solution. DOCA exhibits higher overhead, which is almost five times more than the competitors' one when the density is high. Finally, the computation cost of LOLOCA-Critical and LOLOCA-Badness is higher, but it is kept within reasonable limits.

6 Conclusion and Future Work

In this paper, we proposed "LOLOCA", a localized algorithm for the target coverage problem in wireless sensor networks. LOLOCA exhibits low communication cost by allowing the nodes to keep some information in their memory. We presented two instances of the algorithm using different techniques to deal with the poorly covered targets. The simulation and the comparison results showed that both instances outperform the distributed algorithm of [17] in terms of overhead, while they achieve similar network lifetime performance. However, the computation cost is higher. Our future work includes the use a real experimentation platform in order to evaluate other network characteristics like delay, synchronization, and convergence.

Acknowledgments. This work is partially supported by a grant from CPER Nord-Pas-de-Calais FEDER CIA.

References

1. Deak, G., Curran, K., Condell, J.: A survey of active and passive indoor localisation systems. Computer Communications **35**(16), 1939–1954 (2012)
2. Liu, Y., Yang, Z., Wang, X., Jian, L.: Location, localization, and localizability. Journal of Computer Science and Technology **25**(2), 274–297 (2010)
3. Cardei, M., Thai, M., Li, Y., Wu, W.: Energy-efficient target coverage in wireless sensor networks. In: Proc. of INFOCOM 2005, vol. 3, pp. 1976–1984. IEEE (March 2005).
4. Luo, W., Wang, J., Guo, J., Chen, J.: Parameterized complexity of max-lifetime target coverage in wireless sensor networks. Theoretical Computer Science **518**, 32–41 (2014)
5. Gu, Y., Zhao, B.H., Ji, Y.S., Li, J.: Theoretical treatment of target coverage in wireless sensor networks. Journal of Computer Science and Technology **26**(1), 117–129 (2011)
6. Mostafaei, H., Meybodi, M.: Maximizing lifetime of target coverage in wireless sensor networks using learning automata. Wireless Personal Communications **71**(2), 1461–1477 (2013)
7. Ding, L., Wu, W., Willson, J., Wu, L., Lu, Z., Lee, W.: Constant-approximation for target coverage problem in wireless sensor networks. In: INFOCOM, 2012 Proceedings IEEE, pp. 1584–1592 (March 2012).
8. Cheng, M., Gong, X.: Maximum lifetime coverage preserving scheduling algorithms in sensor networks. Journal of Global Optimization **51**(3), 447–462 (2011)
9. Ding, Y.S., Lu, X.J., Hao, K.R., Li, L.F., Hu, Y.F.: Target coverage optimisation of wireless sensor networks using a multi-objective immune co-evolutionary algorithm. Intern. J. Syst. Sci. **42**(9), 1531–1541 (2011)

10. Gil, J.M., Han, Y.H.: A target coverage scheduling scheme based on genetic algorithms in directional sensor networks. Sensors **11**(2), 1888–1906 (2011)
11. Zorbas, D., Glynos, D., Kotzanikolaou, P., Douligeris, C.: Solving coverage problems in wireless sensor networks using cover sets. Ad Hoc Networks **8**, 400–415 (2010)
12. Hongwu, Z., Hongyuan, W., Hongcai, F., Bing, L., Bingxiang, G.: A heuristic greedy optimum algorithm for target coverage in wireless sensor networks. In: Pacific-Asia Conference on Circuits, Communications and Systems, pp. 39–42 (2009).
13. He, J., Xiong, N., Xiao, Y., Pan, Y.: A reliable energy efficient algorithm for target coverage in wireless sensor networks. In: 2010 IEEE 30th International Conference on Distributed Computing Systems Workshops (ICDCSW), pp. 180–188 (June 2010).
14. Zhao, Q., Gurusamy, M.: Lifetime maximization for connected target coverage in wireless sensor networks. IEEE/ACM Trans. Netw. **16**(6), 1378–1391 (2008)
15. Zorbas, D., Douligeris, C.: Connected coverage in wsns based on critical targets. Computer Networks **55**(6), 1412–1425 (2011)
16. Zhao, Q., Gurusamy, M.: Connected k-target coverage problem in wireless sensor networks with different observation scenarios. Comput. Netw. **52**(11), 2205–2220 (2008)
17. Zhang, H., Wang, H., Feng, H.: A distributed optimum algorithm for target coverage in wireless sensor networks. In: Asia-Pacific Conference on Information Processing, APCIP 2009, vol. 2, pp. 144–147(July 2009).
18. Guo, P., Jiang, T., Zhang, Q., Zhang, K.: Sleep scheduling for critical event monitoring in wireless sensor networks. IEEE Transactions on Parallel and Distributed Systems **23**(2), 345–352 (2012)
19. Bulut, E., Korpeoglu, I.: Sleep scheduling with expected common coverage in wireless sensor networks. Wireless Networks **17**(1), 19–40 (2011)
20. Nan, G., Shi, G., Mao, Z., Li, M.: Cdsws: coverage-guaranteed distributed sleep/wake scheduling for wireless sensor networks. EURASIP Journal on Wireless Communications and Networking 2012(1) (2012).
21. Slijepcevic, S., Potkonjak, M.: Power efficient organization of wireless sensor networks. In: Proc. of International Conference on Communications (ICC 2001), pp. 472–476. IEEE (June 2001).
22. ST: Arm cortex-m3. http://www.st.com/web/catalog/mmc/FM141/SC1169/SS1031/LN1565/PF164485

Connectivity Restoration and Amelioration in Wireless Ad-Hoc Networks: A Practical Solution

Christos Katsikiotis[1,2], Dimitrios Zorbas[1]([⊠]), and Periklis Chatzimisios[2]

[1] Inria Lille, Nord Europe, France
dimitrios.zormpas@inria.fr
[2] Department of Informatics, Alexander TEI of Thessaloniki,
Kentriki Makedonia, Greece
{chkats,peris}@it.teithe.gr

Abstract. Connectivity restoration after a node failure is one of the major issues in wireless ad-hoc networks. In particular, failures can lead to a network partitioning and a huge loss of information. Therefore, a fast mechanism is needed to heal the network between the partitions. In this paper, we consider the scenario where an intermediate node failures and a mobile system is moving autonomously to restore connectivity and provide the best service. We propose a fast connectivity restoration algorithm that is based only on local information. We implement our solution on a real robotic platform and we present some experimental results using a simple case scenario.

1 Introduction

Recently, the use of wireless ad-hoc networks exhibits an exponential increase in different environments and applications. However, one of the vulnerabilities of wireless ad-hoc networks is the appearance of connectivity failures between the network participants that can lead to network partitions and, thus, loss of information. This kind of failures may happen due to the appearance of corrupted nodes or due to their energy exhaustion [1–3].

The purpose of this paper is to present a practical solution to tackle the aforementioned problem. Specifically, we assume that mobile routers are capable of detecting failures and restoring connectivity between one or more routing points. Once a failure has been detected, the mobile router's first objective is to look for neighboring nodes by moving in the periphery of the routing point and stop when the best link quality has been achieved. The router's second objective is to balance the throughput between the two sides in order to avoid bottlenecks. Depending on the application, the mobile router can act as permanent or a temporary solution which restores all or part of the network services, until the corrupted nodes are replaced and the network returns to its normal operation.

The implementation of such a solution poses several challenges since (a) the successor nodes' position is not known in advance, (b) the signal quality is not stable due to environmental changes, and (c) the connectivity restoration must be done very soon without delays. Hence, placing the mobile routers is a fairly complex node deployment problem and constitutes the main focus of the paper.

© Institute for Computer Sciences, Social Informatics and Telecommunications Engineering 2014
N. Mitton et al. (Eds.): ADHOCNETS 2014, LNICST 140, pp. 255–264, 2014.
DOI: 10.1007/978-3-319-13329-4_23

The contributions of our work are:

- we propose a localized solution, called Connectivity Restoration and aMelioration (*CRAM*), to restore connectivity between two network partitions;
- we implement our solution on a real robotic platform taking into account both restoration and bandwidth amelioration parameters;
- we evaluate our approach creating a simple case scenario and present our findings.

The remainder of the paper is structured as follows. In Section 2, we discuss the related work in the areas of connectivity restoration and link quality amelioration. In Section 3 we present the problem and in Section 4 its practical solution. In Section 5, we evaluate our approach and present some experimental results. Finally, Section 6 concludes the paper and lists our future work.

2   Related Work

The problem of failure nodes resulting limited connectivity in wireless ad-hoc networks has recently received much attention in the literature [4–7].

Restoring connectivity by moving some of the network nodes is a research path that has been proposed by many works. In [4], the authors propose the DARA algorithm that moves nodes according to their number of neighbors in order to replace the failed ones. In [5], when a node has become inactive and, thus, causing network partitions, it is been suggested that federating the partitions could restore the connectivity by using the previous route information and moving the nodes. In [6], the authors suggest similar approaches that implement federation on disjoint parts of the network to restore connectivity. Finally, a distributed approach based on battery triggered events is proposed in [8]. Robots are used to replace failure nodes using other nodes in the neighborhood. The connectivity is held by computing a connected dominating set.

Also, remarkable research has been done on finding the ideal position between two nodes to maximize the performance of exchanging data between them. Finding such a position is of a great importance, since the deployment of an extra mobile routing point resolves connectivity. Works of [9,10] recommend the use of the APA algorithm. APA estimates the link quality using either the Round-Trip Time or the Transmission Rate or the Received Signal Strength. The calculations are done locally by an autonomous mobile router. A faster version of APA is proposed in [11] and it is applicable when the distance between the two nodes is known. APA and Fast-APA are evaluated through simulation.

Work of [12] evaluates the implication of the signal strength and data throughput in the estimation of link quality. The signal strength is suggested as a good measure of potential connectivity, while data throughput should be used for ensuring minimum actual data transmission rate. The authors of [13] and [14] conclude that the link estimation is more efficient when several link quality metrics are combined together. However, as explained in survey of Baccour et al. [15], high overhead (memory footprint, computation time) are still open problems, when several link properties are used.

Finally, some works focus on restoring connectivity in disjointed networks ([16–18]), by trying to find the smallest number of deployable nodes using *steiner points* to repair the disruption of network connectivity. The authors deal with the problem of finding the minimum count and the position of relay nodes. The problem is NP-hard and hence they propose the use of heuristics. This type of solutions are centralized.

3 The Robot Redeployment Problem

This paper addresses the problem of network failures which may occur between multiple static stations and cause loss of information. In case of a failure we assume that mobile routers (robots) restore the connectivity between two or more routing points by creating an alternative route between the them.

In this section we model a case scenario which includes a set of stationary nodes that are connected in an ad-hoc network. At some unspecified moment of time, an intermediate node becomes inactive causing a communication interrupt between the rest of the stations. We define a redeployment problem where a mobile routing system is responsible of restoring connectivity providing the best possible network service at the same time.

In more detail, the objectives of the mobile router are to:

- restore connectivity as soon as possible,
- ensure a link quality (between both stations) which is in the worst case equal to h,
- avoid network bottlenecks by balancing the throughput of the links between the two sides.

4 The CRAM Solution

The CRAM algorithm (Connectivity Restoration And aMelioration) is introduced in order to solve the previously aforementioned node deployment problem. CRAM is a localised algorithm which takes into account only neighboring information in order to compute its movement. No global information about the position of the stations is required. The only assumption that CRAM makes is that the mobile router is located close to one of the 1-hop neighbors of the corrupted node when the failure happens. Figure 1 depicts an example of the positions of the devices before the failure.

The algorithm is divided in two phases. During the first phase, a node discovery process is taking place in order to identify the location of the next hop and restore connectivity. Since the next hop is detected, the second phase deals with the amelioration of the link quality between the robot and nodes A and C.

The discovery phase includes several small movements and after each movement the link quality between the router and the routing points A and C is measured. The robot's first movement is to move away from point A traveling a

Fig. 1. Initial network layout

straight line distance equal to r. This distance must be higher than the distance between A–C. The direction of the movement is random.

The robot makes a number of small steps following an almost circular movement around A with radius r. After each movement, it measures the link quality between itself and routing points A and C. The RSSI value is used as a metric of the measurements and it varies between -100 and 0 dBm. When no connection exists, the robot considers a RSSI value equal to -100. Only values above h are considered acceptable, while the rest of the values are discarded. An average value of ten measurements for each link with an interval of dt seconds is considered.

The robot's circular movement can be done either clockwise or counterclockwise. The computation of the next position at which the robot will stop to measure again the link quality is given by Formula (1).

$$(x, y) = (r \cos(i\theta), r \sin(i\theta)), \tag{1}$$

where i is the number of movements and θ is the angle which corresponds to an arc whose chord length (step) is equal to d meters (see Figure 2).

The robot follows a set of rules in order to decide where to move and when to stop moving. First of all, the robot's circular movement continues as far as the RSSI value between the robot and node C is below h. Once the robot computes an average RSSI value above the threshold, it keeps moving, storing in its memory the maximum RSSI value and the position where it was achieved. If during the next movements, the link quality falls bellow a threshold p, the robot returns to the position where the maximum RSSI values was captured. p is defined as the signal attenuation between the current position and the position where the best signal quality was measured.

If no position is found during a full circle with signal level above h, then the robot gives up its effort reporting an error. The maximum number of movements max_i during a full round can be calculated combining the equations in (2):

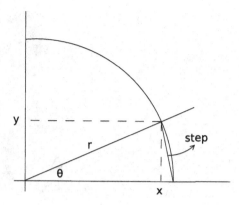

Fig. 2. Computation of the router's next position

$$max\_i = \lceil \frac{360}{s} \rceil, \quad s = \frac{\theta}{180}\pi r, \quad \theta = 2\arcsin\frac{d}{2r}, \tag{2}$$

where s is the length of the arc and θ is the angle in degrees.

The maximum total time of the discovery phase is given by Formula (3).

$$max\_time = \frac{r}{V} + max\_i(\frac{d}{V} + 9dt), \tag{3}$$

where V is the speed of the robot.

At this point the discovery phase has been terminated, giving way to the amelioration phase. This second phase is needed since the robot may be very close or distant to one of the routing points causing link instability. In order to avoid this problem, we use the link amelioration algorithm presented in [10]. The algorithm balances a link quality metric between two sides by applying a step-by-step moving similarly to the circular movement we presented before. The robot's movement is made on a straight line defined by its current and A's position.

According to this algorithm, the mobile router compares the two signals and moves towards to the station with the weakest one. The robot continues moving until the difference between the signals is below a predefined threshold q. In order to avoid network bottlenecks, we use the throughput of the communication channel as metric of our measurements.

5   Evaluation and Discussion of the Results

In this section we evaluate the performance of CRAM by performing a real experiment with three stations and a mobile router. Although, the same experiment has been repeated several times by using different configurations and values, in this section one of the most representative scenarios is employed.

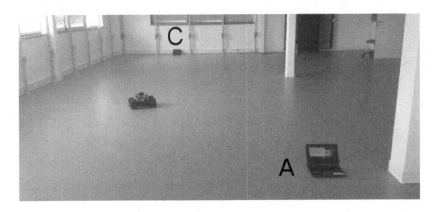

Fig. 3. The experimental setup

The experiment consists of three stationary nodes that are part of an ad-hoc network and a mobile robot[1] which has the ability to move onward and backward as well as to rotate in different angles. All the participants used IEEE 802.11g compatible wireless network cards. The experimental setup is illustrated in Figure 3. In this picture we have excluded the failure node B. The two other stations are placed 12 meters away to each other, the radius for the circular movement is predefined equal to 2 meters and the step d is 1 meter. We also consider a time interval equal to 0.1 seconds between the ten RSSI measurements as well as h, p and q thresholds equal to -65 dBm, 5 dBm and 3 Mbps, respectively. The angle between stations A and C is set equal to 120 degrees. The robot has no knowledge about the position of station C.

We assume that the connectivity between the stations is lost (it has fallen bellow h) and the robot starts moving at that moment of time. In the following lines we present the experimental results derived by the robot's measurements.

As we have already mentioned, CRAM is executed in two phases. During the first phase the connectivity is restored, while in the second phase, the throughput between the two routing points and the robot is improved. Figure 4 presents the positions of the stations as well as the robot's intermediate and final positions. The intermediate position denotes the robot's location after the first phase of the algorithm.

Figure 5 illustrates the robot's movement and the corresponding RSSI values of each step. During the first steps, there is no connection between the router and station C or the link quality is poor (below h), thus, the RSSI value is considered equal to -100. The router detects C's signal after the third step, while the maximum value is measured about 120 degrees away from station A. The signal level at that position is stored and the robot continues its movement. Since after the next step the link quality falls bellow the predefined threshold p, the robot returns to the position where the best signal was captured.

---

[1] http://www.wifibot.com/

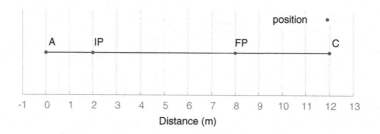

Fig. 4. The distance between the robot and stations A, C throughout the deployment (IP: intermediate position after the circular movement, FP: final position)

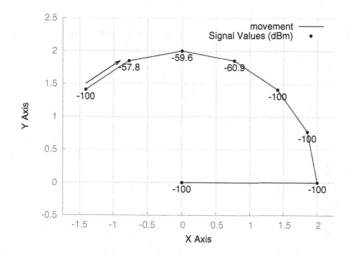

Fig. 5. The position of robot each time

Figure 6 depicts the bandwidth level between the mobile router and the two routing points for the second phase movement. The results show that the movement was completed in eight steps. The robot stops when the two values are below the specified threshold q. We can observe a great improvement in terms of the achieved bandwidth between the initial and the final position.

Finally, the robot's traveling distance during the second phase of the deployment is illustrated in Figure 7. The figure shows that the robot moved 7 times towards the station C and one time backwards in order to find the best measurement. The distance is measured from the point the previous phase was terminated.

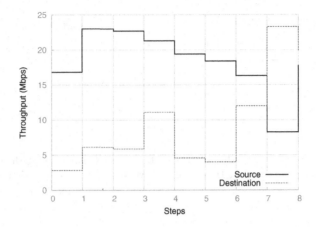

Fig. 6. The signal levels between the router and stations A, C

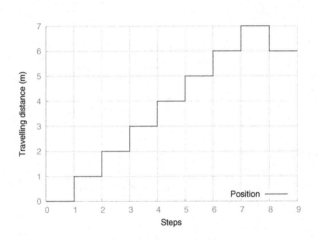

Fig. 7. The robot's traveling distance for each step of its second phase movement

6   Conclusion and Possible Future Work

In this paper, we have proposed an efficient algorithm to restore connectivity between network partitions in a wireless ad-hoc network using another node as an alternative route. The solution is based on local information and its effectiveness is evaluated through experimentation. The results of the experiment are very encouraging and give the confidence that the connectivity between two nodes can be easily restored and ameliorated, thus, we are able to restore the network performance, without the need of robot to take many steps and consume big amounts of energy.

Our future work aims at the extension of the CRAM algorithm by performing more complicated and realistic scenarios. In particular, we investigate the use of CRAM in a multiple routing point layout, where the robot has to restore connectivity between more than two routing points. Furthermore, we are interested in developing a multi-robot system when failures occur further than one hop. In this case, there is a necessity of deploying more than one robot to restore connectivity. Finally, a multi-failure scenario is going to be considered. In this scenario, failures occur in more than one node and the robot is responsible to evaluate the importance of each partition of the network and resolve connectivity by an order of importance.

Acknowledgments. This work is partially supported a grant from CPER Nord-Pas-de-Calais FEDER CIA.

References

1. Marti, S., Giuli, T.J., Lai, K., Baker, M.: Mitigating routing misbehavior in mobile ad hoc networks. In: Proceedings of the 6th Annual International Conference on Mobile Computing and Networking, MobiCom 2000, pp. 255–265. ACM, New York (2000)
2. Li, W., Joshi, A., Finin, T.: Coping with node misbehaviors in ad hoc networks: A multi-dimensional trust management approach. In: 2010 Eleventh International Conference on Mobile Data Management (MDM), pp. 85–94 (May 2010)
3. Srinivasan, V., Nuggehalli, P., Chiasserini, C., Rao, R.: Cooperation in wireless ad hoc networks. In: Twenty-Second Annual Joint Conference of the IEEE Computer and Communications, INFOCOM 2003, vol. 2, pp. 808–817. IEEE Societies (March 2003)
4. Abbasi, A., Akkaya, K., Younis, M.: A distributed connectivity restoration algorithm in wireless sensor and actor networks. In: 32nd IEEE Conference on Local Computer Networks, LCN 2007, 496–503 (October 2007)
5. Akkaya, K., Senturk, I.F., Vemulapalli, S.: Handling large-scale node failures in mobile sensor/robot networks. Journal of Network and Computer Applications **36**(1), 195–210 (2013)
6. Al-Turjman, F., Hassanein, H., Ibnkahla, M.: Optimized relay placement to federate wireless sensor networks in environmental applications. In: 2011 7th International Wireless Communications and Mobile Computing Conference (IWCMC), pp. 2040–2045 (July 2011)
7. Kim, K.H., Shin, K., Niculescu, D.: Mobile autonomous router system for dynamic (re)formation of wireless relay networks. IEEE Transactions on Mobile Computing **12**(9), 1828–1841 (Sept 2013)
8. Magklara, K., Zorbas, D., Razafindralambo, T.: Node Discovery and Replacement Using Mobile Robot. In: Zheng, J., Mitton, N., Li, J., Lorenz, P. (eds.) ADHOC-NETS 2012. LNICST, vol. 111, pp. 59–71. Springer, Heidelberg (2013)
9. Miranda, K., Natalizio, E., Razafindralambo, T., Molinaro, A.: Adaptive router deployment for multimedia services in mobile pervasive environments. In: Proceedings of the Work in Progress session at PerCom (WIP of PerCom), Lugano, Switzerland, March 19-23, 471–474 (2012)

10. Miranda, K., Natalizio, E., Razafindralambo, T.: Adaptive Deployment Scheme for Mobile Relays in Substitution Networks. International Journal of Distributed Sensor Networks (IJDSN) (2012)
11. Razafimandimby, J., Miranda, K., Zorbas, D., Razafindralambo, T.: Fast and reliable robot deployment for substitution networks. In: Proceedings of the 10th ACM Symposium on Performance Evaluation of Wireless Ad Hoc, Sensor, and Ubiquitous Networks (PE-WASUN), Barcelona, Spain, pp. 17–23 (November 2013)
12. Hsieh, M.A., Cowley, A., Kumar, V., Taylor, C.J.: Maintaining network connectivity and performance in robot teams. Journal of Field Robotics 25(1–2), 111–131 (2008)
13. Baccour, N., Koubâa, A., Youssef, H., Ben Jamâa, M., do Rosário, D., Alves, M., Becker, L.B.: F-LQE: A Fuzzy Link Quality Estimator for Wireless Sensor Networks. In: Silva, J.S., Krishnamachari, B., Boavida, F. (eds.) EWSN 2010. LNCS, vol. 5970, pp. 240–255. Springer, Heidelberg (2010)
14. Boano, C., Zuiga, M., Voigt, T., Willig, A., Romer, K.: The triangle metric: Fast link quality estimation for mobile wireless sensor networks. In: 2010 Proceedings of 19th International Conference on Computer Communications and Networks (ICCCN), pp. 1–7 (August 2010)
15. Baccour, N., Koubâa, A., Mottola, L., Zúñiga, M.A., Youssef, H., Boano, C.A., Alves, M.: Radio link quality estimation in wireless sensor networks: A survey. ACM Trans. Sen. Netw. 8(4), 34:1–34:33 (2012)
16. Senel, F., Younis, M.: Relay node placement in structurally damaged wireless sensor networks via triangular steiner tree approximation. Computer Communications 34(16), 1932–1941 (2011)
17. Lee, S., Younis, M.: Optimized relay node placement for connecting disjoint wireless sensor networks. Computer Networks 56(12), 2788–2804 (2012)
18. Lee, S., Younis, M.: Recovery from multiple simultaneous failures in wireless sensor networks using minimum steiner tree. Journal of Parallel and Distributed Computing 70(5), 525–536 (2010)

Author Index